BEHAVIOURAL STUDIES IN HOSPITALITY MANAGEMENT

RITA CARMOUCHE

Department of Food, Nutrition and Hospitality Management

AND

NANCY KELLY

School of Human and Health Sciences
University of Huddersfield, UK

CHAPMAN & HALL

University and Professional Division

London · Glasgow · Weinheim · New York · Tokyo · Melbourne · Madras

Published by Chapman & Hall, 2–6 Boundary Row, London SE1 8HN, UK

Chapman & Hall, 2–6 Boundary Row, London SE1 8HN, UK

Blackie Academic & Professional, Wester Cleddens Road, Bishopbriggs, Glasgow G64 2NZ, UK

Chapman & Hall GmbH, Pappelallee 3, 69469 Weinheim, Germany

Chapman & Hall USA, One Penn Plaza, 41st Floor, New York NY 10119, USA

Chapman & Hall Japan, ITP-Japan, Kyowa Building, 3F, 2–2–1 Hirakawacho, Chiyoda-ku, Tokyo 102, Japan

Chapman & Hall Australia, Thomas Nelson Australia, 102 Dodds Street, South Melbourne, Victoria 3205, Australia

Chapman & Hall India, R. Seshadri, 32 Second Main Road, CIT East, Madras 600 035, India

First edition 1995 and reprinted 1996

©1995 Rita Carmouche and Nancy Kelly

Typeset in Times Ten and News Gothic by Fox Design, Bramley, Surrey
Printed in Great Britain by The Alden Press, Osney Mead, Oxford

ISBN 0 412 60850 2

A catalogue record for this book is available from the British Library

Library of Congress Catalog Card Number: 94-72636

♾ Printed on permanent acid-free paper, manufactured in accordance with ANSI/NISO Z39.48-1992 and ANSI/NISO Z39.48-1984 (Permanence of Paper).

For Ricky and Richard Mazurkiewicz
and for Joan and Fred Kelly

Contents

Series foreword

The Chapman & Hall Series in Tourism and Hospitality Management is dedicated to the publication of high quality textbooks and other volumes that will be of benefit to those engaged in hotel, catering and tourism education, especially at degree and postgraduate level. All the authors in the series are experts in their own fields, actively engaged in teaching, research and consultancy in hospitality and tourism. This is a distinctive feature of the series and each book comprises an authoritative blend of subject-relevant theoretical considerations and practical applications and illustrations prepared by experienced writers. Furthermore, a unique quality of the series is that it is student orientated, offering accessible texts that take account of the realities of management and operations in the hospitality and tourism industries, being constructively critical where necessary without losing sight of the overall goal of providing clear accounts of concepts, techniques and issues. The tourism and hospitality industries are diverse and dynamic industries and it is the intention of the series to reflect this diversity and dynamism by publishing quality texts that embrace topical subjects without losing sight of enduring themes. In this respect, the Chapman & Hall Series in Tourism and Hospitality Management is an innovative venture committed to quality, accessibility and relevance. The Series Editors are grateful to Chapman & Hall for supporting this philosophy and would particularly like to acknowledge the commitment, expertise and insight of the Commissioning Editor, Steven Reed, whose contribution to the realization of the series has been invaluable.

C.L. Jenkins
R.C. Wood
The Scottish Hotel School
University of Strathclyde

Acknowledgements

We would like to express our thanks to the following people. Firstly, we are grateful to our colleagues in the Division of Food, Nutrition and Hospitality Management and in the Division of Behavioural Sciences at the University of Huddersfield for their encouragement of this project. We would like to thank the students in those divisions who have willingly, and sometimes unwittingly, helped us to clarify our ideas and thoughts.

In addition, our thanks go to Roy Wood of the Scottish Hotel School for his encouragement and enthusiasm and to Steven Reed, Jo Koster and Joanna Cooke of Chapman & Hall for their guidance and professionalism.

We would also like to thank MORI for their permission to reproduce material from *Public Attitudes towards Pubs and Leisure*, 1990.

Introduction

The hospitality industry has frequently been described as a 'people' industry. Those people who enter the industry, either through employment or academic study, have some idea that the term hospitality embraces ideas about dealing with people and providing services to paying guests.

For students who intend pursuing management careers in the hospitality industry, the question of how to deal and interact with people will be the very basis of their job. As future hospitality managers, they will find that there are many areas requiring an understanding of human behaviour. Thus, hospitality managers will be confronted with such issues as why some staff are always late for work, why customers choose one hotel rather than another, or why waiters and chefs are often in conflict with each other. The ways of understanding and dealing with such issues form the subject matter of this book.

Even in the early stages of hospitality courses you may have some ideas about how to deal with certain behavioural issues. Indeed, you may have already experienced hospitality organizations in which these issues have occurred. Following on from this, you might have noted specific current management responses to the problems and opportunities that behavioural issues allow.

Whether or not you have direct experience of hospitality organizations, consider the following case, and identify some of the behavioural issues that you think are relevant to the case. Chapter 14 suggests possible answers to this scenario.

BLAIR HOTELS PLC

Jean Smith and Tom Pine were recruited as management trainees by Blair Hotels PLC in October 1990. Both Jean and Tom had graduated from universities in different parts of the country, with the same hospitality management qualifications.

After an 18-month training period covering all departments, and a two-month period in duty management, it was time for the trainees to be allocated permanent jobs within the company. Tom hoped that he would be offered the job of front office manager (which he thought would be a good starting point on the career ladder to general management). Jean, on the other hand, thought that her talents lay in the area of food and beverage and hoped to be appointed manager of the 60 cover *L'Escargot* restaurant.

The general manager, Ralph Green, first called Tom to his office and informed him that he was to be appointed food and beverage manager in *L'Escargot* restaurant. While not being his first choice, Tom accepted that this was an important and high profile role. As Tom left the general manager's office, Ralph Green reminded him that his own first management post had been as food and beverage manager.

When Jean was called to the general manager's office she was informed that she would fill the vacancy of head housekeeper. Upon congratulating her Ralph Green mentioned that the role was ideal for her future, as flexible hours were possible, and housekeeping staff were able to take leave during the school holidays.

After you have read this volume, you might wish to return to this scenario and reconsider your original ideas.

This book is designed to equip students with the skills necessary to analyse and interpret a situation such as that illustrated in the case study above. This will be achieved by providing a foundation knowledge in behavioural studies for hospitality.

USING THIS BOOK

This book aims to introduce the field of behavioural studies to students pursuing courses in hospitality management. As students do not necessarily have any prior training in the behavioural sciences, we recommend reading the chapters in this book in chronological order, so that each set of aims and outcomes is encountered stage by stage.

STRUCTURE OF THE BOOK

The book is structured in three main sections.

In Part One, Chapters 1, 2, 3 and 4 provide a foundation knowledge of the social sciences. These chapters describe the aims, nature, scope and role of the social sciences in aiding an understanding of human behaviour; furthermore, they establish the rationale for including social sciences on courses in hospitality management. Chapter 4 has been specifically devoted to research methods, and can be used as a basis from which to critically evaluate other research, and as a framework to assist you with project and dissertation work on hospitality courses. A series of questions has been included at the end of each chapter, in order to allow you to recap the main points and ideas which have been discussed. Further reading is suggested at the end of each chapter to allow you to extend your knowledge of specific topics.

Part One has been designed to allow you, the student, to use the book for individual study, working through the material at your own pace. Nevertheless it can still be used by the reader to supplement lecture material, and as a basis for group work and student assignments

When Part One has been completed, you should have acquired a foundation knowledge in the social science disciplines, and should understand the underlying principles involved in the social scientific analysis of behaviour in hospitality organizations. You can monitor your own understanding of the material by attempting the question and answer section at the end of the book.

Part Two is concerned with developing social scientific interpretations of a range of hospitality issues. The issues represent a range of topics and areas within the hospitality context, and a multidisciplinary approach is used to interpret and explain human behaviour.

In analysing hospitality issues from a social science perspective, we have found it useful to give students the opportunity to indicate their own understanding of topics. Therefore, we encourage you to write in the spaces in the margins. Once the ideas have been written down, possible responses may be used as the basis for discussion. Lecturers may wish to adopt similar strategies, using students' ideas as the basis for group discussion. This approach indicates the complexity of issues, and serves as the basis on which to introduce theoretical and conceptual treatment of the topic.

At the end of Part Two, you should be able to identify the value of a social scientific analysis of hospitality issues, and should recognize the utility of a multidisciplinary approach to understanding behaviour in hospitality contexts. Similarly, you may at this stage want to interpret the issues from alternative social scientific perspectives.

The final section of this book provides you with a number of behavioural scenarios within the hospitality industry. We have worked though some of the scenarios in order to provide some guidelines for analysis. We hope that by this stage of the book, you will be comfortable identifying the appropriate concepts by which behaviour can be understood and explained, and indeed that you will be able to develop applications of behaviour in the hospitality industry by using multidisciplinary approaches. These scenarios may also be used to supplement group work and group discussion.

At the end of this section, Chapter 15 presents a set of questions and answers with respect to three articles concerned with the hospitality industry; we feel that these will help you to recognize the importance of evaluation through a social science perspective, and will provide a mechanism by which you can monitor your own understanding of the material.

Social Sciences and the Hospitality Industry

The following chapters aim to introduce you to the social sciences. We outline a foundation knowledge of the disciplines of psychology and sociology and present an argument for the inclusion of the study of human behaviour on hospitality management courses. A case is made for the necessity of understanding behaviour using a multidisciplinary, integrative approach. We explain the nature and scope of the social sciences, outlining the role of theories and concepts when interpreting human behaviour within hospitality contexts. The chapter on research methods outlines the techniques that are available to conduct investigations into behavioural issues in hospitality.

Approaching human behaviour in the hospitality industry $\boxed{1}$

Aims

This chapter aims to:

1. introduce you to the nature and scope of the book;
2. outline the case for studying human behaviour in the hospitality industry; and
3. introduce you to the debate surrounding the teaching of human behaviour in the hospitality industry.

Outcomes

At the end of this chapter you will be able to:

1. make a case for the inclusion of behavioural studies on hospitality management courses; and
2. identify the particular approach taken in this book.

THE NATURE OF THE HOSPITALITY INDUSTRY

Despite the long history of the hotel and catering industry, dating back to the inns of the sixteenth century (Medlik, 1978), academic study of the hotel and catering world is relatively new. For example, degree courses in the field in the UK date only from the 1960s and 1970s. This is a very short history indeed, when compared with the 100+ years of academic study devoted to subjects like chemistry.

In terms of teaching degree and diploma courses in the hotel and catering field, the predominant approach has been a multidisciplinary one (Slattery, 1980). This has involved drawing together subjects such as accountancy, law, marketing and personnel management and combining them to form the basis of hotel and catering courses. At the same time, the subjects of hotel and catering operations are underpinned by a set of techniques and practices developed from the origins of teaching hotel and catering as craft-based subjects (Davies and Stone, 1985). The study of human behaviour has also been included as a subject on many hospitality courses (Slattery, 1980).

Many arguments have been put forward for the inclusion within hotel and catering courses of some element of behavioural analysis. The most common argument is the contention that the hospitality industry is a people business (Lockwood and Jones, 1984). Implicit in this view is the notion that hotel and catering work involves the provision of services to paying guests. Whyte (1947), writing in what remains a landmark text, noted that customers consume the restaurant product at the point of its production. What this means is that restaurant meals are produced for immediate consumption on the premises, and are not bought and consumed or used in another context, as is the case with many other consumer goods, for example washing powder, food from supermarkets. The result of this in the restaurant context is that customers are more closely tied into the organization structure than they would be in other organization contexts, such as retailers. Added to this, Smith (1967) has noted that hotel and catering products consist of not only the tangible goods, such as the food and drink, but that they also contain intangible elements such as atmosphere and ambience. Both elements are an important part of a customer's meal experience and it is clear that hospitality staff contribute towards that experience directly. We are asserting, therefore, that staff and customer transactions in the hospitality situation are characterized by a high level of personal interaction, and often a low level of supervision by other staff (Lockwood and Jones, 1984).

By this stage it should be becoming clear that hospitality organizations exhibit features which require an analysis of human behaviour. This is necessary given the direct nature of the relationship between customers and staff. In fact, we can go further and suggest that given the position and role of customers and staff in hospitality organizations, a particular form of organization structure will exist that is not necessarily found in other organizations. This will become clearer if we contrast hotel and catering organizations with, for example, car factories.

In a typical car factory, the following structure might apply between the production of the product and its consumption by customers.

Production line, $\longrightarrow$ Wholesaler $\longrightarrow$ Showroom $\longrightarrow$ Customer
car as product

In this example, contact between the producers of the product and the actual customer does not exist.

However, a typical hotel or restaurant structure would acknowledge the customer at the point of production, as shown in the diagram on the next page.

As we can see, customers are in a more direct relationship with staff in the hospitality context. In the car production process, customers are isolated from the point at which the car is actually manufactured.

Given that this is the case, hospitality organizations exhibit a closer relationship between customer and staff than occurs in other organization types

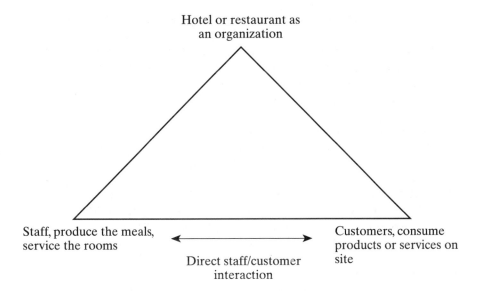

Hotel or restaurant as
an organization

Staff, produce the meals,
service the rooms

Direct staff/customer
interaction

Customers, consume
products or services on
site

(Slattery, 1980). Hotels are not the only organizations in which this relationship is found, however, and it is not strictly true that hotels are unique as some commentators argue (Jones, 1989). What is clear, however, is that service organizations of this type require more detailed understanding of the types of relationships which evolve between staff and customers, and a more detailed understanding of how these relationships are managed. The types of relationship found in service organizations will clearly be related to the organization structure, culture, and company ideology regarding customer management. Thus, we are not saying that all service organizations will be managed in the same way.

At a more general level, hotel and catering organizations require the management of human resources in the same way as other organization types. Textbooks covering hotel and catering courses do include management theories and practices, together with human resource management. Investigations of the customer, on the other hand, are usually undertaken within the framework of marketing. The area of staff–customer relations has usually been the prerogative of commentators within the context of service delivery systems. A notable exception to this has been the work of Angela Bowey (1976), who has undertaken a social scientific analysis of behaviour in restaurants.

As we have indicated there are many areas within the study of hospitality management which require an understanding of people's behaviour. This has been recognized in the design of courses, and some attempt has been made to deal with behavioural issues (Slattery, 1983). For example, issues of staff behaviour, such as motivation, are included in personnel management textbooks for the industry, and thus we have some point of reference from which we can attempt to explain behaviour. Marketing and personnel management are two of the disciplines most commonly used in this context.

It is common practice in these approaches to select concepts and to use these to explain behaviour (Mullins, 1992). Concepts such as motivation are used to try and explain constant lateness for work, or to understand why people work at all. Concepts such as market segmentation are used to try and explain how people can be divided into groups with common goals or needs, in order to explain the demand for hotels or public houses (Buttle, 1986).

The difficulty with these approaches is that the explanations often do not recognize the disciplines from which the concepts came and, therefore, often do not analyse the behaviours or present explanations in an appropriate way. Motivation, for example, is drawn from psychology and social psychology, yet students often study this concept without reference to psychology as a body of thought. Equally, in the marketing example, dividing people into groups and attempting to predict their consumption patterns ignores the whole area of the social and cultural contexts in which choices are made, and ignores the wider societal forces which influence consumption patterns. These are areas which have been a central concern of sociologists.

These examples serve to illustrate that it is not legitimate to use and apply concepts of behaviour to hospitality issues without understanding the wider disciplines from which they are drawn. Before we can understand human behaviour in the hospitality industry, we must first understand some of the central issues and ideas which influence people's behaviour, and the issues which affect the ways in which human behaviour must be studied. As we will discuss, there are many issues and controversies within the disciplines that study human behaviour, and students cannot ignore these if they wish to provide adequate explanations of people's behaviour (Atkinson, McArthy and Philips, 1987). This means, therefore, that students must be introduced to the central concerns of behavioural disciplines. These disciplines are the social sciences, and they have a long history of developing knowledge in order to understand the reasons why people behave in certain ways, in certain situations.

SOCIAL SCIENCES ON HOSPITALITY MANAGEMENT COURSES

The next question which arises is concerned with how the social sciences should be approached and taught on hospitality management courses. This question has been the subject of debate amongst writers within the field of hospitality management. Perhaps the clearest way to present this debate is to categorize the arguments and exponents into two groups: one group we will term the 'generalists'; the other group we will term the 'specialists'.

A crucial theme around which this debate revolves concerns the specific nature of the hotel and catering industry. Even within the multidisciplinary approach in which conventional disciplines, such as marketing, are applied to the hospitality industry, there has been disagreement between authors. This multidisciplinary approach has involved applying general marketing principles to the hospitality context. Some commentators have argued against adopting these generalist approaches, citing the uniqueness of the hotel and catering industry (Nailon, 1982). As a unique industry, it would require specialist knowledge and application. Running alongside this argument, exponents question the appropriateness of transferring knowledge gained in the manufacturing context (which are the origins of those approaches), to the service context (of which hotels and catering are clearly a part) (Nailon, 1982). As such, these authors suggest that studies of hotels and catering and their subject matter, require the development of more specialist knowledge.

In defence of generalist approaches, supporters have argued that developing specialist knowledge of, for example, marketing, might well devalue the discipline base of the subject (Wood, 1983). This is because students would require a sophisticated level of theoretical and conceptual understanding of the discipline prior to being able to develop specialist knowledge. Additionally, specialist knowledge of hotels and catering may lead to a myopic approach, focusing only on the hotel and catering industry, and limiting the scope for comparative analysis with other industries. The generalists rest their case upon the argument that the principles of the discipline are the same regardless of where they are applied.

This debate of generalism versus specialism has also been conducted in the context of teaching social sciences on hotel and catering courses, and it is to this area that we will now turn.

According to Slattery (1983), the value of social sciences for the study of hospitality management rests in their ability to offer explanations and interpretations which are relevant to hospitality contexts. Slattery falls within the specialist approach, for he argues that we cannot simply apply social sciences (or some social science concepts and theories), without taking into account the specific industry context. Indeed, he argues that social science theories must be adapted and refined to provide 'hospitality versions' of these theories. Slattery's approach is echoed by Nailon (1982), who argues for an industry-centred approach to the study of hospitality management.

Writing in opposition to these approaches, Wood (1988) doubts the intellectual rigour and coherence which can be achieved by students selecting social scientific theories and interpretations based upon the criteria of their vocational relevance. Wood is also critical of this as a selective approach in which students are not exposed to the full range of social scientific disciplines. Essentially, for Wood, they do not receive a sufficient foundation in the disciplines prior to evaluating their utility for hospitality management.

Slattery is, therefore, arguing for a specialist social science for the hospitality industry, whilst Wood may be seen to be implying that we should all become social scientists in order to study the hospitality industry. In fact, both of these positions are rather extreme, and we feel neither is necessary nor appropriate for students wishing to understand the behaviour of people in hospitality contexts and organizations.

The debate surrounding the role of social sciences in hospitality courses should not be cast in terms of vocational relevance alone, nor at the level of expertise required to study the social sciences. The central question is concerned more with how well social scientific analysis can explain and account for the behaviour of people in hospitality organizations and environments. This shifts the debate to the area of application, not to expertise or vocational relevance. The primary aim of this book is to offer an applied social scientific analysis of hospitality organizations, their members and customers. This will be achieved by drawing upon social scientific disciplines, and by developing social scientific applications appropriate to students of the hotel and catering industry.

Having outlined some of the features of the debate surrounding the teaching of social sciences on hotel and catering courses, it would be useful for us to clarify our aims and approach.

To begin with, students will be provided with a foundation knowledge of the social sciences which will allow them to understand and explain behaviour in the hospitality industry. We will also encourage students to explore the value of using social sciences in order to develop a critical awareness of studies of human behaviour. This awareness is encouraged both in terms of the theories and concepts that authors use, and the methods that are used to investigate aspects of behaviour. The book is not designed primarily as an aid to management, nor as a problem-solving text. We hope that by reading this text, students will be assisted in making more informed judgements about human behaviour, and will be more able to evaluate approaches offered in other authors' work.

Within the framework of the social sciences, the book concentrates on two core disciplines: psychology and sociology. These two disciplines are selected because they have both contributed to our understanding of individual and group behaviour, and the wider societal forces which influence people's everyday behaviour. By reading this book, students will not become sociologists or psychologists: rather, they will be provided with a range of analytical skills and approaches appropriate to understand, interpret and explain the behaviour of people in the hospitality industry. By focusing on psychology and sociology, we intend to offer an integrated and multi-disciplinary approach. Often it is the case within the social sciences that these disciplines compete in their explanations of behaviour, rather than complement each other. We suggest that to understand human behaviour fully it is essential to adopt a multidisciplinary approach, in which psychological and sociological interpretations are integrated.

By concentrating on psychology and sociology we are excluding a whole range of other social science disciplines that also contribute to our understanding of people and their environments. This is not to deny the importance of those disciplines; it is hoped that other commentators more suited to the task will take up the challenge of discussing these disciplines in the hospitality context. It should be recognized, however, that throughout the book the term social science is being used to refer to psychology and sociology only.

We have already mentioned the importance of interpretation and application in understanding social scientific analyses of hospitality situations and, indeed, this will be a key feature of this book. Social science theories and concepts will be used and analysed in their application to hospitality organizations and the people within them. This means that theory and practise will be integrated throughout the book. We will argue that ultimately the value of social science disciplines, their theories and concepts lies in their ability to explain real situations.

In summary, this book aims to develop students' awareness and understanding of social science disciplines. This will allow students to undertake critical analysis when studying and researching behaviour in the hospitality industry, and will enable them to develop social science applications and explanations of behaviour in the area of hotels and catering.

DISCUSSION QUESTIONS

1. Make a case for the inclusion of the study of human behaviour on hospitality management courses.
2. What is the value of a multidisciplinary approach to the study of human behaviour for a manager in the hospitality industry?
3. To what extent are hotel and catering organizations unique? Discuss the implications of this for an understanding of behaviour in hospitality organizations.

FURTHER READING

Potter, D. (ed.) (1989) *Society and the Social Sciences: An Introduction*, Routledge in association with OU press, London. A useful introductory text to the nature and scope of the social sciences.
Whyte, W.F. (1948) *Human Relations in the Restaurant Industry*, McGraw-Hill, New York. This is a landmark text which identifies issues of behaviour in relation to the restaurant industry in the USA.

REFERENCES

Atkinson, G.B., McArthy, B. and Philips, K.M. (1987) *Studying Society: An Introduction to Social Science,* Oxford University Press, Oxford.
Bowey, A. (1976) *The Sociology of Organizations*, Hodder and Stoughton, London.
Buttle, F. (1986) *Hotel and Food Service Marketing: A Managerial Approach*, Holt, London.
Davies, B. and Stone, S. (1985) *Food and Beverage Management*, Heinemann, Oxford.
Jones, P. (ed.) (1989) Management in the Service Industries, Pitman, London.
Lockwood, A. and Jones, P. (1984) *People in the Hotel and Catering Industry*, Holt, London.

Medlik, S. (1978) *A Profile of the Hotel and Catering Industry*, Heinemann, Oxford.

Mullins, L.J. (1992) *Hospitality Management*, Pitman, London.

Nailon, P. (1982) Theory in hospitality management. *International Journal of Hospitality Management*, **3**, 135–143.

Slattery, P. (1980) The social sciences in hotel and catering undergraduate courses, a review and a position. Paper presented at the international association of hotel management schools symposium on the social sciences in hotel and catering undergraduate courses, 10–12 April. The Polytechnic of Huddersfield.

Slattery, P. (1983) Social scientific methodology and hospitality management. *International Journal of Hospitality Management*, **2** (1), 9–14.

Smith, G.C. (1967) *Marketing of the Meal Experience*, University of Surrey, London.

Whyte, W.F. (1947) The social structure of the restaurant. *American Journal of Sociology*, pp. 302–310.

Wood, R.C. (1983) Theory, management and hospitality, a response to Nailon. *International Journal of Hospitality Management*, **2** (3), 103–4.

Wood, R.C. (1988) Against social science. *International Journal of Hospitality Management*, **7** (3), 239–250.

The social sciences | 2

Aims

This chapter aims to:

1. define the social sciences;
2. illustrate the competing and complementary nature of the social sciences;
3. illustrate the levels of analysis inherent in psychological and sociological explanations of behaviour;
4. locate psychology and sociology in a historical context; and
5. consider the nature/nurture debate.

Outcomes

At the end of this chapter you will be able to:

1. identify and define the aims, scope and nature of the social sciences;
2. compare and contrast social scientific explanations of behaviour with the humanities and common sense approaches;
3. recognize and describe the relevance and utility of different levels of explanation of human behaviour; and
4. describe both sides of the nature/nurture debate, and comment on its relevance to an understanding of behaviour in the hospitality industry.

DEFINING THE SOCIAL SCIENCES

The previous chapter established the case for including social sciences on hotel and catering courses. Before we go on to apply social science disciplines in a hospitality context, we must first of all gain some knowledge of social science disciplines and their central focus and main concerns.

A useful starting point in our discussion is to note that the social sciences are not a totally integrated body of ideas. Quite the contrary in fact, the social sciences are characterized by disputes and disagreements as to the boundaries of their subject matter and the methods of investigation and operation (Open University, 1976). Perhaps this is to be expected, given the complexity of human behaviour, for, as we will discuss, many aspects of social conduct are open to more than one interpretation. Dahrendorf (1968) defines the social sciences as follows

> Social sciences is an ambitious concept used to define a set of disciplines of scholarship, which deal with aspects of human society.

This definition draws our attention to the fact that the social sciences cover a range of subjects. Indeed, many of the social science textbooks define the social sciences as a family of disciplines (Trigg, 1985), an idea which implies that the disciplines have some relationship with each other. The nature of this relationship is found in their common subject matter, that is human behaviour, and the factors and processes which influence that behaviour. Authors disagree as to which disciplines should be included in this family and where the family should begin and end. However, within the literature, the following disciplines are most commonly included as part of the social sciences (Brown and Brown, 1975):

- sociology
- psychology
- economics
- history
- anthropology.

These subjects are considered to be the central, or core, social science disciplines which, from their inception, have spawned sub-disciplines or branches (Trigg, 1985). By examining the list above, it is clear that while the social sciences are concerned with the study of human beings, there are many different types of focus and interest within the social sciences and their sub-disciplines. For example, some social scientists are concerned with specific aspects of behaviour, e.g. the structure of societies; others may focus upon social issues, such as crime (Giddens, 1992). It is also clear that some social sciences are concerned with activities which pervade all social action, such as economics or political science; yet it is just as common for social scientists to take as their subject matter the family, child development or the role of leisure in contemporary society. Indeed, areas of our lives which may seem mundane and ordinary to us are just as likely to be the subject of social scientific enquiry as are the larger social issues, like wars, from which we might feel far removed (Giddens, 1992).

SPECIALIZATION IN THE SOCIAL SCIENCES

The development of specialization within social science can be attributed to many factors (Duverger, 1964). First, the growth in specialization, or sub-disciplines, came about because of the complexity of human behaviour. Given that it is not possible to study every aspect of human behaviour, it makes sense to divide the areas of study. Sub-disciplines allow specialization to occur within the discipline. However, as the sub-disciplines evolve from the same core of knowledge, they hold the same assumptions about the factors which influence behaviour and offer the same types of explanations at similar levels. For example, educational sociology is a sub-discipline of sociology, therefore, an educational sociologist, when investigating behaviour within educational settings, will focus upon the societal influences on education policy, the relationship between gender, the family and schooling and peer group influences upon educational achievement. Similarly, within psychology, psychologists working within the field of organizations will draw upon the individual's perceptions and values about organizations, and will largely explain behaviour in terms of the individual.

A second, and related, reason for specialization is the way in which social sciences have been researched and developed by academics. For example, research funds have been offered in particular areas (Trigg, 1985), which has encouraged the growth of specialisms. As much of research funding comes from government, various governments can influence, to a certain extent, both the direction of research and the types of issues which are investigated. If, for example 'lager louts' or 'football hooligans' become defined as a social problem, this can lead to research in that area. As part of their investigations, social scientists often reach conclusions which are far from popular with governments and policy-makers (Giddens, 1992). This may be one reason why social sciences have not always enjoyed a favourable press. There can be no doubt that while specialization within the social sciences has provided a great deal of knowledge and insight about the social world, it has also had some negative influence on the disciplines.

Specialisms can lead to fragmentation, with the result that artificial boundaries between social science disciplines are created (Open University, 1976). This would be exemplified when economists study the effects of the economy on, for example, international expansion, without regard to the social and cultural contexts in which that occurs. Furthermore, as knowledge becomes specialized, the idea of an integrated body of disciplines moves further away. Not only this, but as specialization occurs, different disciplines may compete to furnish an explanation, i.e. a psychologist's explanation of alcohol consumption as opposed to one suggested by a sociologist. In fact, as we have previously stated, these disciplines should complement each other in order to fully understand and explain complex behaviours.

The diagrams on the next page represent a simplistic breakdown of the core subjects of psychology and sociology.

Within the academic discipline of psychology, the diagrams on the next page show some of the sub-disciplines.

As the book is primarily concerned with the disciplines of sociology and psychology, it is relevant to give closer examination of these subjects.

SOCIOLOGICAL ANALYSIS

At the basic level of analysis, it is often argued that sociology is concerned with the study of groups or social behaviour, whilst psychology focuses upon

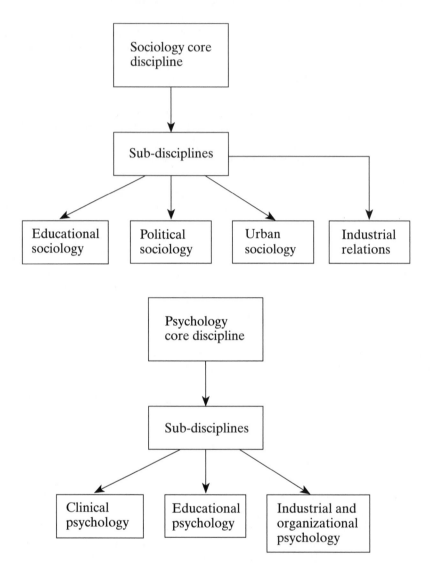

individual behaviour. This is rather simplistic as many of the themes and concerns of psychologists are related to the ways that individuals behave within groups. Sociologists also study individual behaviour in terms of wider societal and cultural influences. Therefore, group versus individual behaviour is only part of the story.

Since its inception, sociology has been concerned to identify and discuss the impact of social processes, and the conventions and organizations which follow from people living and interacting together (Giddens, 1992). This would include the ways in which societies develop and change, the types of social, economic and political institutions which are formed, and the ways of behaving that people adopt as members of a particular society or social group. Sociology is also concerned with the way individuals and social

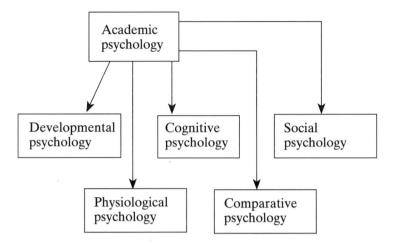

groups manage their day-to-day existence: the resources, social convention, patterns of behaviour and organization, power and authority structures, social and cultural relations. Indeed, sociologists have contributed to our knowledge and understanding of a wide range of areas. Organizations and the authority structures which occur within them have been a key feature of sociological investigation. Similarly, the relationship between managers and workers, and the power structures which support these relations have been investigated within the context of the sociology of industry and industrial relations. Sociological research has also been directed towards leisure behaviour, the social organization of sport, the music industry and the influence of the media on behaviour. It is important to recognize that, as members of society, even our very personal and private forms of behaviour are influenced by social conventions. Giddens (1992) has some interesting points to make on the idea of romantic love and choice of marriage partners. Whilst we might think that choice of marriage partner is an individual decision, it is, in fact, highly influenced by the culture and groups of which we are a part.

In understanding sociological analysis, the key focus that sociologists have are with the wider structures of organization, which influence individual and group behaviour. In examining and explaining behaviour, sociologists would look for similarities and differences in these patterns of behaviour. They seek out the causes of, and influences upon, behaviour in terms of the organization and structure of societies (Atkinson, McArthy and Phillips, 1987). Thus, in essence, sociological analysis focuses on factors outside of the individual, which are a key influence on the types of behaviour which that individual evolves.

Let us take the example of eating. In order to identify the food preference of individuals, sociological enquiry would focus not upon individual food preferences, but upon the factors which have shaped food taste. This would include the early socialization of individuals into food behaviour, the role of peer groups and significant others and the social and economic situation of the individual or group (Mennell, 1985; Mennell *et al.*, 1992).

To undertake sociological analysis, as we will see later, often means that we have to question our 'common sense' views of the world; we have to continually evaluate knowledge and explanation and become critics of what we have hitherto taken for granted (Giddens, 1992). Thus, undertaking sociological enquiry should develop an ability to critically evaluate both knowledge and explanation, bringing us more self-awareness of the social world and our interpretation of social conduct. Added to this, as Giddens (1992) notes, undertaking sociological research provides a means of seeing the social world from a diversity of cultural perspectives, assisting us to dispel preconceived notions and prejudice.

For our purposes in this text, we will demonstrate the value of such approaches, as sociology has furnished many practical applications in studying and understanding behaviour in general and in the context of analysing behaviour within organizations.

PSYCHOLOGICAL ANALYSIS

Turning our attention to psychology, it is clear that psychologists are also concerned with explaining human behaviour. Since the inception of psychology as a body of ideas, the development of sub-disciplines has been common, reflected in the wide range of specialisms in which psychologists work. Within the sub-discipline of clinical psychology, practitioners have contributed a great deal to our knowledge and understanding of behavioural issues, such as the explanation for, and treatment programmes for, phobias, an understanding of depression etc. Similarly, practical applications of other branches of psychology are used in medical practice, education systems and organizations.

The main concern of psychology is with the behaviour of individuals and small groups. An individual's behaviour can be studied in isolation, for example, the investigation of memory processes, or of problem-solving processes; or the individual's behaviour can be studied in the context of small groups and environmental influences, for example obedience to authority, the influence of other people on decision-making tasks etc. To return to the example of food preferences, the psychologist may be interested in an individual's motivation to eat certain foods, the influences on that eating behaviour, the way that the individual perceives the colour, taste, presentation of food and so on. Clearly, the main difference between this and the sociologist's approach is in the psychologist's focus on individual differences. Those individual differences can be studied in terms of both the individual differences between the people in a group, and the ways in which one person may perceive situations differently at different times.

Hence, a key distinguishing feature between sociology and psychology lies not in whether they focus upon individual or group behaviour, but rather in the point at which entry for the investigation begins and the level at which explanations are aimed. Psychologists will begin an investigation of behaviour that will end with explanations of behaviour at the individual level; sociologists, in contrast, will begin investigation and analysis at the level of the wider social unit and its structure. A further example may illustrate the point.

The popular press has recently been giving coverage to car crime in general, and to joyriding in particular. The media attention to this issue has encouraged the view that it is a serious social problem. Academics, in turn, have sought to explain the phenomenon, and this has included comment from both psychologists and sociologists. Sociologists relate this problem to a range of wider issues, such as unemployment, poor social conditions and the membership of sub-cultures. These factors are important for sociologists in the way that young people form values, and it is these 'value systems' that are determining factors in the act of joyriding. Psychologists, on the other hand, whilst recognizing that these issues exist, seek to determine why some individuals internalize those values and commit crimes, whilst others in exactly the same situation do not. A psychologist would be interested, in simple terms, in looking at personality types and the propensity to joyride, or the range of decision-making processes that individuals use in the act of joyriding. This example should illustrate that both types of analysis and levels of explanation are necessary and worthwhile as ways of explaining this particular behaviour.

These then indicate some of the central concerns of sociology and psychology in the contemporary period. However, before we can go on to use these disciplines further in a hospitality context, we must become familiar with the origins and development of the disciplines. These have been important in influencing the ways in which explanations of behaviour are formed.

THE HISTORICAL DEVELOPMENT OF SOCIOLOGY AND PSYCHOLOGY

In order to understand more fully the aims and scope of sociology and psychology, the disciplines themselves must be located in a historical context. By studying the evolution of the social sciences, students will become aware of some of the most important features which have characterized the social sciences in their development to the present day. A key starting point in studying this evolution is the recognition that all social theories and ideas are a product of the time in which they evolved. In using social sciences, therefore, students should not divorce ideas and theories from their historical context.

The origins of the social sciences can be traced back to the moral philosophers of the Greek civilization, notably Aristotle and Plato. However, it was the development of industrialization which established the social sciences as we know them. The industrial revolution brought about new forms of organization and societal structure which required both explanation and understanding (Bottomore and Nisbet, 1978). Before discussing the ways in which social scientific thinkers responded to this, it is important to establish the links between social sciences, natural and physical sciences and the humanities.

The natural and physical sciences have a history dating back to the emergence of natural philosophy (Duverger, 1964). By the period of industrialization, the natural sciences had established a body of knowledge capable of explaining events in the natural world, thus establishing the framework of science through empirical methods and inductive explanations. This led on to the development of laws which could serve as the basis for prediction (Duverger, 1964).

Social sciences evolved within the context of the natural sciences and their origins were closely linked. Just as natural scientists had offered explanations of the physical world, the early social thinkers wanted to apply the same rigour and predictive ability to the study of human beings. It was not unnatural, therefore, that in the beginning, the social sciences drew upon the methods of the natural sciences (Bottomore and Nisbet, 1978). Based upon a doctrine called positivism, August Comte (1830), a founding father of the social sciences applied the methods of the natural sciences to the study of human behaviour (Bottomore and Nisbet, 1978). Thus, the early nineteenth century positive philosophy, or social science (a term borrowed from Charles Fourier (1808) replaced moral philosophy (Duverger, 1964).

The underlying assumption of positivism was that it would establish the study of human behaviour on a scientific basis. This would involve emphasizing the factual as opposed to the speculative, the useful as opposed to the idle, the certain as opposed to the uncertain, the precise as opposed to the vague and the positive as opposed to the negative or critical. The impact of positivism as a method of studying human behaviour shaped the social research of the period, particularly the factual surveys of Booth in the UK and the Chicago school in the USA (both works are the precursors of modern empirical social research). The approach of positivism was also important in shaping the work of Durkheim (1895) and Pareto (1916) (Bottomore and Nisbet, 1978).

However, by the turn of the century, the traditions and approaches of positivism as a method of studying human behaviour were being challenged. The main opponent to positivism was the German sociologist Max Weber, who argued that the positivist traditions drawn from the natural sciences were inappropriate for the study of human behaviour. Weber's criticism centred upon the fundamental difference in the subject matter of the two sciences, one concerned with the study of physical objects, the other with the study of people (Aron, 1967).

Essentially Weber's arguments called for different methodologies for the study of human beings, since they could not be subject to the same approach as physical objects. Weber's arguments clearly had some force, and raised key issues regarding the study of human beings *per se* and regarding positivism as a framework for explaining human behaviour. The first of these key issues recognized that while physical objects only react to stimuli, human beings can act and then change their minds. Indeed, the concept of mind is a key variable which separates people from animals. Furthermore, people are diverse, and so is the range of human behaviour, conduct and emotions which individuals are capable of displaying. Given this diversity, it is difficult to make accurate predictions regarding human behaviour, an issue which is not a central problem for the natural sciences (Winch, 1988). In the natural sciences, conditions can be controlled and held constant and predictions can be more exact; this degree of certainty is not possible when studying human behaviour. Indeed, social science can be compared with weather forecasting, in that social scientists only deal in the probability of outcomes, or the likelihood that outcomes will occur.

An additional key problem encountered when using natural science methods to study human behaviour related to the relationship between the scientists and their subject matter. Two issues were highlighted here. Weber recognized that people's behaviour has a meaning for them, and that researchers cannot impose their own meanings upon this behaviour. The social scientist, therefore, had to develop a set of methods which allowed for this 'interpretative understanding' of the subject, called 'verstehen' by Weber. He also recognized that while researchers studying the physical world may not have had any affinity with their subject, their counterparts in the social sciences formed part of their own subject matter. This could result in the researcher's own values and biases intruding into the research (Winch, 1988). As the later discussion of research methods will show, (Chapter 4) social sciences have become very sophisticated in developing methods to address these problems.

The impact of Weberian sociology, therefore, was to establish a methodological dichotomy in approaches to the study of human behaviour, resulting in two schools of thought – positivism and humanism (Bottomore and Nisbet, 1978). These schools of thought remain part of contemporary approaches within sociological analysis. Since the inception of sociology many camps have developed from positivism and humanism, with the result that sociology has become a multi-paradigm science (Bottomore and Nisbet, 1978). This means that within the discipline there are many competing and conflicting approaches as to how sociologists ought to analyse behaviour, both in terms of the theories of behaviour which are put forward, and the methods and approaches used. This debate has been crystallized in the opposing analyses presented by Weber and Marx, two of the founding fathers of sociology. Readers can follow this debate thoroughly by looking at the further reading. These opposing perspectives are found not only in debates within the discipline itself, but are also conducted within the sub-disciplines.

The history of psychological explanation has been fraught with similar controversies and disputes. Writing in 1890, William James described psychology as the science of mental life. At this time, anyone who was working in the area of the mind could be considered as researching within a psychological framework. The problem with this early focus on studying mental life was that it is not observable; we cannot see the mind, but merely observe the behaviour which follows from mental events. This led to the development of a new paradigm in psychology, namely behaviourism. Behaviourism in fact had, and continues to have, a major impact on psychology as a discipline. J.B. Watson (1913) was the initial proponent of behaviourism and his contribution was to advance psychology from the study of subjective states of individuals via introspection, to behaviours which could be directly observed and measured. This move, Watson hoped, would allow psychology to develop the status of a science, such as physics or chemistry.

B.F. Skinner is, perhaps, the most famous behaviourist. He is well known for his work on learning which he believed occurred through a process of conditioning. Behaviourism remained a key idea in psychology until around the 1950s, when it became challenged by more humanistic ideas and humanistic psychology. The major criticism of behaviourism at its simplest level, is that it does not allow for human agency, i.e. it does not allow for the notion that individuals have some choice or autonomy in their actions, separate from the environment. Indeed for a strict behaviourist, concepts such as the mind, or thoughts, would not be considered worthy of study, and may not even exist. For behaviourists, all our actions are the result of a stimulus-response relationship. Thus, if we are stimulated by the environment, we have to respond; that response becomes learned, the appropriate (or often inappropriate) responses are connected with a particular stimuli and each time that stimulus is presented the same response will be emitted.

In some ways the debate between the behaviourists and the humanists can be addressed via one of the key issues in psychology – the nature/nurture debate.

THE NATURE/NURTURE DEBATE

On the one hand, psychologists who believe in the nature side of the debate would argue that much of our behaviour is determined by individuals themselves, largely by genetic and hereditary factors. On the other hand, psychologists who believe in the nurture side of the argument suggest that all behaviour is the result of environmental influences. Intelligence and personality are key concepts within this debate. In relation to these concepts, the question arises, is intelligence determined by genetic make-up and hereditary factors, or is it largely determined by the environment and the way in which individuals learn through that environment?

This is not an idle debate, for its concerns will influence not only the way that we view people and their behaviour, but also the methods we use to study that behaviour and the resulting analysis of data. Consider this in relation to motivating individuals in the workplace. If you consider that an individual's motivation is largely a function of hereditary and genetic factors, how could you, as a manager, use that knowledge to increase motivation? Similarly, if you think that motivation is largely a function of environmental influences, how could you use that knowledge to increase motivation? In this latter case, it is clear that, as a manager, you would need to investigate the exact environmental influences that act as motivators and attempt to provide these in the workplace. It may be that allowing people to work in groups or as teams will motivate individuals, or that changing the levels of heat in the workplace will achieve the same outcome. There are many theories of motivation and consequent models that suggest how to motivate people. Perhaps the most notable one in a work context is that of Herzberg (1968). Once you have isolated the influences in the environment that are of importance to individuals, it has to be recognized that there may be some that are difficult to change, for example, heat in a kitchen. Similarly, it may become a problem if what motivates one person does not motivate another. As a manager, it would be necessary to evaluate the strengths and weaknesses of change under these conditions.

Students should be able to see that this debate is one of extremes and, for a full explanation of human behaviour, it might be that some integration of the ideas is needed. If this is the case, then the determinants of behaviour are a combination of individual factors and environmental influences. Intuitively, this would seem to be more appropriate than either extreme. If we consider our own behaviours, we like to think of ourselves as having some control over them (i.e. our nature); we can also see, however, that the environment does determine the way we behave in some contexts.

ALTERNATIVE EXPLANATIONS OF HUMAN BEHAVIOUR

Humanities and common sense

Some aspects of the relationship between the natural and social sciences have already been discussed. Weber's contribution to the debate has led us to consider the differences between the natural and the social sciences. However, although we have emphasized some of the differences, we should also recognize the similarities between the two, for these have implications for the study of human behaviour.

Before turning our attention to this issue, however, it is worth identifying some key differences between the social sciences and other perspectives which offer explanations of people's behaviour. One such perspective is provided by the humanities, the other we will call the common sense approach.

The body of academic disciplines, which are regarded as the humanities, concerns itself with the study of human behaviour. Indeed, the humanities have close links with the natural and social sciences because of their origins in moral philosophy (Duverger, 1964). Since its inception, this body of disciplines has grown to include areas such as literature, drama, essay writing and poetry, providing a rich source of information and insight about human behaviour. However, the differentiating feature between the natural and social sciences, and the humanities lies both in the ways in which human behaviour is researched and in the way in which it is understood.

The key point here, is that in the humanities, the approach to the study of human behaviour is based upon personal interpretations and values of the author. Any conclusions drawn thus depend upon that author's perspective, talent and intellect. Given that these explanations and interpretations are essentially those of the author, it becomes difficult to generalize to other people's behaviour. In other words, if an interpretation is based solely upon one opinion, it is difficult to say that it can apply to other people and the way that other people behave. This occurs, despite the fact that a novel often appears to have a universal theme.

Furthermore, in the tradition of the novel, authors are noted for their originality of viewpoints and interpretations, novels generally not involving research methodologies or material that could be tested by somebody else. Replicability and valid research methods are essential to the natural and social sciences (Winch, 1988). As we will see, methods in the social sciences are specifically designed to allow other researchers to test the approaches and the validity of the conclusion.

If we now think about the common sense approach to the study of behaviour, we are in an area where students often experience difficulty. Understanding the relationship between common sense and the social sciences is perhaps one of the first steps in being able to form a social scientific explanation (Atkinson, McArthy and Phillips, 1987). Common sense views of the world are those that we each make and evolve in our day-to-day experience and existence. This again restates the complexity of the social sciences, because the researchers are, in this sense, part of the subject matter. Social scientists exist in the world and form ideas and perceptions as a result of interaction with other people and objects. Clearly, when we undertake social scientific analysis, according to Giddens (1992), research findings both disturb and contribute to our common sense beliefs about the nature of the world.

Social scientific findings do not always contradict common sense views, but they may do so (Giddens, 1992). However, common sense ideas often provide sources of insight about social behaviour. Having said this, we must always ask if our beliefs are really so, if our beliefs about the world are the same as someone else's, if we can predict or understand another person's behaviour as a result of our perceptions.

Additionally, much of what strays into our common sense perspectives about people and events has, in fact, been the subject of social scientific research (Giddens, 1992). Using the example of food preferences once more, we know from sociological research that individual preferences do vary from society to society. In the common sense approach, we may have experienced different cultures, or have discussed the eating preferences of other cultures with colleagues. However, we have to keep in mind the problem of subjectivity.

The use of words, language and value judgements

Further problems exist when using scientific as opposed to common sense terms for explanation. As will be expanded upon later, social sciences often draw words and terms from everyday language. However, within the social science disciplines the terms acquire a precise meaning; they have been defined and classified in a particular way as a description of some feature of social reality. As such, social sciences intend a boundary to be drawn around what can be included within a particular term. This not only legitimately excludes some areas from the research, but it also allows social scientists some consensus as to the subject which is being studied and discussed. Having said this, social scientists may still disagree with the definition of terms, for example the terms personality and intelligence, as implied in psychometric testing for personnel selection, may be defined in different ways by different psychologists.

Within the social sciences, these terms are called concepts and are important in labelling aspects of the social world. When offering social scientific explanations, it is important to ensure that the use of a term as a concept is differentiated from its use in common language; the two may be dissimilar. Consider the way in which you would normally use the terms intelligence and personality. Then consider the following definitions. Consider how the similarities or differences between your definition and that given may result in very different understandings of human behaviour. Intelligence has many definitions supplied by different authors. However, one definition might be that given by Terman – 'The ability to carry on abstract thinking' – cited in Radford and Govier (1980).

Personality is 'The set of individual characteristics which makes each person unique' (Hayes and Orrell, 1987, p. 401). If we now consider in more depth the definition given of personality, if this definition is applied, then how can we say that two people have similar personalities? The issue of defining personality within psychology is, in fact, a complex one. There are many different approaches to personality that depend upon the perspective taken by the author. Similarly with the term 'social class'. In surveys of the term, individuals usually cite accent as an indicator of class membership. However, in sociological studies, the term usually excludes subjective variables, such as accent, in favour of variables such as inequality (Reid, 1989).

A further issue concerning the common sense approach lies in its relationship to opinions. Social scientific explanations and approaches attempt to avoid the inclusion of individual opinions, as they can be biased and one-sided. Opinions often reflect prejudice and false assumptions, the result being that they may be ill-informed, partial and inappropriate. Such an example is provided by the statement 'all waiters fiddle' (this term represents a range of behaviours which can include eating food left over from functions and taking drinks without paying for them; its use varies in different parts of the country, but is described by Mars and Nicod (1984) as pilfering – differentiated from theft).

As an expression of opinion, this kind of approach is intuitive and causes problems when students include such statements in an analysis. It generalizes from particular observations and experiences and perpetuates social stereotypes. Such a statement as 'all waiters fiddle' could in no way be construed as being socially scientific. Consider briefly the problems involved in testing this statement to prove its truth. Every waiter in the world would have to be observed and, clearly, this in itself is an impossible task. Similarly, all waiters would have to be watched at all points in time, just in case their behaviour should change, and they no longer all fiddle. Clearly, a social stereotype has been evoked and a generalization has been drawn from this which is incapable of being tested. Social scientific statements are, by contrast, drawn from testable statements.

Following on from the issue of testability, the common sense approach is linked to the issue of value judgements. People make value judgements when they express a preference or view based upon their own values and beliefs, for example the statement 'McDonald's sells good burgers'. The term 'good' in this statement, is a value judgement, as it implies the values of the speaker concerning burgers. Other individuals may disagree with the statement. The point is that because the term 'good burgers' is an evaluative statement, it cannot be tested or researched, at least not without some established consensus view on what criteria are being implied in the term 'good burger', i.e. is this to do with size, type of filling, etc? A social scientific approach would restate the question in a more testable, non-evaluative way: What are the factors of importance in choosing to eat McDonald's burgers? If this were researched appropriately, it would avoid the problems associated with using terms for which there are no criteria which are open to measurement.

Within the social sciences, when terms include value judgements they are called subjective, that is they include the values of the subject (Atkinson, McArthy and Phillips, 1987). Clearly researching aspects of other people's behaviour and, therefore, their values, requires a great deal more sophistication than the questionnaire approach which is often used by hospitality companies. As we will see later, questionnaires are often an inappropriate research method to gain knowledge about people's values. Yet many research areas require just this type of knowledge to explain behaviour. For example, individuals' perceptions of fast food brands and the values which individuals hold about hotels, all fit into this area of investigation and are necessary areas of research for hotel and catering.

Value judgements should not intrude into the research process or the interpretation of research findings (Giddens, 1992). The history of social scientific research has, in many ways, been concerned with differentiating between fact and value. Factual statements are those which can be tested and proved true or false. It is useful to illustrate this issue with an example: 'How many bedrooms has the London Cumberland Hotel?'

This is a very different kind of statement from those which imply value judgements. The number of bedrooms can be quantified and agreed upon, unlike the goodness of the rooms, the quality of the rooms, or the goodness of McDonald's burgers.

For social scientific research to be adequate, authors may be understandably committed to a particular subject area, holding passionate views about this subject, for example, career progression of female hotel managers. However they must not allow value judgements to bias the research process.

Hopefully, you will now be gaining some idea of what constitutes a social scientific statement. At the same time, some people might doubt the exactness of the social sciences. Given the area of value judgements and the relationship of the researcher to the subject matter it is hardly surprising. Since the outset of the social sciences there has always been debate on the problems of studying human beings, exactly what the relationship between researcher and researched should be, and exactly what constitutes scientific research (Winch, 1988).

In order to answer fully the question of the possibility of a science of human behaviour, we will return to the similarities between the natural and the social sciences. There are two important similarities between these sciences that are of interest to us here: they are both concerned with the use of scientific method, and the use of theory to inform interpretations.

SCIENTIFIC METHOD

Starting with scientific method, both natural and social sciences are involved in observing facts and forming hypotheses to explain them. Also both sciences usually devise experiments or research methods that confirm or reject these hypotheses. The results from such studies lead to conclusions which can be generalized (Winch, 1988).

In the natural sciences the search for cause and effect relationships forms the basis for prediction and the development of laws. We noted the problems of prediction in the study of human behaviour earlier.

Scientific study involves empirical methods backed by unbiased recording and impartial observations. Adopting scientific methods means that the research process is identified and can be replicated by other researchers. As Winch (1988) notes, scientific methods are used by both natural and social scientists, and given that this is the case he sees no reason why the study of human behaviour cannot be considered scientific. Basically, the question of the scientific validity of studying human behaviour depends upon how science is defined.

SUMMARY

By highlighting the differences between the humanities, common sense and the social sciences, we hope to have demonstrated that only the social sciences offer us the possibility of establishing a rigorous basis for the study of human behaviour. Alternative explanations can serve as the basis for further study, but only the social sciences, through their theories, concepts and methods, can provide us with the possibility of more general explanations of human behaviour. This should become even clearer when we consider the role of theories and concepts in the study and explanation of human behaviour in the next chapter.

DISCUSSION QUESTIONS

1. Describe the main focus of the discipline of psychology, and of the discipline of sociology.
2. Identify situations within hospitality contexts where a knowledge of psychology, sociology or both, may be used to understand and explain people's behaviour.
3. What is a value judgement? Describe the utility of a value judgement in understanding behaviour.
4. Compare and contrast explanations of behaviour based in the humanities, common sense, and the social sciences.

FURTHER READING

Gross. R. (1992) *Psychology: The Science of Mind and Behaviour* (2nd edn), Hodder & Stoughton. This is an excellent introduction to the main areas of psychology. The text outlines the nature and scope of psychology, and locates different branches of psychology in relation to each other. It is an accessible book, and widely used as both an A-level and first-year undergraduate text.

Giddens, A. (1992) *Sociology* (2nd edn), Polity Press, Oxford. This is an excellent introduction to the main areas of sociology. It is written in an accessible style, and brings out issues and themes of sociology using everyday examples. Giddens presents his ideas in an interesting manner, and raises crucial debates within sociology again at an A-level and first year undergraduate standard.

Bottomore T. and Nisbett, R. (eds) (1978) *The History of Sociological Analysis,* Heinemann, Oxford. This is a book of readings covering the major strands and themes in sociology. The text aims to outline the historical development of sociology by addressing key areas in a thorough yet succinct manner. It is a useful text for those readers wishing to pursue debates in depth.

REFERENCES

Aron, R. (1967) *Main Currents in Sociological Thought* (volumes 1 and 2), Penguin, London.

Atkinson, G.B., McArthy, B. and Phillips, K.M. (1987) *Studying Society: An Introduction to Social Science*, Oxford University Press, Oxford.

Bottomore, T. and Nisbet, R. (eds) (1978), *The History of Sociological Analysis*, Heinemann, Oxford.

Brown, G. and Brown, L.D. (1975) *A Survey of the Social Sciences*, McGraw Hill, New York.

Dunleavy, P. (1986) *Studying for a Degree*, Macmillan, London.

Duverger, M. (1964) *Introduction to the Social Sciences*, Allen and Unwin, London.

Giddens, A. (1992) *Sociology* (2nd edn), Polity Press, Oxford.

Hayes, N. and Orrell, S. (1987) *Psychology: An Introduction*, Longman, London and New York.

Herzberg, F. (1968) *Work and the Nature of Man*, Staples Press, London.

Mars, G. (1982) *Cheats at work, an anthropology of workplace culture*, Allen and Unwin, London.

Mars, G. and Nicod, M. (1984) *The World of Waiters*, Allen and Unwin, London.

Mennell, S. (1988) *All Manners of Food: Eating and Taste in England and France from the Middle Ages to the Present*, Basil Blackwell, Oxford.

Mennell, S. (1992) *The Sociology of Food, Eating, Diet and Culture*, Sage, London.

Open University (1976) *Social Science: Making Sense of Society*, Open University, Milton Keynes.

Radford, J. and Govier, E. (eds) (1980) *A Textbook of Psychology*, Sheldon Press, London.

Reid, I. (1989) *Social Class Differences in Britain* (3rd edn), Fontana, London.

Trigg, R. (1985) *Understanding Social Science: A Philosophical Introduction to the Social Sciences*, Blackwell, Oxford.

Winch, P. (1988) *The Idea of a Social Science and its Relation to Philosophy*, Routledge, London.

Theories and concepts | 3

CENTRAL THEMES AND ISSUES

The nature and role of theories

One of the key themes that emerges from the historical development of the social sciences concerns the role that theory plays in the understanding, and interpretation, of human behaviour.

One of the first problems that is faced here is concerned with the fact that social scientists are expected to use words and terms that have precise definitions yet, in everyday language, they may have meanings incongruent with these scientific ones (Atkinson, McCarthy and Phillips, 1987). This has already been referred to with respect to social scientific and common sense explanations. For example, ideas about motivation might be described as 'alright in theory but not in practise', 'theoretically speaking' might refer to an idea being thought of in a hypothetical sense.

A second problem is that theory is often used in an attempt to increase the value of a statement. It seems that, somehow, there is more credence to putting forward theoretical propositions than mere facts. Connected to this problem is the notion that some statements put forward as theory are not really theory, but are either statements of simple or complex facts.

A third problem, the opposite of the latter, is that theory is often used to reduce the value of statements by indicating its opposition to practice.

These difficulties can be explained by looking at the historical derivation of the word 'theory'. Williams (1983), traces the development of the word through a number of different stages. The earliest English form of the word – theorique – emerged in the fourteenth century followed by the appearance of the actual word 'theory' in the sixteenth century. The range of meanings associated with the word at that time appeared to include mental conception, contemplation and spectacle. By the seventeenth century, the term theory was used to include the following meanings:

- spectacle – 'a theory or sight';
- a contemplated sight – 'the true theory of death when I contemplate a skull' (Browne, 1643, *in* Williams, 1983);
- a scheme, of ideas – 'to execute their owne theorie in this Church' (Hooker, 1592 *in* Williams, 1983);
- an explanatory scheme – 'leave such theories to those that study meteors' (1638, *in* Williams, 1983).

The distinction between theory and practice became widely known through the work of Bacon in the seventeenth century, where he stated that philosophy is divided into two parts, namely speculative and practical (1657); 'only pleasing in the theory but not in the practice' (1664); and 'theory without practice will serve but for little' (1692) (*in* Williams, 1983).

The nineteenth century saw a further development of the use and meaning of the word, which Williams (1983) identifies as

- a theory is a scheme of ideas which explains practice.

This is important, as it suggests that theory is always, by necessity, related to practice, that there must always be a relationship between actions, observations and explanations of these (Cohen, 1968). If a theory is, indeed, to be seen as a scheme of ideas that explains practice, exactly what does this mean, and why is it important for individuals within a hotel and catering tradition to use theories?

Clearly, a theory is a method or tool for relating facts or observable phenomena, for trying to explain events in the world and human behaviour. A theory, however, must go beyond those facts. If it is to be explanatory in a general sense, it must be about whole categories of events, in the form of general statements concerning characteristics of events. It must be expressed in the form of universal categories and cannot relate to one, or several events only, but must relate to universal phenomena (Cohen, 1968). For example, 'I have seen a leaf falling' is a simple fact, a belief statement concerning the nature of an event which has occurred. 'I have often seen leaves falling' constitutes a more complex fact, stating a relationship between one event and another. In a sense, however, this is still only a belief statement of events that have been observed; it describes events, but allows no prediction or explanation.

In contrast, 'All leaves must fall' constitutes a theory or a theoretical statement. It represents a general proposition about all leaves, which cannot be observed by one person only and which posits a universal relationship between events. From this predictive, universal, statement, hypotheses can be formed and tested.

Essentially, much of the research carried out in the hotel and catering industry is fact-gathering research. Similarly, for example, many of the statistical reports prepared for the hotel and catering industry (Mintel, Euromoniter, etc.) are fact-gathering journals. The major difficulty with these studies is that they are only, and can only be, descriptive. Description does not explain, nor can it predict, future events. Thus, even if we have the results of a study detailing the number of customers entering a particular restaurant on a particular day of the week, what exactly does that tell us? It cannot tell us why those people entered the restaurant, nor can it assist in a prediction about whether or not they will do so in the future.

Therefore, to describe and explain human behaviour accurately, we must use a theoretical perspective. An example of this is W.F. Whyte's (1947) analysis of the social structure of the restaurant. In this study he used the concept of social structure to understand a range of issues influencing the organization and behaviour of people in restaurants. The use of the concept of social structure allows Whyte's analysis to be replicated and tested in other types of restaurant. This approach means that we can make general statements about restaurants and the behaviour of people within them. This would not be possible if observations of behaviour were made without the use of a theoretical framework.

The collection of data en masse with no reference to rationale, or reason for investigation, with no hypotheses to be tested, all too often results in the accumulation of data which are virtually redundant, and which certainly cannot contribute to the formulation or reformulation of theory. Again, this is a feature of many research reports in the hotel and catering industry.

Theories then, are complex sets of interrelated statements which attempt to explain observed phenomena (Cohen, 1968). Theories allow testable predictions to be made or inferred – these predictions are given in the form of hypotheses which are the forms in which theories are tested and proved or refuted. It should be noticed that whole theories can never been tested in research; rather it is the hypotheses drawn from these theories that are tested. A hypothesis is, thus, a statement drawn from the general theory that proposes a relationship between particular events. This can be illustrated by the following examples.

- *Theory:* All leaves must fall.
- *Hypothesis*: Leaf A, or leaves A,B,C on a tree will fall.

- *Theory*: Individuals are motivated to work by money.
- *Hypothesis*: If I pay an individual more money they will work harder.

Again, it is useful to remember that this explanation of theory and hypothesis-testing is not abstract, it is related to everyday life and events. As individuals, we constantly seek universal principles or relationships between events to make everyday life possible. We all have a scheme of ideas which, for example, explains and predicts human social conduct. Thus, I do not speak whilst another is speaking; I do not throw my plate at a waiter in a restaurant and so on. If I and others behave in accordance with this scheme of ideas it will perpetuate itself – my reality testing confirms my hypothesis and scheme. If, on the other hand, individuals behave in such a way as to disprove my hypothesis, it would necessitate a reformulation of a scheme of ideas. Consider, for example, what it would be like to swop cultures for a day, and to experience a set of behaviours never contemplated previously.

Cohen (1968) suggests that there are a number of different types of theory: analytical, normative, scientific and metaphysical.

Analytical theories

These usually occur in the realms of logic and mathematics and are not necessarily connected to reality. They may be said to be sets of statements which, by definition, are true and from which all other statements are denied. It may be useful to remember that a logically valid statement is not, however, necessarily an appropriate one, i.e. all birds can fly; an emu is a bird, therefore, an emu can fly.

Normative theories

These usually elaborate a set of ideal states towards which an individual can, or must aspire. For example the 'subjective expected utility' theory in decision-making, which puts forward an optimal method of human decision-making. It is, again, interesting to note how research progresses here – from a combination of descriptive and normative theories emerged prescriptive theories, i.e. 'decision analysis'. This attempts to incorporate knowledge of individual decision-makers' weaknesses, with conditions of optimal decision-making to culminate in a decision tool designed to aid human decision-makers.

Scientific theory

This is concerned with universal empirical statements asserting a relationship between two or more types of events. This relationship is put forward as a causal relationship, i.e. a hypothesis from a scientific theory would be put forward in the form 'If X occurs then Y occurs', or 'if A then B'. In other words the hypothesis states that 'X causes Y', 'A causes B'.

In many instances, because of the nature of human beings, it is impossible to state a certain causal relationship. Results or possible relations between events would, therefore, usually be expressed in the form of probabilities or levels of significance. One could test the hypothesis 'After ten pints of beer an individual will slur their words', and the result would be expressed as 'Yes to $p = 0.05$'. This means the relationship between beer and slurring words has been demonstrated to within 5% margin of error or chance.

Metaphysical theories

These are, by their nature, not necessarily testable and, therefore, have an ambiguous role to play in scientific enquiry. They concern the nature of knowledge itself and, whilst they may not be subject to empirical testing, are subject to rational appraisal. The use of metaphysical theories may be to direct, define parameters for, and provide ways of, interpreting alternative theoretical perspectives.

Thus the role of theory in the study of human behaviour can be summarized as follows. Theories are a tool by which individuals may investigate, explain and predict events or behaviours. They must relate to classes of phenomena, rather than individual instances, to allow for a capacity for generalization and prediction. In the social sciences, it is not uncommon to encounter ideas which are expressed as theories. Some of these may not actually be theories in the scientifically testable sense, nor may they, in fact, contain any notion of causality. These approaches may come closer to models or perspectives about behaviour. For example, systems theory is widely used on hotel and catering courses. It is used both to study organizations and as an analytical tool for understanding catering operations.

SYSTEMS THEORY IN A HOSPITALITY CONTEXT

Systems theory revolves around the idea that organizations can be seen as a series of interdependent parts. Changes in one part of the system will necessarily have implications for other parts of the system. For example, a hotel as an organization will consist of a series of sub-systems, such as food and beverage, housekeeping, reception, maintenance, etc. Changes in one of those sub-systems (e.g. an unexpected plane cancellation or 100 extra customers requiring accommodation) will bring about changes in the food and beverage and housekeeping sub-system, as they will have to cater for the additional customers. Systems theory, therefore, allows managers to predict in advance what kinds of effects changes in one part of the system may have on the other parts.

Studying hotels as systems also allows managers to take account of the environment in which their hotel is located, as system theory models identify the need for regular feedback into the system from the environment. The models indicate that the system must be kept in a steady state, hence feedback and monitoring will always be necessary. If feedback is not received, the system will not be able to accommodate changes and negative entropy will result. Organisms or systems which do not take account of changes in the environment are called closed systems and their long-term survival or success may be jeopardized by failing to adapt to the changing environment. For example, an organization that does not take account of changing customer tastes or the impact of economic recession, clearly takes the risk of losing its market share.

Studying organizations as systems also allows managers to take an overview of their organization or hotel in relation to problems within the subsystems, e.g. the management of conflict between departments. Additionally, authors of systems models have developed sociotechnical systems, which draw attention to the relationship between work groups and the technical components of the work. This has been important in raising issues of job design and matching particular work groups to the specific technology.

This brief summary of systems theory is designed to show the way in which theories allow the social scientist to abstract the issue from the area of study and to apply it to models which can assist in explanation. The main purpose of this is to allow for some degree of prediction to occur, in the sense that knowing that X will change implies some change in Y.

Using models or theories of behaviour allows us to generalize from one unit or system to another. Thus, we use a theoretical framework to allow us to talk about classes of phenomena, e.g. hotels. This theoretical framework may then show us that the results we find are not universal. Hotels at different market levels, or of different sizes, do not reveal the same patterns, which allows us to refine our theories. Without a theoretical framework to shape our collection of data, we can only collect and analyse data which are relative to the particular sample we are studying. For example, without a theoretical framework, we can observe staff pilfering at a particular hotel, at a particular point in time, but can go no further in generalizing about the phenomenon of occupational theft. However, if we started out with a theoretical framework concerned with the notion of group dynamics in occupational theft, we could use a theory to test the phenomenon in a wider range of hotels, thereby drawing conclusions about pilfering and generalizing to a wider context.

There is a further class of ideas that can be used as tools for investigation and explanation in the social sciences – these are known as concepts.

THE NATURE AND ROLE OF CONCEPTS

Concepts, conceptual frameworks and models are further terms used in the social sciences. Confusion often exists as to the relationships that these words have to theory. Are they the same thing? If not, what differentiates them from theory and how are they to be used? Again, in many senses this confusion is hardly surprising and you will find that these questions form another philosophical debate within the social sciences.

It seems simplest to attempt to elaborate on this debate by summarizing the role of theory, attempting to define what a concept is and by providing the reader with an example to illustrate the points made.

Trigg (1985) differentiates between three key terms, suggesting that:

- theory, in science, refers to a system of laws and hypotheses which attempt to explain and predict observable phenomena;

- concepts are the way we think of things and pick them out; they can be shared and are sometimes identified with words in a language (Dunleavy, 1986);
- 'theory laden' is any word or concept which can only be understood within the context of a particular theory (Cohen, 1968) and cannot normally be used within another theory without a significant change in meaning.

Clearly, all this suggests that concepts are inextricably linked to theory and, in fact, arise out of theories. Concepts, therefore, appear to be a further tool by which we can classify, categorize and label various aspects of human behaviour.

So far we have talked about theories as being schemes of ideas, as being general universal statements suggesting relationships between events in the world of human behaviour. It has been suggested that it is impossible to test out whole theories. Concepts are drawn from theories in an attempt to define parameters or boundaries within which we can investigate behaviour (Dunleavy, 1986). Thus, they are a method of limiting what can be included in particular areas of study. They can be viewed as a tool by which parts of theories can be formulated into testable and manageable chunks, so that specific hypotheses can be formulated and tested.

Just as it is argued that an investigation of human behaviour cannot proceed without theory, it is also difficult to see how investigations into behaviour, and their consequent actions, could be undertaken without the use of concepts. For example, how could an organization expand its markets into different countries without some knowledge of the concept of culture? How could sectors of the brewing industry operate without a knowledge of the concept of leisure? The question of the range and utility of particular concepts will be addressed later, but it is clear that they can encompass a broad range of behaviours and issues (e.g. culture, leisure), or that they can be far more specific and precise (e.g. span of management, authority).

Consider a management problem within an organization – what tools or frameworks can the social sciences offer to assist explanation and prediction of behaviour?

THEORIES AND CONCEPTS IN ORGANIZATIONS

It is difficult to think of any management course which does not include organization theory as part of its syllabus. This realm of knowledge originates from social scientific thought. But what exactly does it mean? What concepts does it include and of what use are they?

The first issue to consider in line with the approach taken in this book, would be organization theory in a historical perspective. However, since there are many introductory texts that give a full account of the historical background of organization theory, it is sufficient for us to say that it is essentially a body of knowledge and ideas used to study organizations, and that the theories have developed hand in hand with management practice over the past century. This is an important point, since it re-emphasizes the argument that theory and practice are necessarily interlinked.

Bowey (1976) defines organization theory as

> The science of human behaviour in organisations, it is concerned with understanding, explaining and predicting behaviour in organisations.

This immediately introduces two questions:

- How do we explain, understand and predict human behaviour?
- What is an organization; how can an organization be defined?

An organization can be seen to be a social scientific concept. It is not merely a building within which individuals are found to be interacting with each other, but rather the term is used to classify and categorize particular forms of activity and particular forms of relationships between individuals. Thus, Buchanan and Huczynski (1985) define an organization as 'social arrangements for the controlled performance of collective goals'.

Silverman (1970) suggests that there are three distinguishing features of organizations:

- an organization is a consciously established artefact with a set of rules and goals which may be displaced over time;
- it is characterized by a pattern of relationships;
- attention is paid to planned changes in social relationships.

The use of the word organization in everyday language gives rise to some of these features and, in a sense, points to the idea that it is, in fact, a concept. It is a label attached to something in the realm of human behaviour that indicates particular forms of activity in particular spheres of life. It can also be seen that the concept of organization itself gives rise to further concepts. Each time this occurs, the concepts become more clearly defined and the boundaries for research become tighter. This is illustrated in the following diagram.

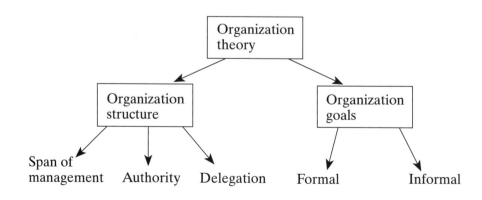

It is worth remembering that these concepts are not divorced from management practice. Organization structure is concerned with the nature of the relationships between individuals within an organization, which leads to such ideas as the organization chart. In addition, organization goals might be stated in the form of management objectives, or in the overall form of the mission statement.

In some ways, this is an example that oversimplifies the nature of the relationship between theories and concepts and their applicability. It would seem to imply a homogeneous, non-conflicting approach to organizations and behaviour within them. However, this would be misleading as there may, in fact, be little consensus as to the nature of concepts other than the words which label them. Again, it should become clear that such dispute is to be expected – a set of alternative theoretical propositions initially will provide very different ideas as to the nature of concepts and the ways in which they should be investigated. Thus, in the case of organizations, students will find that an action theory approach (Silverman, 1970) will emphasize different concepts and techniques for investigation than either a structural approach (Blau and Schoenherr, 1971), or a systems approach, or a contingency approach (Burns and Stalker, 1966).

Students should now understand that a key feature of the social sciences is the way in which concepts and theories are the starting point in explaining behaviour.

SUMMARY

We have described the nature and role of theories and concepts in the understanding and explanation of human behaviour. Theories are causal statements relating various aspects of behaviour that allow us to predict and empirically test behaviour. Concepts are drawn from theories and they set parameters for the analysis of behaviour. Concepts can be seen as labels that are attached to particular forms of behaviour or phenomena, which allow researchers to define and investigate behavioural issues. Crucially the use of theory and concepts in the investigation of human behaviour means that research can be applied in a general sense, rather than to one instance of behaviour in a particular time and space.

Within hotel and catering courses students are required to use concepts to interpret and explain events. For example, within human resource management modules, students will study the size, nature and structure of the hotel and catering labour force. Statistical reports will allow trends analysis to be undertaken in this area. However, when it comes to issues of recruitment and retention, motivation and labour turnover, explanations of both causes and effects cannot be undertaken without reference to conceptual frameworks. Labour market theory can be used to analyse issues such as occupational segregation, skill shortages and employment opportunities with respect to gender and race, for example. Using this approach allows the identification of the cause and effects of issues, such as labour turnover, to be studied. In turn, this will allow students a more rigorous framework within which to develop recruitment and retention strategies in specific sectors of the hotel and catering industry.

It is appropriate at this point to recognize that we are, in fact, presenting only one perspective on the nature and role of theories. We are suggesting that the 'deductive' method in the social sciences is the most appropriate for students on hospitality management courses. There is, however, another perspective on theories which involves inductive explanation. We would suggest that this approach is not appropriate for students in hotel and catering courses; it is identified in the further reading for those who wish to investigate further.

DISCUSSION QUESTIONS

1. Outline the nature and characteristics of theories and concepts.
2. Evaluate the utility of statistical reports in the hospitality industry.
3. 'Academic theory is of little use to a manager within a hotel or catering organization'. Discuss.
4. What is the value of systems theory to the manager of a restaurant?

FURTHER READING

Trigg, R. (1985) *Understanding Social Science*, Blackwell, Oxford. This is an excellent text exploring and discussing issues and themes in the social sciences. Trigg presents arguments surrounding the nature and role of theories and concepts in a comprehensive yet understandable manner.

Buchanan, D.A. and Huczynski, A.A. (1985) *Organisational Behaviour*, Prentice Hall, London and New York. This is a good general introduction to organizational studies.

REFERENCES

Atkinson, G.B.J., McCarthy, B. and Phillips, K.M. (1987) *Studying Society*, Oxford University Press, Oxford.

Blau, P.M. and Schoenherr, R.A. (1971) *The Structure of Organisations*, Basic books, London.

Bowey, A.M. (1976) *The Sociology of Organisations*, Hodder & Stoughton, London.

Buchanan, D.A. and Huczynski, A.A. (1985) *Organisational Behaviour*, Prentice Hall, London and New York.

Burns, T. and Stalker, G.M. (1966) *The Management of Innovation*, Tavistock Publications, London.

Cohen, P. (1968) *Modern Social Theory*, Heinemann, London.

Dunleavy, P. (1986) *Studying for a Degree in the Humanities and Social Sciences*, Macmillan Education, Basingstoke.

Silverman, D. (1971) *The Theory of Organisations*, Heinemann, London.

Trigg, R. (1985) *Understanding Social Science*, Blackwell, Oxford.

Whyte, W.F. (1947) The social structure of the restaurant. *American Journal of Sociology*, pp. 302–310.

Williams, R. (1983) *Keywords* (2nd edn), Fontana, London.

Research methods and their application to the hospitality context

4

Aims

This chapter aims to:

1. illustrate social scientific research methods;
2. identify and illustrate the role of theory in its relation to research methods;
3. provide different examples of methods employed in hospitality research; and
4. provide a worked example of research through the issue of usage patterns of public houses.

Outcomes

At the end of this chapter you will be able to:

1. describe the variety and nature of research techniques;
2. identify the appropriate techniques for different research questions;
3. identify appropriate samples for research investigations; and
4. assess the strengths and weaknesses of different approaches in hospitality research.

RESEARCH METHODS

The previous chapter discussed the role of concepts and theories in investigating human behaviour. It should now be clear to the reader that concepts and theories play a vital role in the research process.

This section focuses on the role of the research methods in undertaking social scientific explanations. This will be achieved by focusing upon the types of research methods which social scientists use, by examining their strengths and weaknesses and by encouraging readers to select appropriate methodologies for the types of hospitality issues they may wish to investigate.

A puzzle

We will begin with a puzzle. You have come home from the pub one evening; it is dark. You enter the house and push the light switch down. Nothing happens.

Write down as many reasons as you can think of which might explain why the light has not come on. Be imaginative. Some of the things you may have written down are:

- wrong house;
- power cut;
- circuits have blown;
- electricity disconnected;
- not paid bill;
- dreaming;
- no light bulb;
- martians have landed and eaten the electricity;
- hamster has chewed through the wiring system.

Clearly, the above are all possible explanations of why the lights are not working. As such, we have been presented with an issue (light not working) and have gone on to generate hypotheses (or possible reasons) for the problem.

Hypotheses

The next step would be to test the hypotheses. In effect, we are trying to establish a relationship between two variables, i.e. no light, wrong house; no light, not paid bill, etc. It can be seen from this example, that there are two very different types of explanations given: those hypotheses that are testable and those that are not. First, we need to determine which hypotheses in the list it is possible to test and then go on to create some way of doing that. Selection of the hypotheses and subsequent testing will, thus, allow us to eliminate them one by one until, hopefully, we find an explanation that is justified. For example, we might test the hypothesis that there is a power cut by drawing the curtains and looking if any other lights are on in the neighbourhood. If there are, we could assume there has not been a power cut, eliminate that as a possibility and, therefore, move on to another hypothesis. Given the fact that we have already discussed the complexity of human behaviour, however, it should be apparent that even for the simplest of hypotheses it will be unusual to totally prove or disprove hypotheses (Popper, 1959).

In a sense, what we are doing when testing hypotheses or the relationship between two variables, is actually dealing with probabilities or likelihoods. Thus, what is the likelihood that A has affected B; what is the likelihood that the light has not come on because of a power cut? In social sciences, this probability is usually assessed as significant if it is likely that 95 times out of

100 this hypothesis is correct. In other words, you can see that even though we suggest a hypothesis is correct, there is still a 5% probability that the relationship occurred by chance.

Once the issue has been clarified, the next step is to select a theory or concept in order to carry out the research. The previous chapter has argued that theory selection is dependent upon the nature of the problem under study and, furthermore, that there is a clear link between the theory chosen and the means employed to test it.

Social scientists have developed a range of approaches and methods to study human behaviour, and we will examine the strengths and weaknesses of these.

TECHNIQUES FOR INVESTIGATING HUMAN BEHAVIOUR

The most commonly used techniques in the social sciences are:

- observation, participant or non-participant;
- interviews;
- questionnaires;
- experiments;
- case studies.

Experiments

Within the context of the hospitality industry, scientific experiments are, perhaps, the least likely techniques to be used. Conducting scientific experiments is, however, the technique which allows the most accurate testing of the relationships between variables. This method, used extensively in the area of experimental psychology, demands that we keep everything constant except the variables that are actually being tested. In other words, if we were interested in testing the hypothesis that drinking ten pints of beer influences reaction times, everything else in the world would be kept constant. The researcher would let one group of subjects drink ten pints of beer and one group not, looking for a difference in the reaction times of the two groups. The research is, thus, changing the **independent variable** (amount of beer drunk) and looking for any consequent change in the **dependent variable** (reaction times).

In the context of a hospitality course, you may become aware of the Hawthorne investigations. In these investigations, the researchers were concerned with examining the relationship between production and the physical environment, following on from the assumptions of Frederick Taylor. Taylor assumed that individuals were mainly restricted in their capacity to work by their physical environment. The researchers in the Hawthorne investigations, therefore, conducted a series of experiments which aimed to establish correlations between variables in the environment, i.e. heat, lighting, length of rest breaks and the productivity rates of the workers. These experiments made an important contribution to the study of human behaviour, since they revealed an interesting phenomenon – it did not appear that any of the variables in question affected productivity rates, since the rates increased no matter what was changed. This seems unusual since workers' rest breaks could be shorter and the temperature colder, yet productivity still rose. This led the researchers to suggest that, in fact, individuals change their behaviour when they are aware that they are being watched (the Hawthorne effect).

These experiments were conducted on a large sample and were replicated many times. However, we would not expect that students engage in this sort of investigation as part of their course. There is, though, the possibility to conduct smaller experiments, for example in training restaurants. It might be useful in understanding the strengths and weaknesses of this technique for students to investigate customers' responses to different types of music, lighting, decor and restaurant layout.

Clearly, experiments can yield valuable insights into human behaviour. Responses from individuals can be evaluated at close quarters and they can give feedback which may be useful to the researchers. On the negative side, experiments do raise issues of both control and ethics. To begin with, it is extremely difficult to control all the variables which may occur in an experiment and, if this can done, it is then difficult to keep them all constant. Second, it is particularly difficult in a laboratory setting to make experiments meaningful and realistic, which brings the technique into question in terms of ecological validity. To use a restaurant example, if we were to investigate the effect of lighting on spend per head, all other variables would have to be kept constant, i.e. sounds, heat and the effect of only light on spend would be measured. Clearly, this will be extremely difficult, as individuals will have different reasons for using a restaurant, may have different disposable incomes and will perceive the conditions in different ways, anyway. This also highlights the ethical problems that can arise with experiments. How ethical is it to subject individuals to different extremes of light or heat? Despite the fact that social scientists have ethical codes of conduct, it is still an important issue to bear in mind with all research.

Observations

Observations are techniques used by both natural and social scientists and occur according to two types: participant observation and non-participant observation.

Non-participant observation is analogous to a fly on the wall. The researcher stands back from the subject to be investigated and observes the behaviour. This can be done either in the full knowledge of the subjects, i.e. sitting with a group, or without the subjects' knowledge via two-way mirrors, for example. This technique can be usefully employed to generate research ideas and form the basis of a hypothesis. For example, by observing social drinking in public houses, we may notice that there is an absence of female customers. This may lead us to hypothesize that female customers do not use public houses in the same way as males. We can now construct a methodology, which would need to be theory driven to allow us to test the hypothesis.

When using non-participant observation, it is usual to record what is observed, which can be done in a number of ways. The researcher can prepare a checklist of anticipated behaviours which will usually have been observed at a pilot stage of the study. As the investigation is underway, the researcher ticks off the behaviours as they occur and, thus, has a record of the number of times certain actions or verbal responses occur. Alternatively, the whole scene that is being observed can be recorded directly by using video equipment, which can later be used for analysis.

There are, of course, difficulties with both types of data collection. In the former instance, it may be difficult for the researcher to actually record all the behaviours as they occur. Even if this can be done, it may be that the researcher unwittingly records only selected items of behaviour, which would then appear over-represented in the final analysis. As a way of trying to overcome this problem, it is often useful to have more than one person present at the observation. A neutral observer and the researcher can independently note their observations, comparing their findings before analysis is undertaken.

In the case of directly recording the scene, it may be that individuals change their behaviour as a result of a camera being present. Methods of trying to overcome this problem include ensuring that the camera is as unobtrusive as possible, or allowing the group to be observed for some time, to get used to the presence of the camera. Examples where this might be an appropriate research technique in the hotel and catering industry may be in observing how many particular groups of people enter units and how individuals react to different forms of service in an outlet.

A major difficulty with non-participant observation involves the notion that individuals may change their behaviours if they are aware that they are being observed. It would be difficult, for example, to investigate the phenomenon of occupational theft using non-participant observation, if the subjects were aware of the observer. As a result, the researcher may choose to use participant observation.

Participant observation is the technique whereby the researcher actually takes part in the behaviour or group that is to be observed. Several examples of this form of research can be identified in the hotel and catering context, e.g. Smith (1981). In this study, Smith became a participant observer of behaviour in a public house in order to investigate issues of social drinking. To undertake such an investigation the researcher has to become a part of the group that is to be observed and, from this position, undertakes the research. There are advantages to this approach. Clearly, it is more likely that a member of a group will experience the whole of that group's activities and that the group will share all their ideas and activities with the researcher. However, there are clearly disadvantages as well. It is difficult for the researcher to remain objective in such situations, as he/she will necessarily develop an involvement with the group over time. It is also difficult to actually record behaviours and actions; often the researcher in this situation will have to carry a notebook around and write down information as the opportunities allow. Of course, the researcher also faces the real possibility of being found out by the group. Consider the dilemma that a researcher would be faced with if the study was concerned with occupational theft and the group discovered that one of their members was, in fact, somebody researching their behaviour.

Observation techniques, alone, do not allow identification of the meanings that individuals may attach to their behaviour. We may be able to observe customers eating in a restaurant 100 times, but still not be able to explain the significance of the meal occasion for them nor their expectations of the products, facilities and services.

Case studies

Most of you will become familiar with case studies as part of your course. Used as a research method in project work concerning hospitality issues, the approach is valuable in assessing areas such as the management of change. For example, a case study approach would be an appropriate method to investigate the impact of a company acquisition upon customers and staff. Ideally, this should not be retrospective, rather the organization should be investigated prior to, during and after the acquisition. In areas in which a process or strategy is being examined, case studies are highly appropriate. The launch of a new lager brand, or fast food item, the introduction of an equal opportunities policy in a hotel company all require analysis of the process of implementation, as well as the final outcome. This is because the process of implementation and how this is conducted is a key factor in achieving the desired outcome.

In the context of conducting hospitality projects, the access required by students to carry out the close investigations necessary for a successful case study may not always be granted. Before embarking upon such a project, researchers should take this into account. Consider, for example, the difficulties that might be encountered should a researcher wish to investigate the decision-making processes within a corporate board of an organization.

It is also necessary to remember the nature of case studies and the levels of explanation that they can offer. Often, unless they are used in conjunction with other methods, care must be taken in generalizing the results. What occurs in one company may be very different from that which occurs in another company. This is also true in transferring statistical analyses, or the conclusion of surveys from one company or country to another. Statistical analyses may be used in this way for comparative purposes, but the cultural context in which the material is gathered should not be ignored. For example, individuals' views about leisure products and leisure behaviour will be influenced by cultural contexts, thus, it would not make sense to make generalizations about superficial similarities between Germany and the UK.

Questionnaires

Questionnaires can be designed in a number of different ways. They can be highly structured, whereby the respondent is required to answer the questions in a pre-determined manner, or they can be loosely structured, whereby the respondent is allowed some freedom to elaborate on their answers. Questionnaires can be posted out to respondents, can be read out to people to gain responses, or can be left in a place where individuals can choose to fill them out. They can be used to gain information from relatively large samples of people and are often used in market surveys, or by hotel groups in gaining information relating to customer satisfaction. The precise format of the questionnaire depends on the information that is required, but one of the major problems with the questionnaire technique is in the development of the questionnaire itself. Questions must be asked in such a way as to elicit appropriate responses without leading the respondent in a particular direction. This must apply not only to the actual questions, but also to the overall structure of the questionnaire. Students are referred to literature on questionnaire design in the references and further reading.

Further difficulties with questionnaires include achieving an appropriate response rate. This is particularly the case with postal questionnaires and where questionnaires are left on a surface for customers to respond to at their will. Consider the number of guests in hotel rooms that will actually fill out a questionnaire; consider why some individuals will respond, but not others. It may be that only those customers with a grievance would respond, thus biasing the hotel's perception of the overall response by all guests. This also raises the question of the validity of the responses to questionnaires. How can the researcher be sure that the respondents are willing to supply all the information that is required, or indeed that the responses are honest ones?

Examples where questionnaires could be used in the hotel and catering context would be situations where a company is trying to estimate the population's awareness of a particular brand, or where organizations are trying to gather quantitative information with regard to the numbers of people using units and their patterns of usage.

Interviews

Just as a questionnaire can be structured or unstructured, an interview can be designed in similar ways. A structured interview occurs when an interviewer has a list of pre-prepared questions, which are asked of the respondent, with little scope for variation or elaboration. An unstructured interview occurs when the interviewer has a number of areas or themes that are to be explored, with perhaps one or two key questions to begin asking individuals about their ideas or opinions. Structured interviews can be used to gain relatively large amounts of information on a range of issues or aspects of an issue from individuals, whereas unstructured interviews can be used to gain in-depth information from individuals.

Again, there are strengths and weaknesses with this research technique. Interviews are similar to questionnaires in that they must be designed in a manner that does not lead the respondent in particular directions and, of course, again, they rely on the willingness of individuals to participate and to be honest in their answers. They do, however, allow the researcher to gain direct access to individuals and to probe answers for more in-depth information which the researcher may not have considered in the original question design.

Examples of situations in which interviews may be used in the hotel and catering context include asking individuals questions relating to their experiences of a service or outlet: asking a population how they consider that a product may be modified or improved.

What we have provided so far is a brief description of some techniques that are available to draw upon in investigations of human behaviour. We have argued that the use of social scientific methods in investigations is imperative to gain a full and informed understanding and explanation of human behaviour. Perhaps the most useful way to emphasize this point is to provide some examples as to how issues in hospitality may be best investigated and interpreted.

Consider the nature of patterns of social drinking in public houses. How might this be investigated? Following the research process outlined previously, the stages described in the next section may be appropriate. The researchers would follow these basic stages:

- *Identification of the issue:* usage patterns of public houses.
- *Development of a general statement:* usage patterns will vary over time and type of customer.
- *Development of hypothesis:* individuals use public houses in different ways.

IDENTIFICATION AND EVALUATION OF POSSIBLE RESEARCH TECHNIQUES

Experiment

This would not be ecologically valid, and it is hard to think exactly what would be tested and with whom in this case, anyway.

Case study

This could be done with one public house only and would clearly, therefore, not give us any generalizable results. It may, however, suggest useful avenues for further investigation.

Observation

Non-participant observation might be undertaken, where the researcher counts the numbers of people entering public houses and at what times. Alternatively, the researcher might observe behaviour from within the public house to ascertain what individuals were doing, etc. Clearly, however, information such as age, social class, occupation could not be determined accurately.

Questionnaire

The researcher might leave short questionnaires for customers to complete. Obvious difficulties include who is filling them in, truth of answers, representativeness of the respondents, etc. Alternatively, the researcher could actually ask the questions of respondents themselves.

Interviews

Used in conjunction with the questionnaire, the researcher can identify a sample of people and ask the questions from a previously compiled short, semi-structured sheet. This semi-structure will allow the gathering of uniform data, i.e. age, but will also allow respondents to add factors that they consider to be important and to elaborate on certain issues.

The unstructured interview may be used further after this initial stage has been undertaken, in order to gain depth on particular topics.

In this case then, the strengths and weaknesses of the various techniques have been identified in order to investigate the hypothesis. It seems most appropriate to use a short, semi-structured interview.

Before embarking upon writing the questions for this interview and putting the investigation into operation, there are a number of key or relevant terms in the research issue that need to be identified and defined. These are the definition of public houses and the definition of customers. This will enable us to consider the sample to be used. In this case, the population, or all the people who could possibly be included, will be all individuals who are of a legal age to drink in pubs.

The sample to be investigated, i.e. those people that will actually be questioned is, therefore, drawn from that population. This sample would be best divided on the basis of age, class and gender. Importantly, given that we are trying to investigate the usage patterns of public houses, it may be crucial to conduct the interviews over different times of the day, as public houses may attract different types of customers at different times and, indeed, different days of the week. This approach is appropriate to this particular case. However, in other studies it might be relevant to ask questions of non-users of the products or services as well as the users.

Questions that we may wish to ask (amongst others):

1. Sex   M/F
2. Age   18–25
           25–35
           35–45
           45+
3. Occupation
4. Marital status
5. Do you visit public houses?
6. Frequency of visits, per week
   lunchtime

early evening

late evening

7. Average spend

8. Reason for visit

business

other

9. Transport   car

                 bus

                 other

10. What drink lager

                 bitter

                 wines

                 spirits

It would be useful at this point for you to reflect upon the exact nature of this investigation.

QUESTIONS YOU SHOULD NOW BE ASKING

1. Is the issue testable?
2. Has the appropriate research technique been chosen?
3. Is the hypothesis answered in some way?
4. Exactly what does this information and these data tell us?

In this case, the answers would be

1. Yes
2. Yes
3. Yes
4. This information will tell us the nature of people using or not using public houses. It will tell us **who** uses, **how many** use, **when** people use public houses. The precise nature of the questionnaire obviously can give more or less detail, but essentially this investigation will provide only a **profile** of users and non-users of public houses.

The results might be, for example, that public houses are most heavily used by single males, between 18–45 years of age, for social reasons, the most popular drink being bitter. Whilst this may be useful information in itself, the point we are trying to stress is that this cannot explain why these patterns occur. The variables have not been isolated and tested explicitly to infer causality. In other words, we cannot say that single males tend to drink bitter in public houses because they want to be macho.

There are, thus, two distinctly different types of issue or problem that can be identified and investigated, those that ask the questions:

1. how many people, what kind of people in terms of age, class and when – which would generate interesting data, but can never explain why such behaviour occurs; and

2. why do those kinds of people engage in such behaviours – which allows explanation.

Clearly, again, it might be that the first investigation is carried out as a precursor to the second, in order to generate ideas and hypotheses.

It is crucial if you are trying to understand human behaviour, or to change human behaviour, to ask **why** people engage in various forms of behaviour. In relation to this example, why are certain people using public houses in certain ways at certain times?

It can be seen that the example so far has given us profiles of usage patterns, but can take us no further. We would not wish to imply, however, that empirical data of the aforementioned type are of no value. Clearly, this information can be of value to brewing companies and public house operators in terms of identifying trading patterns and assisting in the analysis of peak times and troughs in demand. In fact, a great deal of survey research into patterns of usage of public houses is of this type. It can also serve as the basis of hypothesis formation. For instance, in our example, the survey data might reveal that female consumption patterns differ from those of males.

To carry out sociological research to determine why this is so, we must adopt a frame of reference which can lead us beyond descriptive accounts of behaviour. This can be used as an example to generate further ideas.

Consider the possible concepts or conceptual frameworks that might be appropriate to take us further towards explaining why different patterns of public house usage might occur.

- More men than women use public houses – a conceptual framework may be gender.
- More individuals of a higher social class use public houses – a conceptual framework may be social class.

Hence, for explanations of human behaviour, the issue needs to be reformulated, a conceptual framework identified, a hypothesis generated with an indication of causal variables, a technique chosen, data collected and interpretations put forward.

If you refer to Chapter Two on theories and concepts, you will note that the starting point in conducting social scientific research is the adoption of a theoretical framework. In our example, the task is made easier because we have already established our frame of reference in terms of female customers. Following on from this we would examine the theoretical work undertaken in the area of gender. Our main purpose here is to draw upon theoretical analyses of gender which are appropriate to the context of women's consumption. In doing so, we would examine the structures which influence female leisure or, more exactly, non-work time, and female access to public institutions. Thus, we would be investigating the patriarchial and power structures which affect female behaviour and identifying social and cultural barriers which might operate in the context of consumption.

Factors of importance would include

1. the historical development of consumption and the ways in which public houses were historically dominated by males;

2. the acceptability of public houses as legitimate social spaces for women;
3. the role of social drinking in female networks; and
4. the class cultural codes and practices involved in female classifications of particular public house types.

The aforementioned points are capable of empirical testing and are able to furnish a causal analysis of gender dynamics in selecting and using public houses. A further area necessary to consider is the operating practices of brewing companies and the impact of these upon female consumption. These will relate to issues of design, layout, facilities, marketing and targeting.

Understanding the dynamics of public house usage and the barriers to consumption is the starting point in understanding the social drinking patterns of female customers from the operator's point of view. This should be a precursor to investment decisions in relation to refurbishment and marketing strategy. To date, operators initiatives towards increasing female usage have been directed towards the feminization of public houses, rather than focusing upon barriers to consumption, or the strategies that women have evolved to cope with these.

So far, we have assumed that given a conceptual framework with which to investigate an issue, and an appropriate methodological technique, researchers will be able to undertake their analysis. However, the questions then arise – who should be asked questions, who should be surveyed?

SAMPLES

Imagine that you are trying to investigate the hypothesis that male residents in hotels use leisure centres in different ways and for different reasons than female residents in hotels. After you have defined all the key terms (e.g. what type of hotel, what constitutes a resident?) and decided upon an appropriate technique or techniques by which to begin to investigate the issue, it is then necessary to determine exactly who you will direct your questions towards. Once the research question has been formulated, you will be faced with a number of key questions:

- Who do I study or ask questions of?

- How many people do I use in my investigation?

- How do I choose those people?

The answers to these questions are addressed by social scientists in the area of sampling techniques. Some of the more commonly used techniques will be discussed below.

Ideally, the solution in the above example would be to question all residents in the hotel groups you have defined, analysing all those responses. Clearly, though, for anything other than an extremely small-scale question, such as Do residents in Hotel X use the leisure centre in different ways?, this would be an impractical task. If this is the case, the researcher must make some judgements as to who to study and who to leave out. This judgement is premised on the fact that the aim of much social scientific research is to generate explanations that are generalizable. (If the reader refers back to the section on methods, it will be clear that this is not the case for all methods, i.e. case studies.) In other words, a sample of people must be chosen so that their answers are as representative of everybody else as possible.

Already you should be able to see that this may not be an easy task, for even if you have identified groups of people that you wish to question, it might be that asking those questions at certain times of the day will produce different results. Any biases in responses must be eliminated where possible, so that generalizations can be made from examples.

As you would expect, social scientists have devised a number of techniques by which this problem can be solved, and these are known as sampling techniques. There are a number of different sampling techniques, each of which may be appropriate for different investigations: random, stratified, quota and opportunity sampling. Before discussing these, it is appropriate to discuss the nature of the population of the study.

Population

All the possible respondents or subjects of an investigation constitute the population for research. The sample the researcher chooses is drawn from that population. For example, in the above case, the population would be all male and female residents in hotels.

If you were investigating the role of pay levels in motivating staff working in food and beverage departments in three-star hotels, the population would be all staff employed in food and beverage in three-star hotels. Again, however, it is important to remember that for some investigations, the population to study may not be so obvious; it is often easy to miss out some segments of the population. For instance, if you were thinking of building and opening a leisure complex with a swimming pool and were interested in the number and type of customers that might use that pool, you would survey the existing facilities and would probably undertake some investigation of the likely clientele for your pool. This would include questioning people who already use other facilities but, importantly, might also include a general survey of people who do not currently use other facilities.

Once you have identified the population for your research, it is then necessary to draw your sample from that. In other words, from the population, you must narrow the numbers down into a sample of people that will be representative, allowing you to generalize from their responses.

Random sampling

Random sampling simply means that every member of the population has an equal chance of being included in your sample. This can be achieved by a variety of methods, e.g. computer selection, by random number tables, by manual selection. Of course, strictly speaking, if you were to put all the names of the people in your population into a hat, shuffle them and randomly pick out your required sample size, each time you pick one out, it should go back into the pile before you select another one. Otherwise the probability of one name being selected increases each time you remove a piece of paper!

You can probably see that unless your population is a large one, for example the electoral register, and your sample size relatively large also, it may be that random sampling would not produce a representative sample. If you had 100 names in a hat, 50 male, 50 female and wanted to pick 20, a random sample could produce 20 males.

Stratified sampling

In this case, we can partly overcome the difficulty raised above, by arranging the population into strata, taking a sample from each strata. In this way we would randomly select 10 names from the 50 males and 10 names from the 50 females. The categories, or strata, will clearly depend on the research question but, essentially, to be representative, proportions of people should be taken from all strata. If you wanted a representative sample of hotel staff and the staffing was as follows

Food and beverage   50%
Housekeeping   40%
Front office   10%

how would you choose a sample?

If your sample size was 10, it would be logical to choose 5 names from food and beverage, 4 names from housekeeping and 1 name from the front office.

Quota sampling

Here, the population would have been stratified and numbers from each category to be used in the sample would be identified. The major difference between this type of sampling and the above, is that once the strata have been adopted, the techniques of choosing subjects from within those may not necessarily be random. This is often the approach used by market surveys. It may be, for example, that you are required to stand in a particular location, interviewing 20 10–16-year-olds, 20 16–20-year-olds, 20 20–25-year-olds, and so on. If you were to do this randomly, then everyone in those age groups ought to have an equal chance of being asked questions. However, in practice, interviewers will merely ask those people that walk past that appear to fall into those groups and will do that until the quota for that group has been achieved.

Opportunity sampling

As the name suggests, opportunity sampling is a technique whereby the sample would be comprised of anybody that was available at the time. Many student investigations use samples of this nature for practical reasons. If you wanted to test out a new food product or menu in a training restaurant, you may choose a sample of diners according to who was walking past the building at that particular time.

Each one of these techniques will be more or less useful for different investigations and it is always important to recognize which technique is being used and to state the reasons for that. When writing up investigations for a social science audience, it is a requirement that it is written up in such a way that somebody else could pick up the work and replicate exactly the procedure and method.

Once you have the technique for choosing the sample, the next crucial question is how many of the population do you choose? This is a difficult question to answer in general terms. However, one point to bear in mind is that the larger the sample size, the more likely you are to reduce sampling bias. In many cases, the actual sample size will be determined by costs in terms of time or money, but it is important to remember that whatever number you consider appropriate, certain statistical tests that you may want to use to analyse your results can only be performed meaningfully with investigations of a certain size.

SUMMARY

This section has outlined research techniques that students should draw upon when investigating human behaviour in the hospitality context. It has also outlined the ways in which researchers can choose the individuals to be involved in the study. These research techniques have been developed in order to allow replicability in research and to ensure that research is carried out in a logical, rigorous, objective manner. If such techniques are used in conjunction with theories and concepts, researchers will often be able to make more general and predictive conclusions.

DISCUSSION QUESTIONS

1. What are the differences between investigations which can describe human behaviour, and those which can explain and predict behaviour?
2. Identify several pieces of research in the contemporary hospitality industry which have used social scientific research techniques.
3. Take one of those pieces of research and critically evaluate it.
4. Why is it important for research in the hospitality industry to be based on representative samples of the population?

FURTHER READING

Robson, C. (1993) *Real World Research,* Blackwell, Oxford. This is a comprehensive, up-to-date text outlining the methods of investigation in behavioural sciences. It addresses issues in depth and is particularly useful for students undertaking research in applied areas. As well as illustrating techniques, the book also gives advice and guidance on the analysis of data, again in an interesting and understandable manner.

Moser, C.A. and Kalton, G. (1971) *Survey Methods in Social Investigation,* Gower, Aldershot. This text is thorough in its explanations of the nature, design and use of surveys. It outlines the techniques of survey design, the practical factors associated with implementing a survey, and methods of analysis. The book contains information on both questionnaires and interviews.

REFERENCES

Popper, K. (1959) *The Logic of Scientific Discovery,* Hutchinson, London.

Smith, M. (1981) *The pub and publican, a participant observer study of a public house*, Centre for Leisure Studies, Salford University.

Social Scientific Analysis and Hospitality Issues

PART 2

The preceding chapters were concerned with introducing readers to some of the aims, scope and methods of the social sciences. After working through Chapters 1–4 you should now be able to identify the central features of social scientific approaches, such as the concern with theories and concepts, and should be in a position to undertake some critical analyses of the study of human behaviour. Readers should also be familiar with the range of methodological techniques that are available for the study of human behaviour and should be able to identify the appropriateness of specific techniques when looking at particular areas of behaviour within hospitality organizations.

A theme of this book has been to argue for a multidisciplinary approach when investigating issues of behaviour within hospitality contexts. We have demonstrated this so far by integrating sociology and psychology in our approach to behavioural applications of hospitality organizations and their members.

This next section aims to extend this theme by focusing upon a multidisciplinary approach to a range of different hospitality issues. In selecting such issues for study, there are clearly a wide range of topics which we could have included. However, we have tried to focus upon areas which have not yet featured predominantly in textbooks on the hospitality industry. For example, we have deliberately ignored issues relating to human resource management because these issues feature in current textbooks, although they are not usually treated from a multidisciplinary perspective. The range of issues that we have chosen include customer choice, conflict, eating behaviour, discrimination, leisure behaviour and branding.

At the end of this section, we hope that readers will be able to apply similar multidisciplinary approaches to other areas and issues within the hospitality context.

Psychological and sociological explanations in the hospitality context

5

Aims

This chapter aims to:

1. summarize the work covered so far; and
2. highlight and emphasize the argument in favour of social scientific analyses in hospitality management drawing upon work used to understand both customer motivation and the development of hotels in the UK.

Outcomes

At the end of this chapter you will be able to:

1. consolidate your knowledge of the utility of social sciences to hospitality situations;
2. describe the development of hotels in the UK from a sociological perspective; and
3. evaluate Maslow's hierarchy of needs in relation to customer motivation in the hospitality industry.

SUMMARY AND RECAP OF EARLIER CHAPTERS

The value of adopting a social scientific framework or perspective for hospitality management can be summarized in the following points.

1. Social scientific frameworks and approaches provide us with theoretically informed analyses of people's behaviour, in contrast to alternative approaches based on gossip and common sense.
2. Adopting a theoretical framework allows for the testing and analysis of questions and for generalizations to be made for the purposes of analysis. These can be extended to more than one unit, group of customers or set of workers. This avoids the relativistic approaches which are generated from small sample, one-off accounts, solely based upon generating empirical data.

3. Social scientific approaches encourage analysis of behaviour in a rigorous manner. We can use psychological theories and concepts and sociological theories and concepts to investigate behaviour. On occasion, one discipline may be more relevant than another, so that choice of the theoretical framework becomes crucial in understanding and explaining behaviour. Similarly there may be more than one framework within a discipline that is useful in particular situations. Nevertheless, we can also use a multi-disciplinary approach, where both sociological and psychological aspects of the behaviour are investigated. What this means is that we focus upon the complexity of behaviour and avoid reaching for simplistic solutions. Therefore, as researchers, when we adopt a social scientific framework or approach we are able to separate facts from value judgements and develop critical thinking in our assessments of material which purports to explain human behaviour.

4. The ability to develop critical thinking is the basis for the development of analytical skills which should be acquired by students following degree courses. In the present context this can best be illustrated in two ways:

   (a) by examining a framework drawn originally from clinical psychology, but now used extensively both in management and marketing textbooks in general, and in the hospitality industry in particular;

   (b) by looking at the historical development of hotels through a sociological analysis.

MASLOW'S HIERARCHY OF NEEDS AND CONSUMPTION

To begin with, the framework drawn from clinical psychology we refer to is that of Maslow's hierarchy of needs. We have chosen this framework because it is ubiquitous in management education, including within hospitality management education. There are contemporary approaches in this area, however, and Maslow has, in some senses, been superseded. However, we believe that his ideas are still taught on hospitality management courses. Before we analyse Maslow, it is worthwhile briefly outlining his central ideas.

Maslow's approach (1970) to explaining motivation was to argue that individuals were motivated by their needs. These needs were identified as states within the individual which triggered the individual's actions and influenced their subsequent behaviour. When individual's needs were satisfied, they no longer acted as the basis for motivating them. In Maslow's model, needs were hierarchically ordered from basic primary needs at the bottom, to secondary needs at the top. Within the model, therefore, needs occurred in a sequence where one need had to be satisfied before another could take effect as a motivator. The figure on the next page illustrates this hierarchy of needs.

The most fundamental of needs and, therefore, the primary motivator for individuals are their physiological needs. These include the need for air, water, food – all necessary for the survival of the individual. If these remain

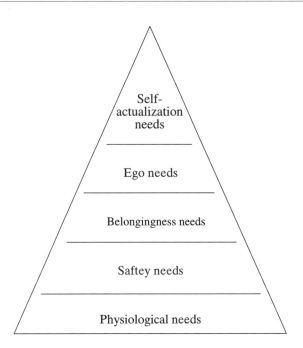

unsatisfied, they will dominate the individual's behaviour and remain the prime factor in motivating that individual. For example, in early societies a motivator to behaviour would have been the need to hunt and gather food. In employment terms, individuals are motivated to work to gain money as a means of securing food. Within the hierarchy, these needs must be satisfied and continue to be satisfied, before individuals become concerned with the satisfaction of other needs. People will eat when they are hungry and may, then, turn to other activities. Once the need for food occurs again, this will motivate individuals to eat once more.

When the means of subsistence have been satisfied, individuals move up the hierarchy, becoming concerned with safety and security needs. In early societies people became concerned with their physical safety and with securing their means of survival. In employment terms again, once employment is obtained, individuals become concerned with the security of that employment and behave in ways to ensure continued access to a money-earning activity. In terms of eating, individuals may be motivated by this need to search for premises with appropriate hygiene standards, or safe buildings. The impact of this need for safety can be demonstrated by people's behaviour in the light of plane crashes or bomb scares. When such instances occur, travel operators undertake measures to guarantee the safety of passengers by, for example, rerouting flights.

The third need that individuals have, once the safety need is satisfied, is that of the need for belongingness and love. This need motivates individuals to form friendships, relationships and group memberships. In employment, individuals may become concerned with the social aspects of work, seeking to be a member of a work group, or social club in the workplace. This was, of course, demonstrated in the human relations school of thought (Mullins,

1992). Team work and groups are extremely important in the hotel and catering industry, if the overall aims of the organization are to be satisfied (Whyte, 1947; Nailon, 1982). Similarly, in terms of consumption, it may be that individuals will be motivated to visit hotels, restaurants or leisure facilities in groups.

The fourth stage or need that individuals encounter is the ego or esteem need. According to Maslow, esteem needs involve the need for recognition, status and achievement. Again, within the employment context, individuals may be concerned with job satisfaction and the intrinsic factors which accrue from work, for example happiness. Herzberg (1968) has shown that these intrinsic factors, such as esteem and recognition, are as important in determining an individual's job performance as the more extrinsic factors, such as pay or number of holidays. Managers, however, have tended to concentrate upon those extrinsic rewards as methods of motivating individuals. Again, in the context of consumption, it may be that individuals will be motivated to use facilities where they consider themselves to be given due levels of respect, or where their achievement and status is recognized by the organization.

The final need that individuals encounter is that of self-actualization. This, in fact, is the only need that cannot be satisfied according to Maslow. With all the other needs, they must be satisfied before the next comes into operation; however, this final need in a sense perpetuates itself. It is difficult to quantify and define this need, but generally it can be seen as the need within people to reach their full potential, to become all that they can become. In employment terms, individuals may be motivated by this need to constantly seek new opportunities or promotions. In consumption terms, individuals will be motivated to seek new patterns of leisure or to experience new forms of behaviour.

Maslow's hierarchy of needs has been used widely in management textbooks to explain the motivation of individuals in the workplace. The perspective has, however, been criticized for the assumption that the needs are ubiquitous and follow necessarily in the sequence that Maslow put forward. Commentators have also noted the problem of generalizing this model to different cultural environments, where people may have very different criteria for assessing the importance of different kinds of activity and behaviour.

Critiques of Maslow's analysis of worker motivation have been undertaken by a range of authors. However, less attention has been paid to evaluating the Maslow hierarchy as an explanatory framework for customer motivation. It is to this area that our analysis will now turn.

Analysing Maslow's hierarchy

Maslow's hierarchy of needs, used as an explanatory model of customer behaviour, is common in marketing circles. Its application to hotel customers is found in the work of Buttle (1988), Greene (1987) and Doswell and Gamble (1981). Applied to customer motivation, the idea is that consumers will convert an unsatisfied need into purchasing behaviour and attain a level of satisfaction. Transferred to the study of hotel customers, need satisfaction is the fundamental criterion of customer motivation and the task for hoteliers is to satisfy the range of needs identified on the Maslow hierarchy. Moreover, the diversity of hotel supply is often attributed to the fact that customers have different needs and, therefore, different types of products satisfy these. For example, Nailon's (1982) utilitarian and hedonistic models indicate this.

Nailon's proposition is that the hospitality industry offers a range of products which relates to the continuum of needs. For example, fast food and motorway service station outlets exhibit the opportunity for the satisfaction of the basic needs of hunger and thirst. A wider range of needs may be satisfied in full service and à la carte restaurants. Nailon claims that the hospitality industry has been more successful in satisfying customers' basic needs than it has the higher-order needs, but that, essentially, customer motivation may be related to a continuum of hedonism or utilitarianism.

This view is rather simplistic, as the extent to which any product or context is utilitarian or hedonistic must rest with the customers' classification. Nailon implies that there is something inherent in the context which works for the customers' needs in this way. Both concepts are highly subjective and customers' motivation and selection make the continuum of hedonism and utilitarianism spurious. Fast food operators, particularly, have a long history of promoting restaurants as fashionable contexts and fast food outlets are often identified as hedonistic contexts by young people.

The proposition that customers are motivated by their needs not only compounds the simplistic models of customer behaviour, but also provides a functional model of hotels. Thus, hotels provide only the functions of eating, drinking and sleeping. The concept of need is limiting because the basis can only be specified when it is linked to biological needs, i.e. food, drink, sleep. The basis of social and higher-order needs, since the role of learning is not discussed by Maslow (1970), is difficult to specify. How are operators able to identify customers' needs *per se*, and at what point are customers on the hierarchy of needs? Furthermore, how do basic physiological needs (which we accept as homogeneous – sleep etc.) become stratified into the diverse range of types of hotel which have evolved to satisfy them? This is evidenced in hotel classification schemes which clearly indicate a range of hotel types. We may concede that customers have needs for the facilities which hotels have to offer, but human motivation and purchasing behaviour is more complex than a needs model allows.

Finally, in the context of commercial provision, customer needs and choices can be open to manipulation by advertizing. The customer needs model, therefore, has brought us no nearer to an adequate explanation of customer consumption in hotels.

HISTORICAL DEVELOPMENT OF HOTELS

Now let us look at the historical development of hotels through a sociological perspective. You should recall from the chapter on the development of the social sciences that we are arguing that social theories are reflected by, and perpetuate, social structures. They do not develop in isolation and they do impact upon behaviours and institutions. If this is the case, it is necessary to try to understand the development of the hotel and catering industry through a historical or sociological analysis.

In tracing the history of human behaviour, we noted that social theories and ideas are a product of the time in which they evolved. That is, they are influenced by the economic, social and political context of society. This point is worthy of note because it applies not only to social theories, but also to social institutions and organizations. Therefore, as students of the contemporary hotel and catering industry, it is necessary for us to know about the key factors which have shaped the industry into its present form and structure.

To chart the historical development of the hotel and catering industry would demand a textbook of its own. Furthermore, there already exist many worthwhile texts which readers are invited to pursue (e.g. Borer, 1972). Our purpose here is to indicate the value of studying the development of the industry from a sociological perspective. Such an approach will focus upon the key factors influencing contemporary hotel supply and identify and explain why hotel provision has taken the precise form that it has. For this to be achieved, we must analyse the relationship between hotels and society.

It will be argued that the evolution of hotel types was influenced by the society of the time and that hotel provision reflected particular features of the wider society.

The evolution of the hotel industry is well documented, having its origins in the inns of English society (Medlik, 1989). However, the provision of commercial hospitality is closely related to the growth of railways and an increased demand for accommodation, which can be traced to the development of industrialization in the UK (Taylor and Bush, 1977).

Inns were socially segregated from one another, aimed at attracting particular social groups. This practice of social segregation was a reflection of the social class structure of the period, in which economic, social and cultural boundaries were clearly evident from the hierarchical structure of society. Royalty and the aristocracy represented the core of landowning interests, whose wealth was based on the agrarian economy, and they dominated the peasantry both economically and politically.

The development of industrialization brought about new forms of class relations. It created wage labour, the emergence of the middle class and some fusion of wealthy industrialists into the aristocracy. These social relations were an important factor in shaping the types of hotels which evolved. This is clearly evident in the growth of railway hotels. Railway companies offered a range of hotel types aimed at attracting the aristocracy and upper class, while at the same time offering small hotels close to stations for commercial travellers. However, it was the luxury hotels which gave the clearest indication of the social relations of the period. Although numerically small, they were important in establishing a type of hotel supply which became important in shaping conceptions about hotels.

Starting with the Savoy company in 1889, luxury hotels aimed to attract the aristocracy and upper class. Architectural styles and furnishings were based upon French models (as France was the style centre of the aristocracy and French was the court language of Europe) (Jackson, 1989). This was an attempt to gain prestige within aristocratic circles. The hallmarks of these hotels were their high levels of personal service, the latest technology, and *haute cuisine* involving rituals of dining evident in French menus. Customer access to these hotels was based on what Bourdieu (1984) has described as 'cultural capital', including manners, dress and speech. This, of course, further served to differentiate aristocracy from other groups in society and helped to bolster their power. What we can identify is a set of behaviours, values and ideas which formed the basis of a culinary culture, thus creating boundaries of inclusion of some groups and exclusion of others. As Riley (1984) makes the point, these hotels reflected the identity of the groups who used them.

Relations between customers and staff were based upon the concept of master and servant, characterized by high levels of social deference (White, 1968). At the same time, staff transmitted the core of aristocratic values, excluding customers who did not possess the appropriate cultural capital. In summary, tracing the relationship between hotels and society demonstrates clearly that hotels are influenced by wider societal factors, often reflecting social relations of the period.

It would be easy to assume that all this relates to the industry of the past, and that the analysis is not relevant to contemporary hotels. However, this dismissal would be premature. The value of undertaking socio-historical analyses in this way is to identify both changes and continuities which have occurred in hotel provision. Clearly, the hotel industry has undergone many changes since the evolution of luxury hotels. The impact of airline travel and with it the growth of tourism and international business markets, have had a significant impact both on the growth of hotels and their geographical locations. Equally important has been the growth of hotel and catering companies and their initiatives in developing hotels for business and conference markets. The growth of leisure in general and the short-break market in particular, have also contributed to changes both in hotel types, and hoteliers' approaches to the market place. Furthermore, a range of new hotel types, from budget to all-suite concepts have been developed (Carmouche and Roper, 1989).

Setting hotels in the wider context, there have also been many changes in society. Changing industrial structures have impacted upon employment trends, firstly in the shift from manufacturing to services and the increase in female employment and, lately, in the increase in unemployment as the UK economy continues in recession. The extent to which the class structure has changed is a matter of debate between social theorists and commentators alike (Giddens, 1973). However, what is certain is that the occupational structure has changed since the evolution of hotels; this has been reflected in hotels and their customer markets.

The provision of contemporary hotels still reflects a hierarchy of supply which is perpetuated by the hotel classification schemes (Carmouche and Roper, 1989). Hotel companies' marketing strategies now reflect the occupational hierarchy, with customers' occupational status being the key determinant of market segregation. Economic exclusion in the form of tariffs is still apparent; however, much less is known about the cultural uses of hotels by particular individuals and groups.

Riley (1984) argues that *haute cuisine* has been stripped of its behavioural trapping in contemporary hotels. Wood (1987) supports this view, arguing that food provision in hotels is now closer to domestic consumption. While the changing structure of hotel supply has impacted upon food and beverage provision, so that French menus and *haute cuisine* are not necessary to the hallmark of luxury hotels, it has not been empirically established that hotel usage is no longer surrounded by cultural codes.

Continuities with the past are clear, with economic exclusion in the form of tariffs, the relationship between hotel types and customer status, the practice of tipping and barriers to female consumption. These are areas which require research to determine the relationship between hotels and society in the contemporary period.

SUMMARY

The aim of this chapter was to demonstrate the use of psychological and sociological analyses in the context of the hospitality industry. The psychological perspective has been shown by the use of Maslow's hierarchy of needs in its application to consumption. This hierarchy clearly has weaknesses when used to understand and explain consumer behaviour, yet the principle of application has been demonstrated. Indeed, the fact that a concept or theory can be shown to have difficulties in explanation may lead to areas for further study and the subsequent reformulation of the theory. The historical development of hotels has been described through a sociological perspective, emphasizing that no social scientific research can be divorced from the time in which it occurs.

DISCUSSION QUESTIONS

1. Discuss the factors which have shaped the evolution of hotels.
2. Evaluate the validity of Maslow's hierarchy of needs for an understanding of worker and customer behaviour in the hospitality industry.

FURTHER READING

Taylor, D. and Bush, D. (1977) *Fortune, Fame and Folly – British Hotels and Catering from 1878 to 1978*. This is a comprehensive account of the historical development of the hotel and catering industry. It locates hotel and catering in a historical perspective, and outlines key factors in the explanation of change in the industry.

Mullins, I.J. (1992) *Hospitality Management, a Human Resources Approach.* This text covers a range of human resources issues particularly in relation to the hospitality industry. It outlines Maslow's approach to motivation, and evaluates this in relation to alternative perspectives on motivation in the hospitality industry. It is written in an accessible style, and contains useful exercises for students in the area of human resources.

REFERENCES

Borer, M.C. (1972) *The British Hotel Through the Ages*, Butterworth Press, Guildford.

Bourdieu, P. (1984) *Distinction: a Social Critique of the Judgement of Taste*, Routledge, London.

Buttle, F. (1988) *Hotel and Food Service Marketing*, Cassell, London.

Carmouche, R. and Roper, A. (1989) Budget hotels, a case of mistaken identity? *International Journal of Contemporary Hospitality Management*, **1**, 28–31.

Doswell, R. and Gamble, P. (1981) *Marketing and Planning Hotels and Tourism Projects*, Barrie and Jenkins, London.

Giddens, A. (1973) *The Class Structure of Advanced Societies*, Hutchinson, London.

Green, M. (1987) *Marketing Hotels and Restaurants into the 1990's*, Heinemann, Oxford.

Herzberg, E. (1968) *Work and the Nature of Man*, Staples Press, London.

Jackson, S. (1989) *The Savoy*, Muller, London.

Maslow, A.H. (1970) *Motivation and Personality*, Harper Row, New York and London.

Medlik, S. (1989) *The Business of Hotels* (2nd edn), Heinemann, Oxford.

Mullins, L.J. (1992) *Hospitality Management, a Human Resources Approach*, Pitman, London.

Nailon, P. (1982) *Theory and art in hospitality management*, University of Surrey inaugural lecture, 4 Feb 1981.

Riley, M. (1984) Hotels and group identity. *Tourism Management,* June, 102–109.

Taylor, D. and Bush, D. (1977) *Fortune Fame and Folly, British Hotels and Catering from 1878 to 1978*, IPC Business Press, London.

White, A. (1968) *Palaces of the People. A Social History of Commercial Hospitality.* Rapp and Whiting, London.

Whyte, W.F. (1947) The social structure of the restaurant, *American Journal of Sociology*, 302–310.

Wood, R.C. (1987) *Some preliminary notes towards a sociology of accommodation management*, Paper presented at the international association of hotel schools symposium on accommodation management, Edinburgh, Nov 26–28.

The management of conflict in service encounters

6

Aims

This chapter aims to:

1. illustrate and explain the concept of attributions and attribution theory;
2. illustrate the utility of attribution theory in understanding conflict in hospitality situations; and
3. describe organization structure and its relationship to understanding conflict in hospitality organizations.

Outcomes

At the end of this chapter you will be able to:

1. describe the nature of attributions and their consequences for behaviour;
2. outline hospitality contexts where a knowledge of attribution theory would be useful;
3. describe the concept of organization structure; and
4. analyse an organization chart and highlight potential areas of conflict, showing the reasons for that conflict.

CONFLICT IN SERVICE ENCOUNTERS

In order to highlight the utility of social scientifically informed explanations of behaviour, it may be useful to create a hypothetical example of a situation that managers and students in the hospitality industry will encounter and have to deal with. We can then present the ways in which the situation may be resolved. In this example, two strategies and courses of action will be outlined, one of which represents the way such issues may often be dealt with in the hospitality industry, and one of which will outline how an explanation and understanding of human behaviour can help resolve situations more appropriately.

You are the manager of a busy restaurant in a hotel. You have walked into the restaurant at 1pm to find that one of your waiting staff and a customer are standing up at the customer's table, shouting at each other. What would you do? Write down the factors that you, as restaurant manager, would take into consideration when deciding what to do. In other words, what would you think about when behaving and deciding on a course of action?

Your list may include some of the following comments or questions:

- Is this customer a moaner?
- What is company policy?
- Is there past experience of complaints in this context?
- Is the member of staff new?
- Is this customer ever satisfied with anything you can do?
- Is this customer a troublemaker?
- You should take the customer aside.
- You should keep calm and not shout.
- Defer to the assistant manager.
- Is this customer stupid?
- Let the staff handle it.

Clearly, this is an issue of customer complaint. Common courses of action in this type of situation are to defer the decisions to someone higher in the organization chain, to intervene in the scene and to argue with the staff, or to argue with the customer. Hence one course of action for you as the manager might be as follows.

You walk to the table and ask both the member of staff and the customer if they would like to discuss this matter in your room. The customer refuses and continues to create a disturbance in the restaurant. You try to get to the cause of the problem by asking both parties about the difficulty, both of whom give opposing stories, the result being that the shouting between staff and customer continues. You send the member of staff away, in front of the customer, and then deal with the customer's complaint – by, for example, reordering a meal, not charging for the meal and so on. You return to the member of staff, and either agree with that version of the story and have a laugh or give the worker a warning about the behaviour.

Let us consider the appropriateness and weaknesses of this course of action. Despite the simplicity of this example, it is clear that there would be several difficulties that occur and arise out of this action. We will try to highlight these in order of the events.

1. You have tried to remove the conflict from the scene by requesting that both parties leave to your room. Whilst this is sensible in that the disturbance is then taken away from the restaurant and no longer involves the other customers, the complainant has refused. This may

cause a problem in that this customer is then in a position to further initiate the action and, in effect, can draw support and power from other customers. Thus an escalation of the problem is likely to occur.

2. You have sent the member of staff away and try to deal with the customer. Assuming that the customer is happy that the member of staff is no longer involved in the problem, you are still dealing with the difficulty in front of other customers. On occasion this may be of benefit, in that they can see that the situation is being dealt with immediately and, presumably, to the customer's satisfaction. However, if the problem then escalates it may be that you would be required to call your superior, thus losing authority. In addition, despite dealing with the complaint, you need not necessarily have actually got to the source or root of it.

3. In dealing with the member of staff, there are a number of considerations to think about. Having a laugh at the customer's expense would send signals to the staff regarding the value you have of customers, and would also be likely to result in some change in the nature of your authority relations with them. It may, for instance, result in you being seen as 'one of the lads', which in other circumstances will make it difficult to assert authority.

   Telling the member of staff off indiscriminately may be inappropriate; the customer may have been complaining unnecessarily and the staff member may have had a legitimate case. However, clearly, the waiter does need some kind of reprimand for letting the difficulty escalate in the restaurant and for engaging in a shouting match with the customer.

Hence, in this scenario, it appears that you have not necessarily got to the root of the problem, you may have lost authority with both staff and customer, and the situation will have had some influence on the other customers in the restaurant.

How can the social sciences help deal with this issue of customer complaints more effectively then? First, it is necessary to view the problem in some kind of framework and, from that, to realize what the influences on behaviour might be, what your objectives are and what the consequent course of action will be.

The situation is clearly one of conflict; it is in this broad framework that the problem can be seen. A realization of this will lead to your primary aim, which is to diffuse that conflict, this in itself leading you to several sub-objectives. These will be:

1. for you as manager to initiate the action – in other words to take control of the situation, attempting to deal with both the staff and the customer in a way that you deem appropriate;

2. for you to minimize the impact of the disturbance on other customers in the restaurant;

3. for you to ascertain the cause of the situation; and

4. for you to act in such a manner that the situation becomes resolved quickly, to the satisfaction of the customer.

Each of these aims and objectives will be influenced by a number of factors, for example by the way in which a customer's views are regarded on a general level, by the way in which you and your members of staff perceive behaviours and the causes of those behaviours.

To consider the first factor, it is often a working assumption on the part of customers and staff that, when dealing with complaints, it is appropriate to act in accordance with the idea put forward by Ritz, that the customer is always right. In the above example, this would have clear implications for the manner in which you as manager treated both the waiter and the customer. However, this statement cannot be accepted unequivocally. There are situations for example, where the customer is making a request, or a complaint that is inappropriate – consider the drunken customer demanding use of the hotel leisure centre, the customer complaining that a bottle of wine was not satisfactory after consuming three quarters of the bottle, a customer in an à la carte restaurant complaining as the meal was not delivered within 4 minutes of ordering. These situations may arise through expectations on the part of the customer that are inappropriate to the context of service, or through expectations that will clearly involve a danger to themselves and others.

This issue is still important though, despite the fact that the complaint or request may be inappropriate. You, as manager, will still be faced with the situation and required to deal with it. It seems then that some reconsideration of the idea that the customer is always right is necessary. If we think about the nature of the hospitality industry it is blatantly obvious that without customers the business would not survive, hence the issue may be best seen as the value that the customer has to the organization. If the customer is seen as having value, then the course of action taken in response to the situation will take account of whether or not the complaint or request is inappropriate. This concept of the customer as value to the organization can be seen to operate in some contemporary organizations where many staff are empowered to deal with customer complaints as and when they arise. For example, a chambermaid may be able to check with housekeeping and reallocate a room to an unsatisfied customer rather than sending them to reception, where the process of reallocation may be much longer. This issue of empowerment is an interesting one, as it raises issues of the nature of the relationship of authority in different sections of the hierarchy and it might be useful to consider it through a framework of motivation.

Attribution theory

The second factor or issue that will influence the way that you will behave and the course of action you will consider is the way in which both you, as manager, and the staff involved perceive the situation. If you return to the original list of considerations that students often give in response to this scenario, you will see that the factors can be split into two categories. There are those considerations that involve comments on the temperament of the customer, i.e. is he/she stupid, a moaner, can never be satisfied; and there are those comments that involve such factors as company policy or the nature of the situation.

In social science terms, there is a theory, derived from social psychology that can inform us about this kind of differentiation of considerations and the way in which these can influence behaviour. This is **attribution theory**. A look at this can illustrate the ways in which different perceptions of the situation in the example may well lead to very different behaviours and courses of action.

Attribution theory (Heider, 1958; Kelley, 1967) attempts to look at the way in which individuals attribute causality to actions, events or objects. In other words, when we experience an interaction with something or somebody, as individuals we try to work out why certain courses of action occur, why things happen in the way that they do and, particular to this example, why people behave in the way that they do. Attributions of this nature are pervasive in our behaviour – consider, for example, the kinds of objects that we act towards as if they had feelings: cars, computers and so on. If our computer is not working we will treat it tenderly, may talk to it, etc. The mere fact that it has broken down and that we attribute feelings to it clearly alters our behaviour towards it. If we do this with inanimate objects, it seems sensible to suggest that we also do it with other individuals or groups (Heider and Simmel, 1944). The important point in relation to the hospitality manager, is the way that we make these attributions, or the things that we see as causes of other people's actions, which will influence the way that we deal with those situations.

When trying to infer causality to particular actions, attribution theory suggests that we can attribute according to two concepts: dispositional attributions or situational attributions. A dispositional attribution would be one where we considered that the individual was the cause of the behaviour, so this may be some notion of personality variable, temperament. A situational attribution would be one where we considered that it was the situation that the individual was in that was the cause of the behaviour. Again, in our example, if we consider that the customer is a consistent moaner, we would be attributing dispositionally; if we consider that the restaurant was overcrowded and service time was taking too long, we would be attributing situationally. Whichever we choose obviously has implications for the way that we perceive the situation and for the way that we will deal with it.

Consider a situation where you are walking outside a pub on a Friday night. It is ten o'clock. An individual opens the door to leave the pub and falls over. A dispositional attribution may be that this person is drunk – a function of the person; a situational attribution may be that the steps outside the pub are greasy – the fall is a function of the situation. What would you do? We are arguing here that the way you would act is dependent on the nature of the attributions that you make. If you have attributed dispositionally, it is likely that you will also think that the fall is the fault of the individual for being in such a state in the first place and may, therefore, laugh and walk on. But if you have attributed situationally, the fall will not be seen as the person's fault, and it may be more likely that you will intervene and assist that person. This is a simplification of the nature and complexity of attribution theory.

There are a number of ways in which we combine information to work out the primary cause or determinant of behaviour where cases are not so clear cut (Kelley, 1967). However, an example like this does illustrate the way that these attributions influence our judgements about other people and the actions that result from this. Similarly, there are a number of fundamental errors or biases in judgements that attribution theory can inform us about.

Errors in judgement

First, the fundamental attribution error. This suggests that when we are looking for the causes of people's behaviour, we are more likely to attribute dispositionally than situationally (Jones and Harris, 1967). This means that as individuals we are more likely to perceive behaviour as intentional rather than as a function of environmental influences.

Second, the 'actor observer' effect. This suggests that when we are looking for the causes of behaviour, we are likely to attribute dispositionally to others, but situationally to ourselves (Jones and Nisbett, 1971). If we go back to the example of the pub on Fridays, if somebody else falls then they must have been drunk, yet if we fall ourselves it must have been the steps that were slippery.

Third, the false consensus bias. This suggests that we assume that other people will behave in the same ways that we do (Ross *et al.*, 1977). For example, in a restaurant we assume that individuals will share our knowledge of the appropriate social codes and will act accordingly.

It would be interesting for students to consider the effects of these biases in different situations, how they influence our judgements of individuals or groups and whether or not we place more value on some information rather than other information.

Going back to the original scenario, it should now be clear that both the issue concerning the value a customer has to you and the ways in which you have attributed the cause of the complaint, will influence the way in which you, as manager, deal with it. It may be that merely understanding these issues and processes will alter the way that you think about situations and the ways in which you deal with them. You do not need a thorough academic knowledge of attribution theory to deal with situations, but an awareness of the fact that the ways in which we infer responsibility for behaviours to either the situation or the individual, clearly plays a role in the way that we behave.

POWER AND AUTHORITY IN HOSPITALITY CONTEXTS

A more structural approach to understanding and explaining conflict in service encounters and organizations might use the concepts of power and authority. Consider the following chart which illustrates one of the possible formal structures of authority within a food and beverage department in a hotel. It may be the case that conflict will arise between staff at different points in this structure, and it is useful to consider the explanations for these within some kind of conceptual framework.

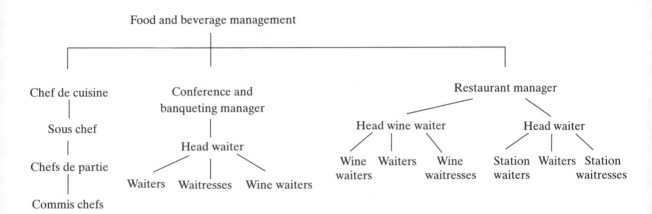

Perhaps the first point to make is that the type of structure outlined in the diagram clearly represents a method of co-ordinating and controlling work procedures. As Weber identified, with the increasing size of organizations it becomes necessary for the management to implement some kind of system whereby they can retain control of work practices and can co-ordinate activities effectively. Weber created an ideal typical notion of a bureaucracy to suggest the most appropriate way of achieving the company objectives. His ideal type was a yardstick that organizations could use to compare their own operating mechanisms against. He did not intend, as is sometimes thought, that all organizations should adhere strictly to the characteristics of his bureaucracy, but suggested that it is likely that all large organizations will display many of those characteristics. Students are referred to texts in the further reading for more elaborate explanations of Weber's ideas with respect to bureaucracy. However, it is relevant here to give a brief description of his ideas.

For Weber, the most rational way to achieve co-ordination and control in large organizations was to adopt a formal structure with clearly defined roles and duties attached to members within the organization. He created the notion of a bureaucratic structure which, as an ideal type of organization included the following characteristics.

1. *Specialization*: Each department, or each section of a department working towards a goal has a clearly defined sphere of competence. In other words, specialist knowledge or skills occur in organizations. In the hotel context this means that the organization is split into different specialist departments; each department may have specialist sections. For example, a hotel will have a food and beverage department, which itself, will have kitchen staff, waiting staff, bars and bar staff.

2. *Hierarchy*: Within an organization there will exist a firmly ordered system of super- and subordination. The departments or individuals at the lower end of the hierarchy are supervised by, and responsible to, those at the superordinate end of the hierarchy. The kitchen and bar staff will be ultimately responsible to the food and beverage manager, the waiting-on staff will be responsible to the restaurant manager.

3. *Rules*: The management of the organization follows general rules. These rules are more or less stable and should occur in such a way as to cover every possible imaginable situation within the organization. These rules are formally written down. There will be codes of conduct concerning dress, the ways in which customers should be served, within what time limits etc. There should be information available about the sanctions should these rules be broken.

4. *Impersonality*: All members of the organization should carry out their duties in an impersonal manner. Everyone is subject to equality of treatment as appropriate to the task. All kitchen staff at the same level in the hierarchy should be accorded the same treatment. Similarly, all customers should be treated equally, regardless of their status or relationship to members of the hotel staff.

5. *Appointed officials*: Individuals within an organization are selected and appointed to the organization purely on the merits of their technical qualifications. They should not be elected to positions within organizations. Management positions should be given appointment by virtue of qualification and skill.

6. *Full-time officials*: Individuals within organizations should treat their duties as a primary occupation. Other activities that members of the hotel engage in, in their out-of-work life, should not impinge on their work life.

7. *Career officials*: The job that an individual is engaged in within an organization should constitute a career. Within the organization there will exist a system of promotion, which will operate according to seniority, to achievement or to both. Members of staff within a hotel should have access to promotion opportunities based on equal and fair criteria.

8. *Public/private split*: Official activity related to the duties within an organization are seen as entirely separate and distinct from an individual's existence in the private sphere.

Whilst organizations in reality may display slight deviations from these characteristics, or might display them at different levels of degree, it would seem that there are some characteristics here which all large organizations display. Similarly, within large organizations it is clear that specialized departments or divisions will also display some of the overall characteristics. Hence, it is possible to treat the food and beverage department as an organization within an organization.

There are two ways of using this notion of organization structure to understand and explain conflict. These are concerned with the notion of rules within organizations and with the notions of power and authority.

A key feature in the co-ordination and control of a food and beverage department is the concept of rules. As Weber suggested, rules will be formally written down, acting as a guide to structure the behaviour of members of the organization. On first joining an organization, or department, individuals should be given documents containing these rules. These may take the form of job descriptions and specifications, duties required, appropriate dress and behaviour codes, disciplinary procedures and so on.

These rules are meant to ensure the smooth operation of the department so that each member is carrying out the appropriate behaviours at the appropriate times. However, as students may be aware, very often within such structures, individual members begin to bend the rules, or blatantly ignore them. This is not always done with the intention of making activities less efficient. Indeed, it is often the case in large structures that rules proliferate and can actually hinder operation. However, this can present a potential source of conflict between individuals. Those in superordinate positions in the hierarchy may expect a job to be performed efficiently and to be performed according to the rules for procedure, whereas those actually performing the job may do so by bending or ignoring the rules. The extent to which this may lead to conflict may depend on a number of factors. The consequences of actions will clearly be important – if an individual has not followed procedure and the consequences are negative it may be that every aspect of the operation will be looked at, and action could be taken if it could be proved that rules have not been followed. If the procedures are not followed and some kind of accident occurs, for example an incident of food poisoning, clearly conflict may occur as the kitchen staff may feel that they are justified in not following rules explicitly as they are under time pressure, without which customers would not be served quickly. The whole issue around rules and the creation of conflict is that rules may not always lead to the most efficient operations in terms of time or finance.

A second way of considering conflict within a department or organization would be to use the concepts of power and authority. Authority can be seen as a legitimated power, i.e. an individual or group can have power which becomes legitimized and sanctioned for use in a wider context, in this case it is termed authority. Authority then is the formally sanctioned use of power by individuals or groups. For Weber, there were three sources of authority.

- Traditional authority was accorded to individuals or groups because of the belief that they had a natural right to that by virtue of their position. For example, the monarchy have authority as a result of their historical position in society.

- Charismatic authority was accorded to individuals or groups based on the belief that they have some unique characteristics or special virtues that give them a natural right. Charismatic individuals in relation to the hospitality industry might include Lord Forte. It is his character that gives him authority.

- Legal rational authority is that accorded to individuals as a result of formal, written rules, the individual's or group's position in an organization hierarchy. Thus, in relation to the hospitality organization, this form of authority would be accorded to a managing director or a head of department.

As can be seen in the diagram of the food and beverage organization structure, some individuals – those at the top of the hierarchy – have more authority than others – those below them. Conflict can occur, however, when members within that structure base their own perceptions of authority on something other than the formal requirements. Or indeed when their perception of the position on formal requirements is different from that of the organization. Thus a chef may be given more respect and may be more effective in co-ordinating and controlling behaviour in the kitchen than the head chef because the rest of the staff see him/her as having more expertise. The assistant manager may be accorded more authority than the food and beverage manager as the staff consider that he/she has more knowledge of the day-to-day operational issues that face them as a team aiming towards some goal.

Clearly, then, there are a number of frameworks that could be adopted when trying to understand the issue of conflict within organizations. Each framework proposed here can give some indication of the possible sources of that conflict and can, therefore, give potential strategies to adopt when dealing with conflict.

SUMMARY

Within hospitality contexts and service encounters, there are many potential sources for conflict. These include conflict between staff and customers and conflict between staff and other staff. Two frameworks have been described that can allow us to understand and analyse conflict. Attribution theory is concerned with the ways in which individuals perceive intention-ality to behaviour, and can thus assist in the explanation of conflict in all behavioural encounters. The concept of organization structure rests on the notion of a hierarchy or authority based on legal rational premises; clearly, individuals within a hierarchy may attribute authority on another characteri-stic, e.g. expertise. Again, this can be used to explain conflict between participants in hospitality contexts.

DISCUSSION QUESTIONS

1. Identify potential areas of conflict in service encounters. What are the possible sources of that conflict?
2. Outline the utility of attribution theory in understanding conflict between staff and customers.
3. To what extent can an organization chart reflect the actual power and authority relationships in a hospitality organization?
4. Why might customers make inappropriate attributions when looking for the reasons why staff behave in particular ways?

FURTHER READING

Eiser, I.F. and Van der Plight, J. (1988) *Attitudes and Decisions*, Routledge, London. The first chapters in this book illustrate the theories and concepts that surround attitudes and attribution theory. The text explicitly links these concepts to decision-making by applying them to particular areas, i.e. health, medical judgement and nuclear energy. It is a useful book for students to look towards when considering the application of theories in everyday life.

Hinton, P. (1993) *The Psychology of Interpersonal Perception*, Routledge, London. This is a thorough and easy to read book looking at the strands within social psychology that address issues of interpersonal perception. The themes and points are illustrated with interesting examples, and the relevance of theories of interpersonal perception to everyday life are made explicit.

REFERENCES

Heider, F. (1958) *The Psychology of Interpersonal Relations*, Wiley, New York.

Heider, F. and Simmel, M. (1944) An experimental study of apparent behaviour. *American Journal of Psychology*, **57**, 243–259.

Jones, E.E. and Harris, V.A. (1967) The attribution of attitudes. *Journal of Experimental Social Psychology*, **63**, 302–310.

Jones, E.E. and Nisbett, R.E. (1971) The actor and the observer, divergent perceptions of the causes of behaviour, in (eds E.E. Jones, D.E. Kanouse, H.H. Kelley, R.E. Nisbett, S. Valins and B. Weiner) *Attribution: Perceiving the Causes of Behaviour*, General Learning Press, Morristown, NJ.

Kelley, H.H. (1967) Attribution theory in social psychology. *Nebraska Symposium on Motivation*, **15**, 192–238.

Ross, L., Greene, D. and House, P. (1977) The false consensus effect, an egocentric bias in social perception and attribution processes. *Journal of Experimental Social Psychology*, **13**, 279–301.

Understanding female customer markets | 7

Aims

This chapter aims to:

1. illustrate and describe the concept of gender;
2. analyse the concept of gender in the context of hotels; and
3. examine the nature of female customer markets.

Outcomes

At the end of this chapter you should be able to:

1. define and describe the concept of gender;
2. outline the issues involved in female consumption patterns;
3. evaluate contemporary hotel companies' strategies in female customer markets; and
4. discuss the implications of the concept of gender for the contemporary hospitality industry.

APPROACHES TO FEMALE CUSTOMER MARKETS IN THE HOSPITALITY INDUSTRY

The demand patterns of female customers for hotel products has been a subject which has frequently appeared in the hotel and catering literature. Early contributors to the discussion, drawn mostly from journalistic accounts, drew attention to the fact that female customers had different demand patterns from male customers, which were not being recognized by hotel companies (Marling, 1983). Following on from these journalistic accounts, hotel companies and related organizations such as Expotel (1993), conducted a variety of surveys aimed at identifying the specific demands from women as hotel customers.

Attention was directed towards what had been a gender bias in the supply of hotel products. This led to the inclusion of a range of facilities and products designed for female customers in an effort to overcome this bias. These efforts included providing skirt hangers, female toiletries, hair driers and more feminine decor in bedroom design for female customers. Some companies established particular programmes for female customers. These were advertised at what was at that time a specialist market. Examples include the Lady Hilton 1979, and the Lady Crest 1983. These initiatives helped signal a recognition by hotel companies that male and female customers had different demands for hotel products and services.

As the female business executive market grew in importance to hotel companies in the 1980s, they expanded their research of this group of customers. Additional research revealed that female customers appreciated the inclusion of gender-specific products (which were appreciated by males as well), but importantly females were still concerned about issues of security and sexual harassment which they experienced in their hotel stays. This harassment came from both male staff and male customers. The response by hotel companies was to embark on a series of training programmes designed to improve the treatment of female customers. Training included staff awareness of the lone female business traveller's situation, involving such initiatives as not giving out room numbers of female customers, not assuming in dining situations that the male would pay the bill, not assuming that lone female customers would want to dine with another person, etc. In some cases, hotel companies took the opportunity to develop the idea of women only floors, and, in other areas, the idea of the female club developed. In the contemporary industry many hotel companies such as Forte and Holiday Inn now have programmes aimed at female customers.

Expenditure on refurbishment programmes for female executives reflected their growing importance as a market segment. It is estimated that the female business market is now at around 25% of business customers in the UK, but is expected to grow significantly by the end of the 1990s (Tunstall, 1989). Clearly issues facing hotel companies in relation to female business markets need to be addressed if this demand is not to be lost to competitors, notably private clubs for women, which are increasing.

One recent survey concluded that the perceptions of hotel services did not vary significantly between male and female customers. Male customers also appreciated increased attention to areas such as security (Lutz and Ryan, 1993). The one exception to this was in the area of hotel restaurants, in which female customers claim to receive inferior treatment compared to their male counterparts. The authors conclude that despite the demand patterns of male and female business customers not differing significantly, hotel companies' initiatives towards female customers should be maintained. This is in order to encourage the recognition by female customers that the companies recognize them as an important group.

Clearly, what has occurred over the years is that hotel companies have made significant inroads towards changing gender biases in the provision of goods and services. They now recognize to some extent that products should reflect the demand patterns for them. At the same time, responses from female customers themselves indicate that their expectations of services go beyond the mere addition of feminine touches, into demands relating to equal treatment with respect to how women wish to use hotels. The result of this is that the discussion of the demand patterns of female customers has shifted away from the provision of female products into discussions of the hotel context and the factors which affect female usage patterns.

This has presented hotel companies with a dilemma, for attempts to alter the hotel context to cater for female consumption patterns have often been regarded by women as both patronizing and paternalistic. Relative to male customers, there is no question that female customers are less experienced hotel users. At present, male customers constitute the dominant customer market. The context of female consumption means that women are entering what has been a socially segregated space, that of one dominated by males (Mazurkiewicz, 1983).

Therefore, to understand the issues affecting female customers' use of hotels, hotels have to be discussed in the wider societal contexts in which they operate. We will argue that the social relations of society are reflected in hotels, and that this is also the case for gender relations.

THE IMPACT OF PATRIARCHY ON FEMALE BEHAVIOUR PATTERNS

The social relations of men and women have attracted much interest within the social sciences. This has resulted in many competing paradigms, all trying to explain gender relations in contemporary society. In fact, a feature of debate which has occurred since the 1970s, is the way in which the social sciences have and, more explicitly, the way sociology as a discipline itself has, marginalized gender as an issue. It is argued that the growth in feminist writings from both psychology and sociology have been responsible for the increased awareness and attention currently being paid to gender issues in their own right.

One approach to explaining gender inequalities has been to trace inequalities to the sexual division of labour which were established in pre-industrial society and have continued into the industrial era (Rowbotham, 1974). It was not the case that industrialization itself created inequalities between men and women, but that it acted as a catalyst to speed up the development of these inequalities and, indeed, to make them more visible. The sexual division of labour is often directly linked to the fact that it is the females in society who bear and raise children. Furthermore, this is natural and right, and women are genetically predisposed to nurture their children. Clearly, the fact that only the female can bear children in itself establishes an unequal balance of power between men and women. As women were incapacitated through reproduction, this established a dependency on males, who were seen as responsible for providing them the shelter and food necessary for survival. From this dependency, men established a greater balance of power in their relations with women and the relative tasks of both sexes were perpetuated as natural and unquestionable.

Established in the pre-industrial era, these inequalities were continued into the industrial era. Industrialization as we have seen created two definite and contained spheres of life with implications for both men and women. The public sphere of life, which included work, the economy and politics, was dominated by males; women were placed in the private sphere of life in which child rearing and domestic responsibilities were expected. In effect, women were excluded from the power structures of society (Rowbotham, 1974).

Social class differences were apparent in the treatment of women within the domestic sphere, but generally women were socialized into roles which reinforced the view that a woman's place was in the home with the family (Cunningham, 1979). There were clearly economic reasons for containing women in the domestic sphere. As Rowbotham notes, they competed with men as cheap labour and, as Marxist feminists would argue, for industry to be profitable it needed a labour force that were looked after in the home. However, these economic structures were supported by powerful ideologies which supported the exclusion of women from the public sphere and, thus, the segregation of the sexes into prescribed roles.

The wider society was characterized by patriarchal structures, in which males dominated females both economically and politically. These structures facilitated male control of women and perpetuated their inequality. Later in the century, the women's movement which had its origins with middle class women, challenged this exclusion. This was done by gaining access to educational opportunities which had previously been denied women and, as a result, gaining entry into male professions, for example medicine. It is interesting to note that medicine was initially a female prerogative; it would be female healers who tended the sick. However, males (notably the church) took the balance of power in medicine by declaring it to be a profession, and barred access to the education necessary for qualification (Rowbotham, 1974).

It is important to recognize that the exclusion of women did not only relate to employment opportunities, but also to female access to areas for consumption. As women were controlled by patriarchal structures this affected their freedom of movement into public areas where males again dominated. (Mazurkiewicz, 1983). Thus hotels and public houses were areas of consumption which belonged in the public sphere and were not available to females (Harrison, 1971). The only way a female could enter such a domain would be in the company of a male companion. The factors which have shaped the evolution of the hotel context as part of the public sphere and, therefore, male, have been an important issue in the debates now surrounding the adaptation of hotel products and services to the growing female business market.

Gender and stereotyping

Running as a parallel to the control of women in public spheres has been the role of advertising in shaping conceptions about male and female behaviour (Ewen and Ewen, 1982). Historically, women have been addressed by advertisers in two ways – one as wife and mother, where a series of products have been gender branded for female consumption, i.e. household goods and food products, and secondly as the target for beauty and diet products. Again, it is interesting to think that this may suggest that women are primarily conceived as physical beings; it is the appearance of women that is all important. Advertising has served to perpetuate sexual stereotypes about women, and again these have been important in shaping conceptions about female behaviour. Advertisers, of course, claim that their adverts merely reflect societal practices but, in continually presenting women in this way, they are in fact reproducing stereotypes. The concerns with diet and beauty are the result of women internalizing males' expectation about them and, therefore, male values about women. Despite the changing role of women in society in relation to their representation in employment, these stereotypes continue to operate. Some recognition of the changes have occurred in advertising, especially commercials which feature role reversal, as, increasingly, advertisers are realizing that gender branding does not always lead to successful selling.

Perhaps it is not surprising, therefore, that hotel company initiatives for female business executives have drawn upon sexual stereotypes and used feminine touches as a means of capturing the market. In this sense, hotels have been reflecting the stereotypes of the wider society.

As women's position in society changes in relation to gaining access to male spheres, organizations like hotels can experience difficulty in changing the context to make it more appropriate for female consumption to occur. It can be difficult to change the connotations and images which surround organizations. As hotels reflect the practises of wider society it is not unusual that these stereotypes will be evoked. Furthermore, it is difficult to control the behaviour of male customers, whose unwelcome attentions remain a source of discontent to female customers (Expotel, 1993). By engaging in what is often sexual harassment of women, male customers and sometimes staff are exercising power from their control of a particular social space. Unaccompanied women can be the target for this treatment in other institutions in the hotel and catering industry, for example public houses and restaurants (Smith, 1982). Hotel companies have, therefore, to attempt to come to terms with the view that male behaviour of this kind is inappropriate in the hotel context. They have to be prepared to discourage such behaviour, reducing the male domination of hotel spaces.

ALTERNATIVE APPROACHES TO FEMALE CUSTOMER MARKETS IN THE HOSPITALITY INDUSTRY

How can hotel companies respond to the demands of female customers? The first point is to suggest that companies must move beyond stereotyping, to identify how women actually want to use hotels. Women are not a homogeneous group and the term 'female business executive' in itself requires more attention. Exactly what does this mean to women, what are their needs, what are their expectations and perceptions? Women from a variety of occupational levels have demands for hotel products and services and these may vary with respect to time and reason for visit. Notice that this may also apply to male hotel users – it may not be appropriate to use such stereotypes in respect of males as groups, either.

Within female business executive markets, women are involved in aspects of networking and, indeed, these ideas have not been explored by hotels. Frequent business travellers may spend evenings in hotels and features such as aerobics classes may be unexplored areas of leisure facilities.

It is also useful to turn our consideration to the ways in which women may try to deal with situations that occur in what we have described as a public sphere, an area dominated by male values and demands. Consider, for a moment, how women may develop personal control strategies.

We have already identified the context of female consumption as a male social space. We have also argued that as a male space, hotels are contexts dominated by male behaviour and this has implications for female customers. One area which deserves analysis and has not yet been discussed in the literature is the way in which female customers negotiate these male territories. To be able to achieve this, we need to focus our discussion on what we will term personal control strategies. This term will be used to identify the ways in which women can successfully use hotels by exercising personal control in the situation in which they are in.

This idea shifts our attention away from both the paternalistic and patronizing approaches which have been used to date in dealing with female customers. It also centres attention on female behaviour and highlights women's input to the situation. In other words, adopting this approach will allow for the notion of women's agency in these situations.

Cavan's (1968) landmark text identified that bars were open social spaces which facilitate spontaneous interaction by strangers. Cavan (1968) is identifying bars as a context in which strangers have legitimately engaged in interaction and conversation with each other, and that this occurs because bars have been identified historically as social meeting places or as entertainment situations and contexts. This means that customers visiting these contexts are open to spontaneous discussions with other potentially unknown individuals or groups.

Additionally, as Spradley and Mann (1975) note in the context of cocktail bars, staff may be legitimately used to facilitate the introduction of strangers. Clearly, the staff are acting as intermediaries in social interaction. This can, for example, occur either whilst customers are awaiting service next to others, or in situations where customers send over drinks to others as a way of being introduced.

In the UK context, Smith (1982) has already indicated the issues experienced by female customers in public houses. Again, as male social spaces, women are required to negotiate a place in them. One control strategy used by women in the context of public houses has been to visit the public house in groups. These groups can either be single sex or mixed groups. Public houses are clearly different from hotels, both in the purpose of visit of customers and in the types of consumption which occur. With the exception of conference markets and training courses, women usually use the business hotel as individuals. In this situation it can be seen that it is more difficult for women to control the space than it is when they are in groups. The result, therefore, is that when women use hotels as individuals, alternative control strategies need to be developed. These might include reading in the dining room – this presents a barrier to interaction with strangers; inviting clients to dinner – in effect they are re-establishing control by actively choosing the other participants in interaction; engaging in leisure activities in the hotel – this avoids the problem by using time in a different way. All these activities can be seen as strategies that assist women in reasserting some control over situations, and they serve to legitimate their presence. To date, hotels have not considered the possibility of providing activities for female customers which would include recognizing those women's presence and control. This has to be an important factor, as the female business traveller is clearly in an occupational sphere where they are able to assert autonomy and control. The exact nature of such personal control strategies is an empirical question which hotel operators need to investigate if they wish to reduce the barriers to female consumption.

SUMMARY

In this chapter we have discussed the concept of gender and identified a relationship between patterns of hotel consumption and gender stereotyping. It appears that these patterns of usage, where women need to actively assert control strategies, are a reflection of wider societal patterns of behaviour. We have indicated that hotel operators need to investigate individual women's interpretations of situations in order to understand and present alternative approaches to catering for the demands of this market. As female business executives exercise power and authority in the occupational sphere, this will govern their expressions of their treatment in the area of consumption. The onus, therefore, rests with hotel companies to resolve the contradictions which are apparent in the treatment of female business executives in hotels.

DISCUSSION QUESTIONS

1. What is the value of the concept of gender when analysing customer usage patterns in a hospitality organization?
2. How can hotel and catering companies overcome gender stereotypes in order to benefit their overall product development? What would be the difficulties in putting ideas into operation?
3. What strategies might female hotel guests adopt when using hospitality services in order to overcome discriminatory behaviour?
4. To what extent do hotel and catering employment patterns reflect a sexual division of labour?

FURTHER READING

Beechey, V. and Whitehead, E. (eds) (1986) *Women in Society Today*, Open University Press, Milton Keynes. A good introduction to the situation of women in contemporary society. The text covers key issues such as employment and stereotyping.

REFERENCES

Cavan, S. (1968) *Liquor License*, Aldine Publishing, New York.

Cunningham, H. (1979) Leisure and the Industrial Revolution 1780–1800, Macmillan, London.

Ewen, S. and Ewen, E. (1982) *Channels of Desire: Mass Images and the Shaping of American Consciousness*, McGraw-Hill, New York.

Expotel (1993) Hotels and the female business traveller. *Dial Magazine*, Autumn.

Harrison, B. (1971) *Drink and the Victorians*, Faber & Faber, London.

Lutz, J. and Ryan, C. (1993) Hotels and the business woman, an analysis of business women's perceptions of hotel services. *Tourism management,* October.

Marling, S. (1983) Always the second sex: the plight of the travelling business woman. *Business Traveller*, March.

Mazurkiewicz, R. (1983) Gender and social consumption. *The Service Industries Journal*, **1**(1).

Rowbotham, S. (1974) *Hidden from History*, Pluto, London.

Smith, M. (1982) *The Publican in Participant Observation*, Salford University, centre for leisure studies.

Spradley, J.P. and Mann, B.T. (1975) *The Cocktail Waitress: Women's Work in a Man's World*. John Wiley, New York.

Tunstall, R. (1989) Catering for the female business traveller. *Travel and Tourism Analyst*, **5**.

Understanding food behaviour

8

Aims

This chapter aims to:

1. illustrate and explain the concepts of social stratification and social class, and to emphasize their relation to food behaviour;
2. provide a description of the nature and role of primary and secondary groups in the shaping of individual food tastes;
3. illustrate and explain the concept of socialization as a learning process; and
4. illustrate how social learning theory can explain the processes by which socialization occurs in relation to food behaviour.

Outcomes

At the end of this chapter you will be able to:

1. define and describe the concepts of social stratification and social class;
2. identify and describe primary and secondary groups in relation to individuals;
3. describe the concept of socialization as a learning process;
4. describe the processes by which individuals can learn food behaviour; and
5. make a case for the integration of sociological and psychological explanations of food behaviour.

Identifying the trends in the eating-out market is an important area of study for both students and hotel and catering operators. By evaluating trends in the eating-out market, catering operators can monitor changes in the popularity of particular food items, identify the spending patterns of individuals and groups and assess the market penetration of particular brands. Continual monitoring of the eating-out market is important for companies to maintain a market share and to identify the impact of competitors. Perhaps even more important to the long-term success of the company is a knowledge of the factors which influence customers' food preferences. Knowing the factors which shape individuals' taste in food allows catering operators to explain why certain trends are occurring. Furthermore, if catering operators can understand how food tastes are shaped, they will be in a better position to understand and predict the factors which influence changes in food behaviour.

INDIVIDUAL FOOD TASTE AND GROUP MEMBERSHIP

Most of us will consider that our tastes in food are individual and specific to us. We may, for example, be able to observe that friends and colleagues display different food tastes from ourselves when ordering from a menu. Therefore, individual differences in food preferences are important to consider if we are to understand food consumption patterns. At the same time, a great deal of our tastes are formed and shaped by our group membership. Hence, it is equally important to consider the impact of group structures in influencing individual behaviour. Within the social sciences the concept of social stratification has been used to identify both the impact of group membership upon individual behaviour, and the way in which the formation of groups may serve as a basis of social differentiation. This concept will, therefore, be drawn upon to assist us in examining the impact of group membership on individual behaviour in relation to food preferences and taste.

Prior to this, we need to establish more generally how group structures impact on individual behaviour. By doing this, we will also be able to identify the shaping and formation of taste and will elaborate upon the processes by which this occurs.

The starting point in the formation of food preferences can be traced to the early socialization of infants. Individuals are born into primary groups which are already established and have already formed ideas about food and food behaviour. Within the primary group, which in most contexts is the family or household, core values about food are transmitted to the young infant. These core values will include not only what constitutes food, for as we will see this in itself is culturally specific, but also a wide range of food behaviour. This includes the names for dishes, the structure of meals and particular codes of behaviour which surround eating. Using the word 'transmitting' does not imply that this is strictly a one-way process, clearly an infant can, to some extent, shape the adults' behaviour by refusing certain food products. Similarly, it is clear that the values that an adult is communicating will, in part, be a product of their own socialization. However, the individual's initial tastes in food are undoubtedly shaped by membership of a group. Many of these core values established in the early socialization of the child will stay with individuals throughout their lives. It is also at this point that food prejudices are passed on to individuals. The shaping of those tastes should, however, be seen as dynamic, both in the sense of the two-way communication process, which will be more deterministic at some points than others, and in the sense that individuals will move through different stages of a life course.

As individuals move into secondary groups, some of their core values about food will be retained, whilst others will be rejected. Secondary groups usually consist of friends and significant others. Consider the case of a child from an ethnic background beginning school for the first time. The child will have established core values about food, but will be subject under this new experience to sets of influences from other pupils and from teachers, although it is only fair to say that school meals have incorporated ethnic preferences into their meals and, indeed, food items offered to individuals at school may not be completely new to them. However, they will face some new items, some will be tried and the individual's food preferences thus widened. This process will continue as the individual's group membership extends throughout their development. First-year students living away from home for the first time may completely alter their food behaviour as a response to peer group influences.

It should be noted that in the process of taste formation, the early stages are the most important in the shaping of tastes. This is when tastes are more volatile and experimentation is more common. When food preferences and, indeed, food prejudices are established in later life, they can be difficult to change. It is for this reason that fast food operators aim their products at young children whose tastes are forming in the hope of establishing future brand loyalty.

In summary, the shaping of individual food taste is a long-term process and is heavily influenced by group membership.

Social stratification

Continuing our theme of group membership, sociologists have long since recognized that societies are not homogeneous in their composition, but rather are characterized by social division and inequality among the population. The concept which sociologists use to describe these divisions is social stratification. This term is essentially a geological metaphor as it implies a series or layer of strata which are hierarchically ordered, as in the arrangement of rocks. The hierarchy indicates that, within a population, individuals have differential access to both economic and social rewards, for example money or prestige.

There have been many attempts made to account for the stratification of societies, yet ultimately explanations return to the possession of power by particular individuals and groups. Discussions are then based around the ways in which this power can be used and can perpetuate inequality. Two points are relevant here. First, we must recognize that it is not only that social differentiation occurs in societies, but that it has important implications for individuals. Belonging to a particular group or stratum is important in terms of an individual's access to rights and privileges. Therefore, second, we could divide society up in relation to a host of criteria. We could, for example, divide according to the colour of people's hair. However, what really matters is the differences that are socially significant in the ways in which people are treated. We must also recognize that social stratification is not inevitable in societies, it is created by individuals within those societies. As such, those forms of stratification can be changed.

Within the sociological literature it is commonly accepted that societies are stratified on a host of criteria. The main criteria that sociologists identify are social class, gender, age, race, culture, education and occupation. Contributions from American sociologists add income and status to this list.

The German sociologist, Max Weber, identified that societies are usually stratified according to more than one criterion, which he termed multidimensional stratification. Since Weber's writings, it has become accepted among social scientists that social class, gender, age and race are universal forms of social stratification. That is, they are found in all societies. Whilst this is certainly the case, he should perhaps also have added that the importance of the stratification criteria depends upon the social context in which they occur. For example, race can be seen to be the most important criterion of social stratification in South Africa, whilst in Ireland it may be that religion is the most important criterion. Implicit within the concept of social stratification is the idea that individuals within a stratum possess a common attribute, be that male/female, young/old, etc. If these attributes are common, it may, therefore, be possible to attempt to predict how individuals in particular strata will behave in particular circumstances.

Now that we have established the concept of social stratification, we are in a position to be able to evaluate its utility for understanding individuals' food preferences. First, let us use the concept of social class.

Social class

There are many approaches within sociological literature to studying the concept of social class. Marxist contributors focus upon the structure of societies in relation to individuals' location in relation to the means of production or the means of producing wealth. Marxist commentators argue that ownership of the means of production, i.e. the place where wealth is created, places individuals in a particular location with regard to power. Those that own the means of production have power over those that do not. Hence, this approach to social class is, therefore, based upon social relations between groups. Within Marxian approaches, therefore, social class identifies the particular structural location of individuals in relation to each other. Marxian approaches to the concept of social class differ from those of stratification theorists.

Stratification theorists recognize that there are variables that are important in determining an individual's life chances, these of course, being occupation, age, gender, etc. If this is the case, they can then empirically identify groups who share a common position on these variables and these become termed social classes. It has been usual to identify an upper class, middle class and working class grouping within this approach.

Current approaches by stratification theorists accept that the class structure is more fragmented and group boundaries are more difficult to identify. When it comes to empirically testing these contemporary ideas, occupation tends to be the variable used as a symbol of an individual's social class. This is because for most people, their occupation is the main determinant of their life chances. Occupations are stratified in terms of the rewards which accrue to them, occupation remaining the backbone of the reward system (Parkin, 1974).

Despite the different approaches to analysing social classes (and these are not insignificant), commentators accept that social class position is important in behaviours with regard to food consumption. Mennell's (1985) analysis has shown that food tastes are shaped by social experience and that historically an individual's location in the class structure has had an important impact on food preferences.

Tracing the development of food consumption, Mennell (1985) notes that those at the top of the class structure were able to procure a wider range of ingredients and develop a particular pattern of food consumption. These food patterns acted to socially differentiate them from other groups in society and, indeed, to establish boundaries between classes. *Haute cuisine* is historically associated with the upper class, whilst peasants developed a different range of recipes and dishes.

Food consumption behaviour has always been linked to status and particular foods have been accorded high status because of their price, scarcity or association with particular groups. Contemporary surveys of food consumption continue to note the impact of social class differences in eating patterns. This occurs despite the fact of availability and price. The same ingredients can be turned into very different dishes, for example beef may be cooked in cream as the basis of a stroganoff, or eaten as a roast.

Gender is a further factor in assisting us to identify behaviours related to food consumption. We have already noted that historically, women's location in society placed them in the domestic sphere of the home and the family. Within the domestic context, cooking has evolved within households and, in popular conceptions, it is strictly a female activity. Surveys of household behaviour indicate that women continue to be in the majority when it comes to shopping and providing food for the household. What is interesting is the different status attached to cooking if it is conducted outside the domestic private sphere. With some notable exceptions, cooking in the public sphere is usually conducted by men, or chefs, and clearly the terms chef and cook carry different status. This must be taken as another indication of the separation of tasks within spheres of life, indicative of the way in which employment is, and continues to be, engendered.

Given the different relationship to food which women and men have had historically, it is not surprising to find gender differences in the selection of menu items (Ball, 1992). Added to this, we have already remarked on the way in which advertising works to reinforce male values about women in relation to appearance. This has stimulated the growth of an industry devoted to diet products, for which women still remain the main targets. Consider, for example, the number of slimming products advertised just after Christmas, or just before traditional summer holiday times. Think about these adverts and their target markets.

Within the framework of social stratification, age has been identified as a variable on which social divisions occur. In most societies, different rights and privileges are related to different age groups. For example, individuals in the UK must be 18 years old before they can legally consume alcohol in a public house. Again, we need to emphasize here that this is, in fact, a social construct. What constitutes young and old can vary across cultures, across time and across different societies. In the USA, the legal age for consuming alcohol outside the home is 21.

In relation to behaviours related to food consumption, age will clearly restrict diet at the extremes of very young and very old. In both cases, it may be that other people are required to feed an individual. However, age groups have been identified by both fast food and brewing companies as the target market for certain products. Within the fast food industry, young children are targeted by using role models, for example the promotion of food with 'Turtles' or 'Sonic the Hedgehog'.

From about 1970, UK brewing and retail companies identified youth markets for their products. Consumption patterns of young people can be used to express an identity and can be used to express a differentiation from their elders.

Any discussion of food consumption and behaviour must take account of the role of culture. This is a rather complex concept, but for our purposes we will adopt the definition established by anthropologists, that culture is 'a way of life of a group'. Anthropologists recognize that different societies have different cultures and food consumption is part of that culture. Food behaviour can be seen to be culturally specific. Levi Strauss (1978) argued that individuals take substances from nature and call them food. This can be demonstrated in France, where people eat horsemeat, or in Eastern cultures where dogmeat is often eaten.

Cultural patterns of food behaviour relate also to the structure of meals. This refers to issues of whether food is eaten in different courses, as is common in western Europe, or whether all the food is brought to the table at once, as is common in Chinese culture. It is interesting here to notice that as Chinese cuisine is served in many UK restaurants, it is served in courses. So, whilst the actual food remains Chinese, the manner in which it is served changes according to the culture in which it is served. As hotel and catering and fast food companies expand to the international environment, a knowledge of the cultural patterning of food is essential. There are many examples of UK companies adapting menus for international markets in the UK context, i.e. Hilton's approach to the Japanese market.

Racial differences are closely linked to culture when analysing food behaviour. Britain is often referred to as a multi-racial society, and this is meant to indicate that the society is made up of a range of groups with different heritages and ideas about food. Thus, we can identify specific food items among, for example, Chinese or West Indian groups. Racial and ethnic differences result in a wide variety of foods becoming available in the UK and are clearly connected to the growth of ethnic restaurants, such as Italian, Chinese and Mexican.

Religion can also be identified as a variable influencing food behaviour, and is closely related to race and culture. Religious taboos surround food in relation to the types of food that can be consumed, who should prepare and cook the food at what times and in their significance for the group. It should be becoming clear that when we study food we cannot divorce it from the social and cultural environment in which it is shaped.

The discussion, so far, has identified the social and cultural determinants of food preferences. Sociological approaches are concerned with the meanings and values which are attached to food. The roles of food in the structure of group life, for example the function food serves in establishing group boundaries and in socializing with friends, are all relevant to understanding food behaviour.

Within the hotel and catering industry, the context of food consumption is also important as restaurants pay attention to the environment in terms of layout, design and ambience. This can be used to reflect the purpose for the visit, i.e. entertainment, business, celebrations, etc. Often the context can be as important a factor in motivating customers to use the restaurant as can the food, i.e. TGIs.

One final area which has to be addressed when discussing the shaping of food tastes is the food manufacturing industry. Food manufacturers compete for a share of the highly profitable food market. As such, innovators of new products are important in gaining market share, which can stimulate developments. Advances in food technology mean that foods need not be seasonal and pre-prepared meals compensate for a lack of skill. This results in a situation in which customers can try dishes at home prior to ordering them in a public context. This serves as a means of reducing the risk of dissatisfaction. Food manufacturers are, therefore, able to perpetuate and influence the tastes of groups within the population. Efforts may be made in this respect to dictate fashions in food and patterns of consumption.

Thus far, we have concentrated on the impact of taste formation within the structure of group membership. This has been drawn from our framework of social stratification and has been useful in identifying the impact of group membership on individual tastes. The concept of social stratification does, however, mask the differences which we can find within groups, because as a concept it is rather static. Added to this, stratification theorists attempt to predict the behaviour of people by placing them in a category – age, gender, etc. – and assume a homogeneity of behaviour which may not be found in practice.

In an effort to address this problem, it may be useful to turn back to the concept of socialization, focusing upon individual differences in food behaviour.

INDIVIDUAL DIFFERENCES IN FOOD BEHAVIOUR: SOCIAL LEARNING THEORY

If we return to the concept of socialization, that process whereby individuals take on the values of the group to which they are a member, then essentially food habits must, in some way, be learned. As we have stated, an infant is born into a primary social group and it is, therefore, logical to consider that the early socialization will occur within this group. The early work in understanding social learning came from Bandura (1973), in the area of moral development. Indeed, students may be familiar with that work in relation to the arguments that are used with regard to the impact on young children of watching violence on television. However, it seems that social learning theory can also account for the socialization of food preferences.

Social learning theory attempted to explain both social and moral development in children and suggested that both are learned using the same mechanisms. Essentially, social learning is an observational kind of learning where children learn behaviours by watching others perform them. This learning can occur through two mechanisms: identification and imitation; reward and punishment.

Imitation and identification

Imitation occurs when infants and children directly copy another's actions. Clearly this copying behaviour involves the learning of very specific sets of skills, involving both the child and a role model from which to copy. It seems sensible to suggest that many behaviours may be learned in this way, including the codes that surround eating behaviours and those that structure meals within the primary group. Children will be taught how to use a knife and fork, for example, by copying the actions of a role model. If this is the case, there are a number of points that need to be made with regard to who and why children will engage in this imitating behaviour. First, with regard to the model that children will copy, the role model does not necessarily need to be a human being (Gross, 1992). It is often the case that the most important models will be siblings or adults who form the primary group. However, children do copy the behaviours of cartoon characters, characters from books, etc. Second, with regard to the question of why children copy some models rather than others, there are a number of points to be made.

1. It seems that children will be more likely to imitate behaviour that they perceive to be appropriate (Bandura, 1973). In the context of Bandura's work, this was connected to the idea that aggression was more likely to be imitated if the role model was an aggressive male, than if it was an aggressive female. Somehow, then, children seem to have a perception of sex role appropriate behaviours.
2. Children will be more likely to imitate behaviour that they perceive as relevant to them. Hence, for Bandura, boys were more likely to imitate the aggressive male model than were females. It may be important in learning social behaviour then, that the child perceives some kind of similarity between themselves and the role model. Again, this has implications for the ways in which gender-stereotyped behaviour will be imitated by children of different sexes.
3. Warm and friendly adults are more likely to be imitated by children than unfriendly ones (Yarrow, 1961).
4. More powerful role models were imitated quicker than were less powerful ones. Clearly, this raises the question of the child's perception and definition of power (Bandura, 1973).
5. The consistency of the role model's behaviour influenced the imitation.

By taking all these factors into consideration, it becomes clear that children can learn eating behaviours from role models and, indeed, these role models can be members of the primary group. However, role models can vary over time and space depending on the factors outlined. Hence, two children within the same primary group may learn slightly different eating behaviours simply by imitating two different people.

Observational learning is not, however, simply about copying the behaviours of other people; children do, it seems, have the ability to take on a whole role or whole set of behaviours from a role model. They do not only copy specific sets of behaviours. This involves the concept of identification. A child may begin by imitating a role model; however, once this process occurs, the learning may become internalized and the child will actually identify with the role model. This means that the child models itself on the whole person. Again, this may demonstrate how certain food preferences come to be learned in children. A role model may show preferences for certain kinds of food, or for eating at certain times during the day; these will then be taken on by the child. Clearly, identification will occur over a much longer time period than imitation and is likely to be influenced by factors such as the gender of the role model, the status of the role model and so on.

Rewards and punishments

Within social learning theory, learning is also influenced by the rewards or punishments that occur as a result of behaviours. Actions and behaviours that are positively reinforced are more likely to be repeated than those that are punished or ignored (Bandura, 1973). Again, much of the work here has been done with aggression as a form of behaviour. Hence, a child is more likely to repeat an imitated behaviour if that is accompanied by praise or some kind of reward rather than if it is ignored or punished. Within this notion of reward or punishment, it seems sensible to suggest that even within the same primary group, two children of similar ages may be rewarded or punished in slightly different ways. If this is the case, some kind of differential socialization is occurring. This means that even when children display similar behaviours, they can be treated slightly differently by the models in the primary groups, therefore learning different sets of behaviour.

Clearly, the ideas of social learning theory can inform us about the ways in which children can learn eating behaviours and learn the social codes that surround eating in a given society. They allow us to understand the ways in which children learn from the primary social group, and the factors which children seem to take into account when developing their learning. As such, eating behaviours are learned by children by various processes and from various role models. Therefore, it is only to be expected that individuals will indeed show differences in food preferences and eating behaviours.

SUMMARY

In this chapter we have presented theories and concepts that may be used to understand and explain food behaviour; that is the development of individual food preferences and the codes of conduct that surround patterns of eating behaviour. The concepts of social stratification and social class have been used to provide ways of understanding how factors such as culture, age and religion shape individual and group food behaviours. The concept of socialization has been used to provide a way in which membership of primary and secondary groups influences food behaviours. Clearly, again, it is the integration of wider social influences such as culture, and the processes by which cultural values can be transmitted, i.e. via social learning theory, that is important. Both the social, structural and individual variables need to be taken into account when attempting to analyse and explain individual food preferences and food behaviours.

DISCUSSION QUESTIONS

1. Identify the factors that influence the development of individual food tastes.
2. How might these factors operate in the shaping of food tastes?
3. Describe the concept of social stratification, and give another example of a situation in which it could be usefully applied to an analysis of the hospitality industry.

FURTHER READING

Murcott, A. (ed.) (1983) *The Sociology of Food and Eating: Essays on the Sociological Significance of Food,* Gower, Aldershot. This text is a very useful collection of readings, covering a variety of topics affecting food behaviour. The sociological significance of food is clearly demonstrated in relation to food in work settings, the meanings attached to food, and the social relationships which underpin food behaviour in domestic settings. Values attached to food behaviour are included in discussing the menus chosen for wedding receptions in the commercial context.

REFERENCES

Ball, S. (ed.) (1992) *Fast Food Operations*, Stanley Thornes, Cheltenham.
Bandura, A. (1973) *Aggression: A Social Learning Analysis*, Prentice Hall, London.
Gross, R. (1992) *Psychology, Science, Mind and Behaviour*, Hodder & Stoughton, London.
Levi-Strauss, C. (1978) *Myth and Meaning*, Routledge and Kegan Paul, London.
Mennell, S. (1985) *All Manners of Food: Eating and Taste in England and France from the Middle Ages to the Present*, Blackwell, Oxford.
Parkin, F. (1974) *Social Analysis of Class Structure*, Tavistock, London.
Yarrow, L.J. (1961) Maternal deprivation. *Psychological bulletin*, **58**, 459–490.

Choosing a fast food brand | 9

Aims

The aims of this chapter are to:

1. consider a sociological contribution to the issue of fast food consumption;

2. consider a psychological contribution to the area of fast food consumption;

3. evaluate sociological and psychological approaches to fast food consumption; and

4. illustrate the value of a multidisciplinary approach in the understanding and explanation of fast food consumption.

Outcomes

At the end of this chapter you will be able to:

1. describe the factors that a sociological perspective would use in the explanation of customer choice of fast food brands;

2. identify and describe the strengths and weaknesses of an individual decision-making approach to the explanation of customer choice of fast food brands; and

3. make a case for the integration of psychological and sociological explanations of fast food choice for operators in the hospitality industry.

FAST FOOD CONSUMPTION: PSYCHOLOGICAL AND SOCIOLOGICAL EXPLANATIONS

Attracting customers to buy and consume products is a key concern of producers and marketers in the hotel and catering industry. Contemporary approaches to the issue have involved attempts to classify the needs of customers using the Maslow hierarchy or by drawing from demographic and statistical data produced by marketing and consumer organizations.

The problems with these approaches have already been identified and discussed. Suffice it to say here, that they are limited to either providing descriptive and positivistic accounts of customer behaviour or suggesting frameworks which are incapable of empirical investigation.

Following the approach outlined in the book, a case will be made that social scientific approaches to answering questions of consumer choice and decision-making have more to offer than other approaches in assisting operations to understand the complex nature of customer behaviour.

Let us start our investigation with the question of why customers select particular fast food brands. Using a social scientific approach directs us first to ask which particular social science discipline is appropriate to the task. Clearly, there are many possibilities. To start with, we need to determine whether the focus of our enquiry should be concerned with individuals' perceptions of fast food brands and the factors which determine these, or whether we want to identify regular and consistent patterns of behaviour which can be traced to particular social groups. The latter approach is clearly identified as falling within a sociological framework.

This section will look at this issue from both a sociological and a psychological perspective.

SOCIOLOGY AND FAST FOOD CHOICE

For a sociologist confronted with the issue of consumer selection of fast food brands, the starting point would be to consider the factors which influence eating behaviour and the choice of eating venue. A key issue in this respect would be to consider how tastes are shaped and formed, and the role of group membership on those preferences. Using this approach, the individual's taste and selection is not a random process, although we acknowledge that fast food outlets might encourage a degree of impulse purchasing with regard to time and convenience for the consumer.

Clearly, to be of some value to fast food operators we need to furnish an explanation of behaviour which might go beyond the impulse purchase, and provide one which can establish a basis in which regular consumption patterns by individuals and groups can be identified.

The process by which tastes are shaped has already been discussed. The key variables which were identified in this process were social class, race and culture. It is clear, therefore, that an individual's group membership will be important in the process of eating behaviour in general, and in fast food consumption in particular. For our research topic, therefore, we have moved our discussion from an idea about consumer choices into a concept based upon group membership and group relations. Our hypotheses can now be concerned with the impact of group membership upon the selection of fast food brands.

The concept of group membership will require more elaboration to include the types of social groups to which individuals belong, the social networks in which individuals are involved, and the ways in which these operate in shaping customers' conceptions about food. This will involve such notions as the appropriateness of fast food outlets as an eating venue with the group, the ways in which fast food brands are classified in particular ways within the group, and the occasions on which fast food outlets may be classified as inappropriate and outside the range of venues considered by groups. Crucially, these classifications will be formed with respect to social class, gender, age and race. It may be the case that fast food outlets are not considered appropriate eating venues by some groups. Alternatively, fast food outlets may be identified as meeting venues for certain social groups. Again, we want to stress that the success of fast food brands depends upon a regular volume of customers who can form the basis of a stable market. Fast food operators cannot develop products based upon the individual conceptions of a disparate range of customers.

Thus we are now at the stage in the process where we need to identify and empirically test the social classifications of particular groups who use fast food outlets. We will need information regarding:

1. the reasons why particular groups use fast food outlets; and
2. the significance of fast food outlets within the wider framework of the eating behaviour of the group.

This will allow us to identify the role of fast food outlets within the eating behaviour of particular groups, and will allow us to avoid the collection of descriptive categories of customers which we often find in demographic approaches.

Now that the conceptual framework has been established, the next step is to select an appropriate research methodology. Since our task is rooted in customer expectations and evaluations of brands, we need a method which will capture this. Thus, we are involved in the 'why' type of question and, therefore, require an approach which goes beyond the collection of statistical data. Our research methodology will involve a qualitative approach and, in this context, interviewing is an appropriate research method to be able to determine the factors underlying customer selection. We can proceed in the stages of research as follows.

- Select sample and fast food brands.
- Select sample of customers.
- Interview customers.
- Analyse operating practices and objectives of fast food brands.
- Relate data to framework.

In designing the interview schedule, questions should cover areas of patterns of usage. These will include who influences the choice of eating venue, the significant group, individuals in the decision-making process and the ways in which consumption may be a function of group membership. Equally important will be the occasions in which fast food outlets are selected in preference to other restaurant contexts. This will direct us to the role of fast food in the consumption habits of the sample. Furthermore, the aims of a qualitative approach will be to identify the underlying values about brands and the extent to which these can be differentiated among specific social groups, acting to influence their consumption patterns.

In a research topic of this nature, we must include the role of fast food operators in the consumption process. This is because operators themselves attempt to influence consumption and selection both through their marketing and advertizing strategies, and their conceptions of the individuals and groups whom they seek to attract. Operators also seek to influence customer choice through the use of branding. Brands are positioned so as to manipulate the needs and demands of special groups. This is achieved through the design and layout of the facility, the visual display of products, and the association of the products with role models. Fast food operators consider the consumption process to be influenced by the concept of impulse purchasing, structuring their approach to capitalize on this. The research must, therefore, include the wider context of consumption and examine the role of fast food operations in influencing the selection process of consumers.

The practical applications of the sociological approach are the ability to furnish an analysis of consumption which is theoretically informed and, therefore, capable of being generalized to more than one unit and one occasion. It also avoids a reductionist view which relates consumption to prices, time available and convenience. This latter approach is of limited use in understanding the process of customer consumption. Whilst these variables may be important for impulse purchasing, fast food operators are also concerned to establish brand loyalty among customers and, therefore, require a means by which more stable and regular patterns of usage can be identified. From the point of view of operators who seek knowledge of the behaviour of specific groups, this sociological approach offers a testable framework to enable the consumption process to be identified, understood and evaluated in ways which are not possible in alternative approaches.

What we have suggested, therefore, is that a sociological analysis of the choice of fast food brands would focus on social relations and networks and the role that these play in consumer choice. Key variables include gender, race, age and social class.

A second way one could analyse the choice of fast food brands is by using a psychological perspective. One such perspective could be a decision-making approach.

INDIVIDUAL DECISION-MAKING APPROACHES TO FAST FOOD CHOICE

Given a choice to make between two or more restaurants or food outlets, an individual may make that choice by undertaking a rational decision-making procedure. This may entail carrying out an analysis according to 'subjective expected utility theory' (SEUT), 'multi-attribute utility theory' (MAUT), or a decision analysis.

To begin with in this example, we shall highlight a possible scenario using SEUT and 'multi-attribute utility decomposition' (MAUD) – the model derived from MAUT. SEUT and MAUT are psychological theories from which we can generate decision-making models that premis themselves on a rational decision-making principle. This principle suggests that individuals, when faced with a choice between two or more alternative courses of action, will make that choice by considering and maximizing utility. In other words, given two alternative courses of action – to go to McDonald's or go to Burger King – an individual will weigh up the pros and cons of each in relation to some values or utilities that are to be achieved, and will make the choice in terms of the place that offers the highest value.

Subjective expected utility theory (SEUT)

When considering the alternatives of Burger King or McDonald's, there are a number of phases that a decision-maker must go through.

1. *Identify the relevant decision-maker.* In this case it would be the individual involved: however, things may not always be so simple. If, for example, a family was considering dining out, it might be more complex trying to identify the decision-maker – it could be the parents, children or another.

2. *Identify the courses of action available.* Again in this case, the alternatives identified are the two outlets. (There is of course here the problem of how these are chosen, it may be that a decision strategy is required to do this!)

3. *Identify the relevant uncertainties in the world.* These are the factors that might influence the decision – in this case, possibly time, food preference, quality of food, choice of menu, etc. In this instance, we can assume that the uncertainty with regard to the choice is the time factor involved in being served. The decision-maker must now identify exactly what those time factors may be, or must try to anticipate the likely scenarios with respect to time. It might be that there are three possibilities envisaged:

   (a) there will be no queues and food will be served immediately;

   (b) there will be large queues and, therefore, considerable delay in being served; and

   (c) the outlet will be closed.

4. *Create a matrix that includes all the relevant information.* This will be set out in the following way.

	(a)	(b)	(c)
McDonald's	1	2	3
Burger King	4	5	6

Combining the alternative courses of action (the two outlets), with the possible states of the world (a, b or c), means that there are 6 possible outcomes or consequences envisaged – shown by numbers 1 – 6.

In cell 1, an individual will have chosen McDonald's, there will be no queues and the food will be delivered quickly. In cell 6, the individual will have chosen Burger King and the unit will be closed.

5. *Input values to the matrix.* Once the matrix has been drawn (the number of cells varying with the number of alternatives and likely states of the world), the decision-maker must then *input values to each cell*. The decision-maker will have a preference for some of the alternatives and outcomes and, at this stage, a numerical value must be assigned to those values. This is normally done on a scale of 1–100, and the utilities or values are supposed to be relative to each other.

   Thus, going to McDonald's with no queues may be of maximum value to the decision-maker, worthy of assigning a value of 100. Going to Burger King when there is a queue may still have value, but only a third of that in cell 1; therefore, it is assigned the value of 33. This procedure continues until each cell has been assigned a numerical utility.

   The matrix may then look like this:

McDonald's	100	60	0
Burger King	70	50	10

6. *Consider making a decision based on the number of decision strategies available.* A decision could now be made based on the information analysed so far.

   (a) An individual can choose the option which gives the outcome with the highest value – in this case, cell 1 with a value of 100; therefore, McDonald's would be selected. This is the **maximax strategy**.

   (b) An individual could choose the alternative which creates the best of a bad job, i.e. choose the cell which is next to the least in value. This would be cell 6, with a value of 10 utiles and Burger King would be selected. This is the **maximin strategy**.

   (c) A further strategy might be to sum the utilities of each alternative – McDonald's would achieve a utility of 160, Burger King a utility of 140, therefore, McDonald's would be chosen.

We can see that in some circumstances these do represent ways that we make decisions. We do on occasion just go for an alternative that appears to offer us the highest potential value, or the alternative that appears to offer us at least something if all else should fail. However, the crucial fact that is missing in these decision strategies is the likelihood of certain states of the world occurring. For example, given a particular time of day that the decision-maker is choosing to eat, a reasonably accurate prediction can be made about the likelihood of an outlet being closed. Similarly, given past experience, either direct or indirect, a decision-maker will have subjective judgements about the likelihood that queues will occur in outlets.

7. *Assign numerical figures that reflect the likelihood of the states of the world occurring.* In other words, the decision-maker is now asked to assign

probabilities to the uncertainties identified in stage 3. These probabilities are normally expressed as values between 0 and 1, and again need to be relative to each other and sum to 1. Thus, the decision-maker here may judge the following probabilities

- Scene 1 – there are no queues – probability=0.4;
- Scene 2 – there are queues – probability=0.5;
- Scene 3 – outlet is shut – probability=0.1.

8. *Calculate the 'subjective expected utility' (SEU)*. The decision-maker has all the relevant information needed to calculate the SEU. This is really only a function of the utility or value of each alternative outcome, combined with the likelihood that that outcome will occur. It is calculated by working out the sum of the utility and probability for each event.

$$\text{SEU McDonald's} = (100 \times 0.4) + (60 \times 0.5) + (0 \times 0.1)$$
$$= 40 + 30 + 0$$
$$= 70 \text{ utiles.}$$
$$\text{SEU Burger King} = (70 \times 0.4) + (50 \times 0.5) + (10 \times 0.1)$$
$$= 28 + 25 + 1$$
$$= 54 \text{ utiles.}$$

9. *Choice*. Since the expected value for McDonald's is greater than that for Burger King, the rational decision for the individual to make is to go to McDonald's.

There are a number of points to make about SEU as a decision-making process. First, it is meant to be a prescriptive theory for choice. There are a number of fundamental premises that SEU and decision theory are based on and, if these are appropriate, then the decision-maker ought to abide by the prescription for choice, even if that goes against intuition or 'what the decision-maker really wanted to do'. These fundamental principles or axioms are decidability, transitivity, dominance and the 'sure thing' principle. Students are referred to Wright (1984) for an explanation of these. In fact, the fundamental assumptions have been shown to be inappropriate in certain circumstances, hence the prescription for choice may not always be appropriate.

Second, it is a subjective utility measurement – the values and probabilities that one decision-maker inputs may not be the same as another decision-maker. Two individuals may well arrive at a different choice given the same alternatives in the world. Similarly, the subjective estimates and value judgements may be inaccurate in reality, i.e. an individual's estimates may not be a true reflection of reality. This is not a problem, since it is the perception of the decision-maker that is important in determining the choice. What is actually true may influence our decision-making, but equally what we believe to be true will influence our choices. Clearly, given that it may be more than one decision-maker involved in the decision of where to eat, this fact alone may cause some difficulty. The subjectivity of the process has often been criticized by students, but it must be remembered that this was, in fact, the intention of the theory.

Third, SEU represents the decision at a particular point in time. The individual assigns values and probabilities that may have changed by the time the group is standing outside the outlet, hence the process would have to be restarted. Taking a snapshot of reality in decision-making may not be appropriate, particularly where the nature of the world can change so rapidly.

Given some of these points, however, we can see that this may represent one way in which an individual could choose to aim for one fast food outlet rather than another. The psychological research that surrounds this approach is largely concerned with demonstrating the appropriateness of the four fundamental principles that underlie the theory, and with the cognitive mechanisms and processes that individuals use when assessing value judgements or probability judgements.

Despite the theoretical and descriptive difficulties of these approaches, this information in itself may be of value to a hospitality manager. For instance, if probabilities (in this case the likelihood of queues) are judged primarily on the basis of past experience, a manager may want to create an environment where queues appear to be smaller than they really are, or use strategies where food comes at a discount if a certain waiting period had been encountered. Even so, there is information available on heuristics and biases that suggests that when we make such probability judgements we use strategies that simplify the nature of the information. Whilst these strategies allow us to make accurate judgements most of the time, they also lead, on occasion, to systematic errors or biases in judgements. It might be that knowledge of these errors would be advantageous. Students are referred to the further reading for information on heuristics and biases.

The above example is, in fact, a fairly simplistic representation of the decision problem regarding which fast food outlet to choose. The utility of each outcome is a general statement of value and it might be that there are complex factors that constitute this value. The SEU calculation that we have used has allowed only one dimension of uncertainty to be introduced. The assumption here is that all other variables and factors are included in the assigned values given so, for example, the quality of the food is taken into consideration in the overall utility figure.

There is, however, a second decision strategy that might be employed given the alternative courses of action, which takes into consideration the issue of multi-attribute utility situations. Thus, this strategy (MAUT) recognizes that there may be more than one variable over which the value of the outlet is to be evaluated. As with SEUT, there are a number of phases that the decision-maker will negotiate.

Multi-attribute utility theory (MAUT)

1. *Identify the decision maker.* In this case the individual faced with the choice of outlets.
2. *Identify the alternative food outlets which are to be compared.* This again might be McDonald's, Burger King, Pizza Hut.

3. *Identify the dimensions on which each alternative is to be compared.* For an accurate comparison, and one in which variables do not overlap with each other and thus contribute to the total utility more than once, each dimension must be isolated and different from the others. This is achieved by a process of triadic comparison.

In this case, to elicit the dimensions, one would ask the decision-maker to think of ways in which McDonald's and Burger King were similar, but different from Pizza Hut. The answer may be food product. The process would continue: in what ways are McDonald's and Pizza Hut similar, but different from Burger King? The answer may be presentation of food. This continues until all the dimensions that are important, but different from each other, have been worked out.

Assume that the dimensions of importance are

- Price
- Presentation of food
- Speed of delivery
- Cleanliness
- Image.

4. *Assign a weighted value to each of the dimensions.* We now have the alternatives that are to be compared and the criteria that are important in making that comparison. Clearly, however, some of those dimensions will be more important than others, so weighted values must be assigned. This is normally done by ranking dimensions in order of importance, then assigning them relative values which will sum to 1.

Dimension	Rank	Value
Price	Rank 1 (most important)	0.5
Presentation	3 =	0.1
Speed of delivery	Rank 5 (least important)	0.05
Cleanliness	Rank 2	0.25
Image	3 =	0.1

From this, it can be seen that to the decision-maker, price is twice as important as cleanliness, while speed of delivery is half as important as presentation.

5. *Assign a value for each alternative on each dimension.* Again, this is normally done on a scale of 1–100, and the values ought to be relative to each other. The decision-maker must then consider the value McDonald's has on a scale of 1–100 regarding price, presentation, speed, etc. The following matrix can be produced.

	Price	Presentation	Speed	Cleanliness	Image
McDonald's	80	60	50	60	50
Burger King	70	50	50	60	40
Pizza Hut	60	60	30	70	70

Hence, Pizza Hut has twice the value in the price category as it does in the speed category, Burger King and McDonald's have equal value for speed and presentation.

6. *Carry out the MAUT calculations.* The decision-maker must combine the importance of each dimension with the actual value on all dimensions for each alternative, i.e. the multi-attribute utility (MAU) for each alternative is calculated by the sum of dimension weighting and value for each combination with each alternative.

$$\text{MAU McDonald's} = (0.5 \times 80) + (0.1 \times 60) + (0.05 \times 50) + (0.25 \times 60) + (0.1 \times 50)$$
$$= 40 + 6 + 2.5 + 15 + 5$$
$$= 68.5 \text{ utiles}$$

$$\text{MAU Burger King} = (0.5 \times 70) + (0.1 \times 50) + (0.05 \times 50) + (0.25 \times 60) + (0.1 \times 40)$$
$$= 61.5 \text{ utiles}$$

$$\text{MAU Pizza Hut} = (0.5 \times 60) + (0.1 \times 60) + (0.05 \times 30) + (0.25 \times 70) + (0.1 \times 70)$$
$$= 30 + 6 + 1.5 + 17.5 + 7$$
$$= 62 \text{ utiles}$$

7. *Prescription for choice.* Since the highest utility value in this case is that of McDonald's, with a value of 68.5, this is the outlet that should be chosen.

MAUT is based on the same premises as SEUT and, therefore, should be treated with the same amount of caution when considering the prescription for choice. However, it should be possible to see that in many instances we do make decisions by going through a process like this, even if we do not necessarily input the actual numbers and carry out the calculation. Indeed, consumer magazines that compare and contrast different consumer items use this procedure when evaluating them, e.g. *Which?* magazine.

The difficulties of numerical attribution have been considered with respect to SEUT and MAUT and, in fact, even if the final option is rejected, it is often thought that merely carrying out the process of breaking down the decision into its component parts will benefit the decision-maker. The operationalization of SEUT and MAUT – decision analysis – which is used in business and can be seen in many marketing texts, is often thought to improve decision-making by 'dividing and conquering'.

It is useful to consider the dimensions that were important to the decision-maker in this above MAUT example. Some of the factors were readily quantifiable, e.g. price, yet others were not, e.g. image and cleanliness. Again, this does not constitute a real problem because it is the decision-maker's perception of those things which are important.

These techniques were intended to be prescriptive and the major criticism of these approaches to decision-making is that they do not actually describe the real process of decision-making that individuals go through. It is useful here to re-emphasize the point that in the above examples, this criticism is probably an accurate one; it is unlikely that you would go through the process of SEUT or MAUT to decide where to eat. The fast food operators' notion of the impulse purchase is probably of greater influence. However, these techniques may still inform us of decisions involved in forming brand loyalties. It may be, for example, that past experience of queues in outlets, or the cleanliness of the outlet has contributed to a multi-attribute decision, which may then influence overall decisions on brands. However, in other cases, e.g. investment decisions, whether or not to merge companies, etc., these techniques may be descriptive of at least some of the process. It is interesting to note that in such cases, not only are the risks of alternatives high (hence possible payoffs or values), but also that probabilities and values are probably more readily quantifiable, through market analyses and projections.

The value of these ideas and theories to the hospitality manager is the same in both cases. Research into any kind of decision, and the process involved, may give coherent indications as to appropriate planning and behaviour. To assume that individuals choose fast food outlets on a whim, or according to the proximity of the outlets, would be misguided without empirical foundation.

As students will have seen, SEUT and MAUT can be used to prescribe and analyse individual decision-making strategies and processes. They may have weaknesses as far as their ability to describe everyday decisions goes but, as illustrated, they can be used to provide investigators with some information about decision-making processes. Thus, they can provide information about the ways in which individuals access information and how that information may be evaluated and processed. Kahneman and Tversky (1979) did, in fact, recognize the weaknesses of SEUT and attempted to overcome these in their proposed 'prospect theory'. Students are guided to the further reading section.

As can be seen, multi-attribute evaluations can often by used when making choices between products or services where more than one criterion is of value to an individual. However, it seems that SEUT may be far too simplistic for the consideration of everyday choices. It is a static model and can really only incorporate one dimension of uncertainty into the calculations. If you consider the decision-making situations that you find yourselves in, it is likely that the alternatives, criteria for choice and uncertainties would be more complex than this.

Decision analysis and the decision to expand a product range

It is useful to consider another model or aid to decision-making – that of decision analysis. Decision analysis is the way in which SEUT and MAUT are integrated in order to provide another prescriptive model for choice. Students may encounter examples of these decision aids in accountancy, marketing or business texts. It is important to note that whilst these may illustrate the models, they rarely comment upon the assumptions that underlie them. In other words, they cannot comment upon the weaknesses of such models arising from the nature of the fundamental axioms.

In any decision analysis, there are a number of stages that a decision-maker would go through. Since the model is based on SEUT and MAUT, it is not surprising that these stages are familiar.

1. Identify the decision-maker/s.
2. Identify the alternative courses of action.
3. Identify the criteria on which to compare the alternatives.
4. Identify the relevant uncertainties.
5. Represent the decision problem in the form of a decision tree.
6. Assess the decision outcomes. For this, use MAUT.
7. Assess the relevant uncertainties. For this, elicit probability figures.
8. Evaluate the alternatives. For this, use SEUT.
9. Carry out a sensitivity analysis. Work out the extent to which the figures would need to be changed in order to produce a change in the final prescription for choice.
10. Follow the prescription for choice.

The starting point and the structure that will determine the level to which the problem is addressed, is the design of the decision tree. This will illustrate the alternative courses of action, which will lead to a finite number of outcomes. The outcomes are then compared as a function of utility on the dimensions that are important. Probabilities are elicited at the points of uncertainty, and the decision-maker is then in a position to combine the information using SEUT to arrive at a prescription for choice. Calculations should begin by rolling back from the outcome end of the tree, as some of these calculations may produce utility figures that will be used at earlier uncertainty points in the tree.

Consider the following example. A company is in the process of deciding whether or not to expand its product range. If it decides to expand, then it can either develop a completely new product or it can modify an existing one. The company is concerned about the length of time these developments will take, the financial cost in terms of immediate outgoings and, of course, the predictability of the outcomes. They are also concerned with whether or not the staff within the company have the ability to develop the product. What should they do?

This is a relatively simple example, but is worth using to illustrate the idea of decision analysis as a decision aid. Let us follow the decision stages.

1. *Identify the decision-maker/s.* The directors of the company.
2. *Identify the alternative courses of action.* (a) To keep the old products only; (b) to develop a completely new product; (c) to develop a product that is a modification of an existing product.
3. *Identification of the criteria on which to compare the alternatives.* (a) Time; (b) financial cost in terms of immediate outgoings; (c) predictability of the outcomes.
4. *Identification of the uncertainties.* The likely success of the product in terms of the company's ability to develop it.
5. *Representation of the problem.* This involves designing the decision tree incorporating all the courses of action and outcomes that result from those. Squares represent the points of choice, circles represent the points at which uncertainty occurs and ovals represent the outcomes. This tree will be explained and elaborated upon as we get to the seventh stage.

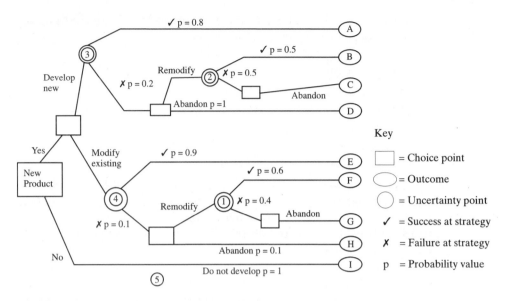

6. *Assess the outcomes, using MAUT.* The criteria of importance, their rankings and relative weightings are as follows:

Criteria	Rank	Weighting
Immediate financial cost	1	60
Predictability of outcome	2	30
Time	3	10

The position of each of the outcomes on these dimensions is perceived to be:

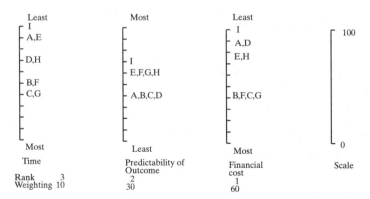

Hence, the multi-attribute utility (MAU) for each outcome can be calculated.

$$\text{MAU A} = (10 \times 90) + (30 \times 40) + (60 \times 90)$$
$$= 900 + 1200 + 5400$$
$$= 7500 \text{ utiles}$$

$$\text{MAU B} = (10 \times 50) + (30 \times 40) + (60 \times 50)$$
$$= 500 + 1200 + 3000$$
$$= 4700$$

Students are referred back to the example of MAUT to continue the calculations here; the results for the remaining outcomes work out as

MAU C = 4600
MAU D = 6400
MAU E = 7500
MAU F = 5300
MAU G = 5200
MAU H = 7300
MAU I = 9100

7. *Assess the uncertainty figures, eliciting the probability figures.* At uncertainty point 3, if the decision is to develop a new product, and then to develop a completely new product, the likelihood of success is estimated at 0.8, and the likelihood of failure at 0.2. If the development works, then outcome A occurs.

If it does not work, the company is then faced with a choice of whether or not to abandon the idea, or to have another go by modifying an existing product. It is thought that a complete redevelopment of a new product would be too time consuming. If the decision is to modify, the likelihood of success of that is 0.5, and the likelihood of failure is 0.5. Having failed once, the estimate of success is thus reduced. These alternatives lead to outcomes B and C respectively. If, on the other hand, the choice is just to abandon the whole idea, then that will lead to outcome D and, in effect, the old product will be the only one used now, and that will still have a utility.

At uncertainty point 4 the option is to choose to develop a new product, but to do that by modifying an existing one. If this choice is made, again there is the uncertainty of the ability to do this. If we follow this route, the probability of success is estimated at 0.9, and the probability of failure at 0.1. The probability of success here leads to outcome E, and as this is higher than with the completely new product, we might expect that this company has had past experience of development of products, and they have largely been more successful with modifications of existing products.

If that modification fails, they are then faced with the choice of abandoning the idea, which will lead to outcome H, again still with a utility.

Or they could decide to remodify. In this case the probability of success is estimated at 0.6 leading to outcome F. And the probability of failure as 0.4 leading to the decision to abandon the idea which leads to outcome G. Clearly again here, failure to modify the first time means that the company is less certain about its ability to remodify.

And finally of course, the company could make the choice not to develop the product in the first place, and since they know they have the ability to do this, the probability value is 1, and this leads to outcome I.

8. *Evaluate the alternatives, using SEUT.* Remember that SEUT is a function of the combination of probability and utility and, in effect, what we need to work out is the SEU for the alternatives; (a) stick to the old product; (b) develop a completely new one; (c) develop a new one based on

modifications to an existing one. We really need the SEU values at points 3, 4 and 5, and we should opt for the alternative that gives us the highest value. If students examine the tree now, it is clear that the SEU figures at uncertainty points 1 and 2 will give us utility values that are needed for SEU at 3 and 4, hence these will be worked out first.

$$
\begin{aligned}
\text{SEU 1} \ &= \ (\text{Utility F} \times 0.6) + (\text{Utility G} \times 0.4) \\
&= \ (5300 \times 0.6) + (5200 \times 0.4) \\
&= \ 3180 + 2080 \\
&= \ 5260
\end{aligned}
$$

$$
\begin{aligned}
\text{SEU 2} \ &= \ (\text{Utility B} \times 0.5) + (\text{Utility C} \times 0.5) \\
&= \ (4700 \times 0.5) + (4600 \times 0.5) \\
&= \ 2350 + 2300 \\
&= \ 4650
\end{aligned}
$$

$$
\begin{aligned}
\text{SEU 3} \ &= \ (\text{Utility A} \times 0.8) + (\text{SEU 2} \times 0.2) + (\text{Utility D} \times 0.2) \\
&= \ (7500 \times 0.8) + (4650 \times 0.3) + (6400 \times 0.2) \\
&= \ 600 + 930 + 1280 \\
&= \ 8210
\end{aligned}
$$

$$
\begin{aligned}
\text{SEU 4} \ &= \ (\text{Utility E} \times 0.9) + (\text{SEU 1} \times 0.1) + (\text{Utility H} \times 0.1) \\
&= \ (7500 \times 0.9) + (5260 \times 0.1) + 7300 \times 0.1) \\
&= \ 6750 + 526 + 730 \\
&= \ 8006
\end{aligned}
$$

The utility of staying with the old product will be

$$
\begin{aligned}
\text{SEU 5} \ &= \ (\text{Utility I} \times 1) \\
&= \ 9100
\end{aligned}
$$

9. *Sensitivity analysis.* This stage of the decision analysis is really a final check on the whole procedure. It essentially involves working out how the figures included in the analysis would need to be changed for the final prescription to change. The end to the decision analysis becomes the prescription for choice.

10. *Follow the prescription for choice.* In this case, the company should not develop a product of any kind, but stick with the old one. The utility for outcome I, combined with the probability of success in terms of ability to do it, is higher than for any other combination.

Again, there have been criticisms of decision analysis as an aid to decision-making. Obviously, it remains a static model, while the environment in which decisions are made may be dynamic. Similarly, it works on the assumptions that underlie SEUT and MAUT and we have discussed the problems with these. However, the strengths of the approach seem to lie in the fact that merely carrying out the process can make considerations more explicit. It can mean that alternatives are not forgotten and that criteria which are important in making a decision are recognized. Indeed, it may be that carrying out such an analysis will reveal the necessity for more environmental analysis or more explicit information generally. At the very least, such an analysis will allow the identification of relevant issues and information.

SUMMARY

What we have tried to do in this section is suggest that both sociology and psychology have something to offer to students in their understanding of customers' selection of fast food brands. A sociologist would be interested in looking at the ways in which variables such as race, gender and age influence the purchase choice, while a psychologist would be interested in the ways in which individuals access and select information relevant to that choice, and the ways in which they might then evaluate that information. An example of a decision analysis has been presented in order to suggest how subjective expected utility (SEU) and multi-attribute utility (MAU) could be used in more complex planning decisions. Our central point is that this multidisciplinary approach can give students a better explanation and understanding of behaviour and, indeed, that it can offer fast food operators some ideas about the way in which their customers behave and the reasons for their purchase behaviour.

DISCUSSION QUESTIONS

1. Make a case for the use of a multidisciplinary approach to understanding why customers choose particular fast food outlets.
2. In what other situations might a decision-making approach be useful within a hospitality context?

FURTHER READING

Graves, D. and Lethbridge, D. (1975) Could decision analysis have saved Hamlet? *Journal of Management Studies*, May, 216–225. A lighthearted look at the practical application and use of decision analysis.

Cooke, S. and Slack, N. (1984) *Making Management Decisions*, Prentice Hall, London. This is a useful text for undergraduates on management courses. It outlines areas of decision-making and uses applied examples in order to illustrate themes and issues.

Wright, G. (1984) *Behavioural Decision Theory*, Penguin, Harmondsworth. This is an excellent text outlining the main ideas and principles behind decision making and evaluates different approaches. It is short, clear, and uses everyday examples.

REFERENCES

Kahneman, D. and Tversky, A. (1979) Prospect theory: an analysis of decision under risk. *Econometrica*, **47**, 263–291.

Wright, G. (1984) *Behavioural Decision Theory*, Penguin, Harmondsworth.

Race and discrimination in the hospitality context

10

Aims

This chapter aims to:

1. define the concepts of race, prejudice and discrimination;
2. consider racial discrimination in the UK in a historical context;
3. discuss the Race Relations Act and its operation in terms of the role of legislation in changing behaviour; and
4. identify social scientific explanations for stereotyping, and its relation to an analysis of race in the contemporary hospitality industry.

Outcomes

At the end of this chapter you will be able to:

1. compare and contrast the concepts of race, discrimination and prejudice;
2. apply sociological and psychological explanations of racial stereotyping to patterns of employment and behaviour within the hospitality industry; and
3. discuss the relationship between attitudes towards race and behaviour in interactions in hotels and catering.

In 1991, the Commission for Racial Equality published the results of an investigation into employee recruitment and selection in the hotel and catering industry. The study revealed that ethnic minority employees were disproportionately concentrated in unskilled jobs within the industry. Consequently the report indicated that racial inequalities were a feature of the hotel and catering industry. Many reasons were advanced to explain the concentration of ethnic minorities in unskilled jobs, such as the image of the industry, the recruitment practices of employers, a lack of ethnic minority applications and, finally, racial stereotyping.

The image of the industry has been the subject of discussion over the years (Corcoran and Johnson, 1974) and has prompted many studies by the hotel and catering industry's training board (now the Hotel and Catering Training

Company). Recruitment methods of hotel and catering companies have also been discussed in the literature (Mars and Mitchell, 1976; Wood, 1992). The practice of racial stereotyping has, however, received far less attention from commentators, and issues of race in general have not been systematically discussed within the hospitality literature. To be able to understand and explain why racial stereotyping occurs and to consider its implications, we must address the issue within the wider concept of race relations.

The study of race relations is a legitimate subject matter for social scientific analysis as it is concerned with the kinds of social relations which exist within and between groups in a population (Rex, 1986). Furthermore, the field of race relations requires a multidisciplinary approach in order to explain the societal structures and forms of organization which contribute to discrimination and racial inequality. At the same time, we need to identify the attitudes and belief systems of individuals, as these may serve to perpetuate racial inequalities.

In attempting to understand the issue of race, therefore, both sociological and psychological contributions to the field of race will be discussed. It is worth noting at the outset that the subject of race is a complex one, and a comprehensive coverage of the area is outside the scope of this text. What we will attempt to do is to identify some of the central issues in the study of race, and assess their implications for understanding race and ethnicity in contemporary society and, in particular, in the contemporary hospitality industry.

THE CONCEPT OF RACE

An appropriate starting point in our analysis is to trace the evolution of the concept of race and to clarify the terms of race, ethnicity, discrimination and prejudice.

Race and biology

Early approaches to the study of race identified the concept in biological terms. Within these approaches race became a category in which groups of a population were differentiated from each other on the basis of phenotypical markers, or differences in physical appearance, notably skin colour, pigmentation (Van der Berghe, 1986). These early approaches were often used to justify inferior treatment of one group by another (Rex, 1970).

Following the Second World War and the ideas about race which had influenced the treatment of Jews in Germany, UNESCO commissioned a team of biologists to give an exact scientific meaning to the term 'race' (Baker, 1974).

The biologists working for UNESCO (1952) concluded that the human species had a single origin and that races were statistically distinguishable groups only. The investigation further concluded that the recognition of racial differences did not correlate with behavioural or physiological differences which had previously been used to justify the unequal treatment of some groups by others (Rex, 1986).

Categorizing groups in terms of racial differences did not, however, explain why inequalities in the treatment of different groups were a feature of many societies. This led sociologists and psychologists to enter the field of studying race.

Race and colonialism

In seeking to identify the origins of the racial domination of one group by another, it is important to note that the specific causes of racial domination are not universal. In fact, the practice relates to specific historical periods and sets of social relations (Rex, 1970). For example, racial domination can be related to a country's colonial past. As Rex (1970) suggests, many European countries took territory in the New World and functioned by dominating the native population. This extended to the creation of low wage slave labourers necessary for the acquisition of the resources of that country. As Africans, for example, were physically different from Europeans, they were subject to different sets of laws, which established a system of domination by the colonialists. Britain's colonial history fits into this pattern. The history of slavery has been well documented – basically slaves were treated as a commodity which could be bought and sold, and as a group which had different laws and rights applied to them. Slave owners, therefore, dominated and exploited the slave group. The issue here is that racial domination created a situation in which Black Africans were differentiated on the basis of race, so that they came to occupy different positions in the social order from their White masters (Rex, 1970). These different positions in the social class structure resulted in unequal treatment economically, socially and politically. Once these practices become established in societal structures, they are difficult to change. Clearly, those in the position of power are hardly likely to relinquish that power particularly if that also means relinquishing a means of acquiring wealth. Modood (1992) suggests that when some groups gain economic advantage, racial discrimination and prejudice can continue, and even become heightened. The relationship between race and social class is complex, and has been the subject of debate within sociology (Rex, 1986; Wolpe, 1986). Within sociology then, it is important that the analysis of social class structures do not marginalize the concept of race.

We can observe already that studies of race include both the ways in which societies are organized with respect to power and domination, and at the same time the belief systems of individuals. Within the UK context, discussions of racial discrimination are often attributed to the patterns of immigration which can be traced to 1948, with the arrival of many immigrants from Jamaica. These immigrants filled the unskilled positions and accepted jobs which were difficult to fill by White workers and White nationals. From this period until about 1958, demand for labour outstripped supply and immigrants filled these jobs (Braham, Rhodes and Pearn, 1981). This was not only at the unskilled level, but also in areas such as the National Health Service. The early waves of immigrants resulted in a concentration of particular groups in particular geographical areas of the country, usually where labour was required (CRE, 1985). Thus, for example, the growth of certain groups can be correlated with the nature of the textile industry in Yorkshire. Immigrants often experienced problems in housing and tended to colonize certain districts of towns, producing enclaves or pockets within the towns where certain groups were concentrated.

In later years, Britain opened its doors to commonwealth immigrants escaping political persecution. However, in Britain, the economic conditions changed and employment opportunities were not as plentiful. Ethnic groups were blamed for levels of unemployment in some areas, and prejudicial feeling saw them identified as scapegoats. It is often the case that minority groups will be reacted towards in this way in times of economic difficulty. In some political quarters, Britain's economic problems were attributed to the perceived high levels of immigrants and ethnic groups. In fact, in 1988, the ethnic minority population was still only 4.7% of the total UK population (Haskey, 1990).

So far, we have discussed a situation in which the phenotypical and physical characteristics between groups in a population are the basis for unequal treatment. It is now recognized by commentators that 'race' as a biological concept is insufficient to explain the complexities of race relations in contemporary society. Therefore, having established some of the contextual features of racial domination we can now turn to the contemporary treatment of the issue, which will involve some analysis of race and ethnicity.

Race and discrimination

In 1976, the Race Relations Act established the legislative context for the treatment of racial groups. Within the act, race referred to biological differences and it was deemed unlawful or illegal to discriminate on racial grounds with respect to the following: colour, race, ethnic or national origin.

A racial group was defined as a group of persons defined by reference to colour, race, national or ethnic origins. The Race Relations Act included and defined the concept of ethnicity. Within the terms of the act, a group can be defined by reference to its ethnic origins if it constitutes a separate and distinct community by virtue of characteristics which are commonly associated with common racial origins. This means that the term ethnicity is being used in a much wider sense than simply a racial or biological category. For a group to constitute an ethnic group, it must regard itself and be regarded by others, as a distinct community possessing certain characteristics. This was established by Lord Frazer in Mandela vs. Dowell-Lee 1983. The characteristics that ethnic groups must have are:

- a long shared history;
- a cultural tradition of their own;
- a common geographical origin or descent from a small number of common ancestors;
- a common language not necessarily peculiar to the group;
- a common literature peculiar to the group;
- a common religion different from that of neighbouring groups; and

- a sense of being a minority or being oppressed or dominated within a larger community.

Within the UK, the following ethnic groups have been identified: West Indian, African, Indian, Pakistani, Bangladeshi, Chinese, Arabs, mixed race, other (Haskey, 1990). As is indicated, the concept of ethnicity is a much wider concept than the biological definition of race. Contained within the concept of ethnicity are the values, traditions, religious practices and behaviour patterns of particular groups.

Ethnic groups have cultural practices and ideas which may appear alien to the host culture (Modood, 1992), and these can serve as the basis of discrimination. Within the context of the hospitality industry, the cultural values and traditions of particular groups must be recognized and accommodated if discrimination is to be avoided.

The introduction of the Race Relations Act was clearly a recognition that racial discrimination was practised in all aspects and areas of society, from employment to education and housing. Underpinning the legislation was the view that in a multicultural society, equal opportunities should be afforded to all citizens. The question that now needs to be addressed is how effective can legislation be in outlawing discrimination?

Thus far, we have traced the origins of racial domination and discrimination to the structures of society and to historical contexts. Examining the structure of contemporary society, it is clear that institutionalized racism can be found in the UK. This refers to the policies which possibly unintentionally, produce unequal opportunities and consequences on the grounds of race or ethnicity. When this situation occurs, these institutions (such as education and the media) can reproduce racism over time.

Within organizations, this may involve cases of dress which are inappropriate to particular racial groups, or a lack of understanding of the religious and cultural beliefs of groups. Clearly, these policies are linked to prejudice whether or not the organization is aware. Part of this prejudice may be the belief that ethnic groups should assimilate into the host culture and adopt the same cultural patterns and behaviours – a requisite for equal treatment. In fact, maintaining particular codes of dress, particular codes of food preferences and behaviour are important aspects in the construction of identity among ethnic groups. Often, maintaining specific social networks within the group can serve as a buffer against prejudice and discrimination (Modood, 1992).

Prejudice occurs when we impute characteristics to people or groups which we believe them to have, and which may be false. This is the basis for racial stereotypes, which can become perpetuated through the media and social life.

Institutionalized racism related to inequality and power in organizations also serves to perpetuate that power. This can be found in direct discrimination in which people may be discriminated against on the basis of colour, or in indirect discrimination in which individuals may be asked for characteristics which are not actual requirements for the job. For example, individuals' applications may be rejected on the assumption that they have insufficient command of the English language. Within the wider context of society, if discrimination operated in education and training, individuals would be excluded from particular occupations because they did not have the qualifications for the job.

More subtle forms of discrimination may be practised in situations in which staff responsible for recruitment reject applications because of dress codes which they perceive may not be acceptable to other staff or to customers. This can be regardless of an individual's ability to perform the job successfully.

Legislation can have some impact upon outlawing direct discrimination, even though this may be difficult to prove. Individuals have redress through the legal system and employers can incur penalties for acting in an unlawful manner. In the context of discrimination, the Race Relations Act is seeking for a behaviour change to take place, and it can be effective in reducing discriminatory practices. Discrimination, therefore, is concerned with the behaviour of individuals in specific contexts, and it may be that we can attempt to change an individual's behaviour by legislating against direct discrimination. However, changing an individual's attitudes is much more difficult. Within the hospitality industry we must address the problem of discrimination, and companies should incorporate equal opportunities policies. At the same time we must understand the ways in which prejudice is formed to enable prejudicial attitudes to be eliminated.

ATTITUDES AND RACIAL PREJUDICE

Racial stereotyping was demonstrated as early as 1933 by Katz and Brady, when they undertook a study with students in order to discover whether racial stereotyping occurred and, if so, what stereotypes were being attributed to which groups. They found that students were willing to attribute stereotypes to particular people despite the fact that they had not met anyone from that race. Similar studies were repeated in the 1950s and 1960s and they found that, although subjects were less ready to display stereotyping as quickly, they were in fact still evident. In other words, as time went on, it seems that people had perhaps become more aware of the concept and implications of racial stereotyping, but in fact still engaged in such actions.

If we consider exactly what stereotyping is about, however, it becomes clearer why individuals may use such attributions. A stereotype can be seen as a way in which individuals attribute actions and characteristics to other individuals or groups of people based on a fairly small number of actual characteristics. We tend to see other individuals or races of people as having certain characteristics and, on the basis of that knowledge, we predict and anticipate their actions. Whilst these stereotypes can lead to negative consequences where, for example, individuals create and use stereotypes that are inaccurate or inappropriate and are detrimental to their perceptions of others, they are also useful ways of categorizing people's behaviour and actions. If, as individuals, we had no way of predicting and anticipating behaviours before they occurred, we would have to treat every encounter with people as a new one. Stereotypes, therefore, allow us to interact with individuals or groups of people without any previous extensive knowledge of them.

There is little doubt that individuals do use stereotypes and, indeed, are prepared to attribute characteristics to others on the basis of limited knowledge, such as race. If this is the case, clearly it becomes a problem when racial stereotypes are used and form the basis for racial discrimination.

Within psychology, there are a number of explanations for the development and use of racial stereotypes. Weatherley (1961) suggested that when individuals or groups experience frustration and anger, and that cannot be placed onto the object which caused it, then the group will look for somewhere or somebody else on which to place it. In other words, in situations of frustration, individuals may turn to find a scapegoat. This scapegoat can either be another individual, or a group or race of people. It can be seen that the feeling and discrimination experienced by certain races in the UK in the 1980s and 1990s was, in fact, a demonstration of scapegoating. Groups of UK nationals experienced anger and frustration as a result of changes in the economic climate, and other groups were blamed for these conditions.

A second explanation for racial discrimination and prejudice came from Adorno and Frenkel Brunswick (1950) in their work on the 'authoritarian personality'. They were interested in particular types of behaviour that occurred during and after the Second World War, and essentially wanted to argue that there is a particular personality type that predisposes individuals towards prejudice. They suggested that individuals who possess an authoritarian personality are likely to display a number of behavioural characteristics; these included lack of independent thought, a need for very strict discipline and law and order, a belief that things are valid only from their point of view, a support for traditional morals and a prevalence to be critical of others and not of themselves. It is easy to see that a person holding such beliefs is likely to hold negative opinions and impressions of other races, and that they are likely to be translated into actions i.e. they will demonstrate hostility and discrimination to other races. There are many issues that such a concept raises, for example, how does such a personality come to be formed in the first place. Adorno and Brunswick believed that part of the answer to this question lay in the ways in which individuals had been brought up. Authoritarian parents were likely to have authoritarian children, largely as a result of patterns of socialization, which would perpetuate the cycle. Similarly, can this propensity for an authoritarian personality be measured and, if so, what are the implications of that? Adorno and Brunswick believed that it was possible to measure this personality type, and he developed an 'F scale' with which to do so. The implication, if this is correct, is that recruitment and selection procedures ought to include some method of determining whether or not individuals are likely to exhibit authoritarian and potentially racially discriminatory behaviour.

This raises the important issue of the relationship between an individual's thoughts and feelings about behaviours or races of people, and their actual actions towards them. If we consider the three-component model of attitudes outlined at length in Chapter 13, we can see that this would suggest that individual's can hold beliefs and values that are negative towards an individual or race, but not actually behave in a discriminatory manner. Organizations have developed policies which attempt to prevent racial discrimination, therefore preventing behaviours towards groups of people which are inappropriate based only on the grounds of race. It would be almost impossible, however, to legislate for the holding of a belief or value.

SUMMARY

This chapter has examined the concepts of race and prejudice, and their relationship to discriminatory behaviours. The major concern regarding race in relation to the hospitality industry has been with regard to patterns of employment and employment practices. Examples of both sociological and psychological explanations have been represented in an explanation of racial prejudice and students are encouraged to evaluate the strengths and weaknesses of these. It is clear when taking this approach, that defining and legislating against discrimination on the grounds of race is possible, but also that influencing the underlying attitudes and stereotypes of different races may be more difficult. It may be in the future, that more research will be undertaken to investigate race and consumption patterns. Furthermore, within the hospitality industry the success of equal opportunities policies will be dependent upon recognizing and understanding the concepts of ethnicity in relation to employees' behaviour. The study of race and ethnicity as applied to the treatment of customers in the hospitality industry is an area which has not yet been fully researched.

DISCUSSION QUESTIONS

1. What is racial stereotyping?
2. To what extent is an understanding of the concept of race useful in the context of (a) employment patterns in the contemporary hospitality industry; (b) the analysis of consumer behaviour?
3. Evaluate the utility of the concept of attitude in dealing with racial discrimination in the hospitality context.

FURTHER READING

Commission for Racial Equality (1991) *Working in hotels; report of a formal investigation into recruitment and selection*. CRE London. This report identifies the situation of ethnic group employment patterns in the hotel industry. It includes recommendations for recruitment and selection practices, for positive action and for training within the hotel companies.

Rex, J. (1986) *Race and ethnicity*. This is a good introductory text which explains the concepts of race and ethnicity and identifies the historical roots of discrimination.

REFERENCES

Adorno, T.W. and Brunswick, F. (1950) *The Authoritarian Personality*, Harper & Row, New York.

Baker, J. (1974) *Race*, Oxford University Press, Oxford.

Braham, P., Rhodes, E., and Pearn, M. (1981) *Discrimination and Disadvantage in Employment. The Experience of Black Workers*. Open University Press, Milton Keynes.

Commission for Racial Equality (1985) *Ethnic minorities in Britain, patterns of settlement*, CRE, London.

Commission for Racial Equality (1991) *Working in hotels*, CRE, London.

Corcoran, J. and Johnson, P. (1974) The image of four occupations. *HCIM Journal*, June, 13–19.

Haskey, J. (1990) *The Ethnic Minority Populations of Great Britain: Estimates by Ethnic Group and Country of Origin*. Office of Population Census and Surveys.

Katz, D. and Brady, K. (1933) Racial stereotypes of one hundred college students. *Journal of Abnormal and Social Psychology*, **28**, 280–290.

Mars, G. and Mitchell, P. (1976) *Room for Reform?* Open University Press, Milton Keynes.

Modood, T. (1992) Cultural diversity and racial discrimination in employment selection, in *The Limits of the Law, Studies in Labour and Social Law*, (eds B. Hepple and E. Szyszczak), Centre for the Study of Race Relations Law, University College London.

Rex, J. (1970) *The Concept of Race*, Weidenfeld and Nicolson, London.

Rex, J. (1986) *Race and Ethnicity*, Open University Press, Milton Keynes.

UNESCO (1952) The race concept, results of an enquiry, UNESCO, Paris.

Weatherley, D. (1961) Anti-semitism and expression of fantasy aggression. *Journal of abnormal and social psychology*, **62**, 454–457.

Wolpe, H. (1986) Class concepts, class struggle and racism, in (eds J. Rex and D. Mason) *Theories of Race and Ethnic Relations*, Cambridge University Press, Cambridge.

Wood, R.C. (1992) *Working in Hotels and Catering*, Routledge, London.

Investigating the branding of products and services: the role of the consumer

11

Aims

This chapter aims to:

1. introduce the concept of branding;
2. describe the historical reasons for the development of branding within the UK hotel and catering industry; and
3. consider social scientific techniques by which operators in the hospitality industry can identify the important characteristics of brands that individuals hold.

Outcomes

At the end of this chapter you will be able to:

1. describe the nature of branding in the hotel and catering industry;
2. identify a number of hard and soft branded products and services within the hospitality industry;
3. describe the relationship between an individual's personal constructs about products and their perceptions of brands; and
4. evaluate the strengths and weaknesses of a personal construct psychology approach to an operator interested in the development of branded products or services.

Companies are often involved in product innovation. This might be a new restaurant concept, a new type of drink, a new leisure idea. How do they go about this? Unless the idea is completely novel, it is likely that there will be products of this type already in the market place. Therefore, the product will have to compete with those existing products. In these circumstances, how can the company be sure that the product will be successful?

The launch of new products usually involves the marketing department within companies, and the first stage in the process is usually to conduct some market research to identify or confirm a gap in the market. As part of the marketing strategy, it may be decided to launch the product as a brand. You will already be familiar with some brand names, even though you may not yet be familiar with the process of branding and how and why it works .

If you wrote a list of well-known products, your list would probably contain such names as Coca Cola, Kelloggs, Levis and Marks and Spencers. These products are brands, are the leaders in their product class. Their names have become so well known that they are synonymous with the product. Thus, Coca Cola is a soft drink which is known worldwide by its brand name. If therefore, through the process of branding, products can become so well known as to be synonymous with their name, perhaps branding could ensure the success of the new product?

Of course, it is not that simple, and the possibility of the product becoming a brand leader is not at all certain. Furthermore, there may also be aspects associated with the product which make branding difficult to achieve. For example, can a new restaurant concept be treated in the same way as a soft drink, or are there fundamental differences between the two things?

To be able to answer the question it is necessary to identify and discuss the underlying principles involved in branding.

THE CONCEPT OF BRANDING

Clearly, brands are closely tied up with products and cannot easily be separated from them. However, it is a mistake to assume that brands are only found in the area of consumer goods. In fact, the process of branding has been applied right across the spectrum of financial services, retailing and in hotels and catering.

It is commonly held within marketing circles that products exist to meet the needs of consumers. When several companies offer rival products, one way to distinguish your product from that of the competitors is through the process of branding. An influential exponent of the value of branding is Professor P. Doyle. He defines branding as

> A name, symbol, design or some combination which identifies the product of a particular organisation as having a sustainable differential advantage. Differential advantage means simply that customers have a reason for preferring that brand to competitors' brands. Sustainable means that the product cannot easily be copied by competitors. For example, often by creating barriers to entry, by developing an outstanding reputation or image for quality service or reliability. (Doyle, 1989)

From this definition, it is clear that the success of brands depends upon their ability to be perceived by consumers as having particular characteristics. It is the consumer who must perceive the differential advantage of one brand over another, and it follows, therefore, that the criteria for the success of a brand is not what the producer puts into the brand, but what the customer gets out of it. Thus, in theory, the development of brands should start with a knowledge of customer perceptions and classifications of products. The criterion of importance, or the differential advantage which the product has for the consumer, needs to be known. This, in turn, means that operators need to identify these attributes among the intended markets for the product. They must also have a means by which they can identify the attributes which individual consumers hold, so that the brand can be targeted to them.

In practice, it is often the case that product brands will be developed to fill a gap in the existing provision of the company's portfolio, rather than as the result of a systematic research of consumer behaviour. This may be one reason why, in the context of the hotel and catering industry, brand loyalty among customers is low (Tarrant, 1988).

Turning our attention to the issue of branding specifically in the hotel and catering industry, the concept has received much attention in recent years. The introduction of brands to the hotel and catering sector, however, is not a new idea and can be traced to the involvement of multinational hotel companies in the UK industry in the 1950s and 1960s (Littlejohn and Roper, 1991). What is more recent is the proliferation of brands across the various sectors of the industry, evident in the growth of public house brands, e.g. Millers Kitchen, Brewers Fayre, and in the themed restaurant sector, e.g. TGI and Harvester restaurants.

There are many reasons for the introduction of branding by UK hotel and catering companies. To begin with, the competitive environment of the industry means that growth and profitability are likely to be achieved by increased market share, rather than by development of completely new markets. Branding, it can be argued, assists this process as brands seek to develop customer loyalty. Closely related to this is the idea of the competitive advantage offered by brands in terms of product consistency and the opportunity to develop critical mass, as brands can be exported to different geographical locations and environments (Renaghan, 1993). Furthermore, the branding process can also be used to restructure a portfolio of diverse products, as has been the case with the Forte company.

In developing brand strategies, hotel and catering companies have focused on the development of product brands with the result that UK hotel and pub retailing companies now offer a portfolio of brands within their current provision (Slattery and Johnson, 1991). Underpinning the approach is the idea that specific brands communicate a consistent message to specific customer groups and assist with consumer choice. Branding is, therefore, held to assist with the process of market segmentation, and targeting as consumer demand is matched to brand type. An additional advantage of the process of branding lies within the area of franchising, an important feature of the UK hotel and catering industry (Khan, 1993).

Operators argue that quality assurance is easier to achieve as tight brand specifications are laid down to facilitate the consistency of the product

(Renaghan, 1993). Clearly, from the point of view of hotel and catering operators, branding is an important area worthy of investigation. Yet, to date, much that has been written about branding has focused upon product brands, with far less attention being paid to the role of the consumer in the branding process. Contributions from academics within the hotel and catering field have also neglected the role of the consumer in the branding process. Where branding has been discussed by this group, it has been confined mostly to debates surrounding the appropriateness of branding for service as opposed to manufacturing products. The argument centres on what is perceived to be a crucial difference between manufacturing and service characteristics.

The argument runs that factors which apply to product brands are not the same as those which apply to service brands. For example, the tight specifications necessary for product consistency cannot be achieved in services or service products. This is because those services are thought to contain aspects which are intangible and difficult to reproduce. A restaurant product is made up of more than the food and beverages which customers consume. It also consists of such things as atmosphere, ambience, and, of course, customer and staff interaction. These, it is argued, are difficult to standardize and reproduce in the same way as a soft drink or lager. The fundamental difference between the two is the way in which the environment of product brands can be controlled. The production of Coca Cola occurs in a controlled environment, whereas in restaurants the product is delivered by intermediaries which can affect its consistency.

It is often argued that because of the necessity for standardization needed for the product consistency which is achieved in brands, hotels cannot be subject to the branding process in the same way as consumer goods. Hotels vary in their geography, size, type, market level and specific customer mix, thus making the standard, consistent experience of the consumer difficult to achieve. Running as a parallel to this, Slattery and Johnson (1991) differentiated brands to be of two types, hard and soft brands. Hard brands are the closest to the branding of consumer goods or products. Standardization of the product or hotel can only be achieved when it is a new-build hotel, as it can then conform to the specification in architecture, product facilities, design and decor. An example of a hard brand would be Travelodge, the budget chain owned and operated by the Forte company.

Soft brands, by contrast, are when companies assign their units the same name, signage, menu and product range, and perform to the same established specifications without the standardization in architecture, size and type. Within the industry, the approach of soft branding is defended on the grounds that as long as the product is consistent in standards, it needed not be standardized in every aspect.

Operators also argue that branding provides the opportunity to develop individual marketing programmes for their brands, which can allow them to match trading pattern similarities. It is also recognized that companies involved in the branding process also require some form of brand management system to ensure quality control. This is to prevent the most negative aspects of branding from occurring – that one bad experience of a unit within a brand can mean that the consumer has a negative view of the entire brand.

As we have demonstrated, the process of branding is a complex one, with many pitfalls along the way. The situation is compounded when hotel and catering companies attempt to export their brands to the international context. This is an extremely complex issue; suffice it to say that environmental conditions are even harder to control (Lewis and Chambers, 1989). Consider the situation of McDonald's in Moscow, and EuroDisney in Paris. In the former example, McDonald's have had to become involved in growing the correct potatoes to produce the standard French Fries. For the operations of EuroDisney, the impact of the environment upon the concept was under-estimated in relation to both the cultural values of the French nation, and the location of the theme park.

Given the complexities involved in the branding process, it is perhaps not surprising that the role of the consumer has been neglected. Yet, as we argued at the beginning, without an understanding of how brands are per-ceived and the images and connotations which are attached to them, the differential advantage discussed by Doyle cannot be known. Furthermore, without this knowledge, operators have no guarantee that their brands will be appropriate for the various individual consumers. Thus, what needs to be known is the process by which customers classify products and imbue them with meaning. Within the social sciences individuals' classifications and perceptions of products can be studied. It is to this subject that we will now turn in relation to the issue of branding.

Much of the traditional market research undertaken to investigate characteristics that customers find important in products or services uses some form of structured questionnaire. Again, many of us will have been asked to participate in such questionnaires either at college, or by interviewers on the street.

INDIVIDUAL CUSTOMER PERCEPTIONS OF PRODUCTS OR SERVICES

In the context of a company wanting to investigate the potential with regard to a new brand, one may get a brewing organization asking individuals if they recognize various brand names of lagers, bitters or spirits: asking how they compare on price, taste, availability, image, colour, fizziness, etc.; and asking how often such product types are consumed. Alternatively, a retailer may ask individuals if they recognize various brand names of outlets or services, how they compare on price, standards, consistency of service, and how often such services or outlets are used.

Such questionnaires often include attitude scales so that the individual's attitude towards the products or services can be scored. Popular attitude measurements include the Likert Scale and the Thurstone Scale. If used appropriately, these can reveal a positive, negative or neutral attitude towards the target object. Students may remember that the relationship between attitude and behaviour is not a simple one and, indeed, it would be a nonsense to undertake such an investigation without a knowledge of the concept of attitude, its nature, functions and processes with regards to purchase behaviour. Similarly, it is worth re-emphasising the point that these techniques must be utilized thoroughly and rigorously if they are to reveal meaningful results. Both the Likert and Thurstone Scales can, in themselves, require a great deal of research and preparation.

Since it is likely that we are familiar with such types of investigations, it is worth considering the precise strengths and weaknesses of these when involved in the context of trying to launch and brand a new product or service. Remember the information that is required: exactly what criteria do individuals perceive to be important with respect to particular products or services?

It seems that the research outlined could allow the researcher to discover individuals' familiarity with brands, and could allow the identification and description of individuals' attitudes towards characteristics or products. Fundamentally though, those products and criteria have been provided to the individual. The writer of the questionnaire suggests the products to be considered, and further suggests the characteristics or criteria of those products for the individual to evaluate. Again, consider the difficulty here, given the original question.

How is it possible to know whether the suggested products and criteria are compatible with those that the customer might supply given the opportunity? How can the questionnaire writer know that the objects and characteristics are the appropriate ones to be asking questions about? Undoubtedly, individuals will answer such questions, but they may also have alternative products and criteria which they consider to be important. To be fair, many questionnaires will allow some consideration of this by leaving space at the end for further comments, but it may be that individuals are not explicitly aware of some of the issues and criteria important to them, hence a difficulty in commenting upon them arises.

If this is the case, it becomes necessary to identify and use information-gathering techniques that are almost completely customer or individual led. It would be far more sensible to ask the individual to provide both the list of products or services which are recognized as brands and which are to be compared, and to identify the criteria which are important to them.

PERSONAL CONSTRUCTS

There are a range of such techniques developed from a branch of psychology known as 'personal construct' psychology. Simply and briefly, according to personal construct psychology, individuals are active in their perception and behaviour within the world around them. They do not merely react to events and actions around them, but seek to make sense of the world and act accordingly. Individuals do this by developing and using a system of personal constructs. Personal constructs are bipolar in nature, and can be general or very specific in nature. For example, an individual may have a construct of happy/sad, and one of right/wrong. These constructs are developed through our experience in the world and are organized hierarchically. That is, a system is composed of superordinate constructs at the top, which may be abstract in nature, and have far-reaching consequences through the rest of the system, or subordinate constructs below, which may be more concrete and more specific in nature.

Through our everyday interactions and experience, we constantly test the appropriateness of this system of constructs and revise it when necessary. Hence, Kelly's (1955) well-known metaphor of 'Man the scientist'. Our system provides us with hypotheses and guidelines for action, which we use in our perceptions and actions. Should our expectations be inappropriate, we consider the utility of particular constructs. It is worth noting here that this does not necessarily mean that we are aware of our constructs, in fact it is unlikely that we will be aware of some of the more superordinate ones. However, they do allow us to predict and anticipate actions, behaviours and consequences.

Clearly individuals will have constructs concerning the nature of other people, and the nature of behaviours in interaction, but in the context of branding, it is also possible to hold constructs about objects, products or services. The task, therefore, arises to identify those constructs.

Identifying constructs that are important to customers

One technique that can be used is that of the triadic comparison, which has been briefly mentioned in connection with MAUT. It will be useful to elaborate this with regard to branding, to illustrate how characteristics and criteria of products can be identified. The first stage would be to ask an individual to name three or more of the type of product or service of interest. For example, assume that you are interested in developing a new brand of lager. The individual being questioned might identify 5 different brand names of lager:

- Heineken
- Carling
- Budweiser
- Fosters
- XXXX

It is important to note that these products have come from the individual; they have not been suggested by the researcher.

The second stage is then to find out the criteria which individuals find important with respect to these brands of lager. In personal construct terms, you need to elicit the constructs which individuals use with regard to those objects. Consider three products at a time, e.g. Heineken, Carling and Budweiser, and ask the question 'In what ways are two of those things similar but different from the third?' Thus, how are Heineken and Carling similar, but different from Budweiser. The individual's answer might be that Heineken and Carling are cheap, while Budweiser is expensive. This produces the first construct elicited from those three products:

- expensive/cheap.

This is potentially one criterion which the individual finds important in their perception of brands of lager. Let us compare another of the lagers: How are

Carling and Budweiser similar but different from Fosters? This time, the comment might be that Carling and Budweiser are strong in alcohol while Fosters is weak. Another construct created from those three products is:

- strong/weak.

The process would continue until all combinations of products have been tried. The criteria of importance to individuals will then have been elicited. Notice that even for 5 products, as in this example, there is a large number of possible combinations of products to consider, e.g. 1/2/3, 1/3/4, 1/4/5, 2/3/4, 2/4/5, 2/1/4, 3/4/5.

Thus, for this individual, there are a number of constructs that are important when considering lager brands. These may be expensive/cheap, strong/weak, fizzy/flat, light/dark, bottled/on draught, and it is possible to state which pole of those constructs is preferred, e.g. cheap lager is preferred to expensive lager, or bottled lager to draught lager, etc. It is useful to notice that the information on which the comparison is based may actually be incorrect: Budweiser may be cheaper than Heineken. The method, nevertheless, reveals characteristics that the individual feels are important, e.g. price.

Following this, what information is now available, and what does it tell us? With this example, what is currently available are the constructs with respect to brands of lager. Clearly, producing a product or new brand line on this basis would be inappropriate. A sample of individuals would have to be consulted and their constructs elicited. This could, of course, potentially result in a large number of different sets of constructs or criteria – a set for every individual asked – and this is in the nature of personal construct psychology. Indeed, the constructs individuals use to anticipate the world are personal to them. However, it is likely that commonalities will occur, perhaps around price or strength, and it is, therefore, possible to set out all the responses and look for those commonalities. There are inherent difficulties in doing this sort of clustering within personal construct psychology, as students can discover in the further reading. However, sensible ways of doing it in this context might be to ask the sample themselves to create common groupings. That is, ask the sample to look at all the constructs elicited, and put them in common or appropriate groups. Thus, the constructs expensive/cheap, costly/average, clearly relate to price, while the constructs strong/weak, gets me tipsy/doesn't, potent/normal, clearly relate to strength. Therefore, a list of the criteria that individuals find important in brands of lager might now be price, strength, fizziness, colour, presentation.

It seems sensible to suggest that, of itself, this information has little utility. What would be the point in knowing the criteria that individuals find important without knowing the relative importance of those criteria. It would be of little use creating a product that was cheap but very low in strength if customers consider strength to be more important than price. The task is, therefore, two-fold. The criteria of importance do need to be identified, i.e. the constructs, but the relative importance of these also need to be identified.

There are many techniques that could be used here. At its simplest level, it may be easiest to ask the individuals to rank them in order of importance. Thus, for a given sample of people, both sets of information are now available to the manager or operator. We would argue that this information, because of the way it has been elicited is of more value than the traditional questionnaire. All the relevant information on which to consider a new brand has been identified and, crucially, it has all come from customers. The criteria of importance and their relative weightings are available, and those which allow the creation of a differential advantage can be considered.

The next stage for brewing companies is to focus upon the commonalities that can found amongst customer perception in relation to the product attributes of lager. This will be a precursor to establishing target markets for the product. Lager brands are aimed at national markets, achieved both by high expenditure on advertising and by gaining shelf space in supermarkets and in the off-licence trade. In this context, the markets can be very wide and impulse purchasing may apply. However, the long-term success of the product requires groups of customers to be identified in order that the brand can (a) gain an established market of consumers; (b) advertise and target appropriately; (c) and that changes in brand loyalty can be monitored. Furthermore, the context in which the product is consumed needs to be included in the analysis, as does the impact of social groupings on the individual's choice.

SUMMARY

This chapter has considered the nature of branding and the role of branded products and services within the contemporary hospitality industry. We have argued that if an operator is to fully understand the characteristics of products that customers find important, then it is crucial to adopt a research strategy that elicits all that information from individual consumers. We have suggested that using a framework of personal construct psychology would allow operators to do this. There are difficulties here, notably in the generalization of one customer to another, but again, the integration of psychology and sociology can go further in considering and investigating the concept of branding than single disciplinary approaches..

DISCUSSION QUESTIONS

1. Outline the nature and role of branding in the hotel and catering industry.
2. Why is it important to consider the perceptions of the customer when investigating the branding of a product or service?
3. What are the strengths and weaknesses of adopting different social scientific techniques for eliciting customers' perceptions of products or services.

FURTHER READING

Baum, C. (1989) Trusthouse Forte pushes more branding of hotels. *Hotels and Restaurants International*, February, 38–42. This article discusses the development of international brands of Trusthouse Forte (now Forte plc).

Burr, V. and Butt, T. (1992) *Invitation to Personal Construct Psychology*, Whurr, London. This book is an accessible introduction to the psychology of personal constructs. It illustrates ideas using everyday situations and examples, and has a section on measuring personal constructs.

Murphy, J. (ed.)(1987) *Branding: A Key Marketing Tool*, Macmillan, London. This is a useful introductory text in the area of branding. It includes the history of branding, the legal aspects of branding and the use of logos. It covers branding in relation to the service industries.

REFERENCES

Doyle, P. (1989) Brand building. *Marketing*, July 6, 25.

Kelly, G. (1955) *The Psychology of Personal Constructs* (Vol. 1), Norton, New York.

Khan, M. (1993) International restaurant franchises, in (eds P. Jones and A. Pizam) *The International Hospitality Industry, Organisational and Operational Issues*, Pitman, London.

Lewis, R.C. and Chambers, R.E. (1989) *Marketing Leadership in Hospitality: Foundations and Practices*, Van Nostrand Reinhold, New York.

Littlejohn, D. and Roper, A. (1991) Changes in international hotel companies strategies, in (eds R. Teare and A. Boer) *Strategic Hospitality Management*, Cassell, London.

Renaghan, I.M. (1993) International hospitality marketing, in (eds P. Jones and A. Pizam) *The International Hospitality Industry, Organisational and Operational Issues*, Pitman, London.

Slattery, P. and Johnson, S.M. (1991) *Quoted Hotel Companies: the World Markets*, Kleinwort Benson Securities, London.

Tarrant, C. (1988) Understanding the hotel guests: the role of research in the development of hotel marketing and segmentation programmes. Paper presented at the seminar on tourism research, Anticipating and Responding to Change, Nicosia, Cyprus 4–7 May, pp. 51–73.

Understanding leisure behaviour 12

Aims

This chapter aims to :

1. illustrate the historical context and development of the concept of leisure;

2. consider qualitative and quantitative approaches to the study of leisure;

3. outline and evaluate three frameworks in which leisure behaviour can be understood; and

4. consider the contemporary leisure industry.

Outcomes

At the end of this chapter you will be able to:

1. define and describe the concept of leisure;

2. critically evaluate qualitative and quantitative approaches to the study of leisure;

3. describe the strengths and weaknesses of the models of work/leisure relations, leisure and the life cycle, and leisure and class culture; and

4. outline the contributions of such models of leisure behaviour for leisure operators in the contemporary hospitality industry.

THE MEANING OF LEISURE

Think about what you understand by the term leisure, write down the activities that you consider to be leisure activities. Some of the activities that you have noted down may include sleeping, eating out in a restaurant, reading, going to the park, listening to music and swimming etc. It is useful to try this activity in a group, comparing the lists that individuals come up with. You may not have a problem in constructing your own list, but you may find that your list differs from that of other people.

When individuals begin to compare lists, often what one individual defines as leisure another individual will define as work. Thus, for example, catering students may define cooking a meal for friends as work, whereas other students may consider this activity to be leisure. Similarly, a music student may consider playing an instrument to be work, whereas someone else may consider that to be leisure. There is the possibility also, that such students would define activities as a combination of work and leisure.

Clearly, this exercise demonstrates the fact that leisure means different things to different individuals: defining leisure is not as simple as it may appear. Contained in many individuals' definitions of leisure are issues about leisure being the ability to please oneself, having freedom from work tasks and pressures, activities that allow some element of choice. Also, as you may be able to see in your original list, when individuals define leisure, they often do so by contrasting it to other forms of activity, notably work.

The relationship between leisure and other areas of life has been an issue which has attracted much interest from social scientists (Parker, 1983; Clarke and Critcher, 1985; Moorhouse, 1989). Attempts to examine this relationship have also contributed to our knowledge about leisure, and individuals' views on it. Perhaps it would be useful in investigating the concept of leisure, to examine the historical context in which leisure has evolved.

HISTORICAL DEVELOPMENT OF THE CONCEPT OF LEISURE

It is commonly accepted that the idea of leisure evolved with the development of industrialization (Cunningham, 1980). In pre-industrial society, life was regulated by the seasons, and work and play were carried on in the same place. There was no clear division between work and non-work. A shift from an agrarian to an industrial mode of production, in effect, meant that life became separated into two spheres (Burns, 1969). One sphere involved work activity, in which activity was regulated and conducted in a defined place and within defined time periods, and in the other, time was left over from work.

Initially, this time left over from work became a vacuum into which the sphere of leisure was created. Therefore, the idea that leisure is time left over from work has its origins in the period of industrialization. Leisure then grew up with the connotation of free time and this idea still features in many of the contemporary discussions about the subject. It is interesting to note at this point, that right from the outset in industrialization, this free time became the space and time where consumption occurred. Burns (1969) makes the point that the industrial economy relies upon establishing consumers for the products of the new technology. Of interest to us is the fact that one of the first industries which grew up to facilitate consumption, comprised the drink shops and gin palaces, which were in effect the forerunners of contemporary public houses. It is significant for us to realize two points from this: that leisure is an important area for the development of commercial interests; at the same time, it is an important area of consumption.

Since the period of industrialization, many commentators have sought to classify the concept of leisure (Dumazadier, 1974). The original idea of leisure as the time left over from work has been challenged for its neglect of the sets of work and domestic obligations which occur after work is completed. Parker (1983) expresses this as follows.

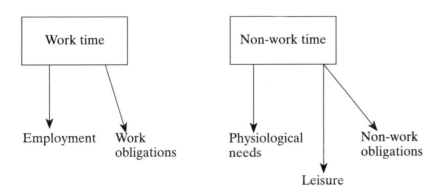

The argument that work and leisure are dichotomous is now brought into question, largely because of the range of activities which individuals engage in after work. However, an important strand within the study of leisure argues that leisure is about freedom from constraint, as the diagram above indicates. This may be represented in the way that you first conceived of leisure, and it would be a common sense view of leisure which we would expect individuals to put forward. In this view, leisure is the time when we choose what we want to do. Commentators (Roberts, 1978) have found this a useful approach when dealing with the problem of one person's work being another person's leisure. This can be demonstrated with such activities as DIY, keeping fit or playing sports.

Within these approaches to leisure, therefore, leisure involves individual definitions, perceptions and values. Leisure can only be studied in terms of what it means to the individual. Roberts, a supporter of this approach, does not see any problem with defining leisure. He claims that individuals themselves will know when they engage in a leisure activity. Whilst the importance of individual perceptions and values about leisure cannot be ignored, if we take the idea of leisure as being only a subjective one, that is only how individuals perceive it, this makes the area of leisure difficult to study. The nature of this difficulty arises in relation to being able to provide a concept of leisure. A conceptual treatment of leisure will allow us to establish ideas about leisure which are empirically testable and can serve as the basis for comparative analysis. Students should be able to see that if we reduce the study of leisure to the subjective states of individuals, this would produce as many definitions of leisure as there were individuals.

To avoid this, the area of leisure requires analysis which can account for the values and perceptions which individuals hold about leisure, while at the same time establishing a conceptual basis for the subject. This will allow the wider factors which shape perceptions of leisure to be studied and integrated into the analysis. We will now move from discussing leisure at the level of the individual to discussing the wider framework of leisure and society in the contemporary period.

Within the UK economy, the leisure industries make a substantial contribution to the gross national product (GNP). These leisure industries contain a diverse range of companies, all competing for the leisure pound of customers. Included within the leisure industries are public houses, theme parks, nightclubs, hotels, restaurants and casinos. In order to win a share of the leisure spend of customers, leisure operators need to understand the concept of leisure and the factors which influence the demand patterns of particular individuals and groups.

Apart from leisure operators, there are many additional parties interested in the field of leisure. The State, for example, is an important provider of leisure in the form of leisure centres, recreational grounds, parks, museums and the arts. Government bodies are interested in collecting information about a wide range of leisure behaviour in order to allow planning for leisure provision, e.g. social trends. A second source of interest in leisure is the many commercial organizations who are involved in conducting market research into leisure activities. These organizations compile statistics covering a wide range of leisure activities from watching TV, to attendance at spectator sports, to the popularity of particular leisure activities. These statistics are drawn upon by leisure operators and are often used as the basis for predicting changes in market behaviour. Examples of commercial organizations involved in the collection of leisure statistics are Mintel, Euromonitor, J. Walter Thompson and the Henley Centre for Forecasting. In addition to the commercial organizations, the field of leisure has been the subject of much sociological enquiry. Contributions from sociologists have, however, focused on a different range of concerns from the commercial and marketing organizations. Sociologists have been concerned with such issues as the role of leisure in society (Clarke and Critcher, 1985), the effects of work on leisure behaviour (Parker, 1983) and the impact of leisure upon particular social groups, such as women (Deem, 1986), the retired and the unwaged.

Students approaching the field of leisure are, therefore, confronted with a wide range of sources with which to study the topic. Further investigations of these sources reveals that the information supplied is often contradictory and in some cases confusing. In an effort to aid understanding of the topic of leisure, this section will attempt to categorize some of the approaches available and, in turn, examine their strengths and weaknesses. For the purposes of this discussion, approaches to leisure will be divided into two types: those that are quantitative and those that are qualitative.

QUANTITATIVE APPROACHES TO LEISURE

These are characterized by the collection of statistical data. This approach is commonly practised within commercial organizations (e.g. Mintel) and the statistics form the basis of reports which usually cover such areas as the frequency of customers engaging in particular leisure activities, the participation rates of various groups in the population. Two key areas covered by most of the commercial organizations are the amount of money and time which individuals have available for leisure pursuits. Thus, for leisure operators this information is very valuable in identifying trends which may be occurring in particular areas of leisure behaviour. For example, both Mintel and the Mori organization collect statistical information about the frequency of drinking in public houses. This information may then be used by pub retailing companies to identify changes in pub visiting.

There is no doubt that statistical information and approaches are useful to gain some idea about what people generally do in their spare time. Furthermore, statistical analysis can help in the generation of hypotheses for research. However, used as a basis to explain leisure activities and behaviour, these approaches are very limited. The limitations stem from both the methodologies used to compile the data and the underlying assumptions which they make about human behaviour. The methodologies usually consist of questioning samples of the population about their leisure pursuits. Often, the pursuits will not be related to the wider context of people's lives or their overall leisure behaviour and, therefore, the importance of this activity within wider leisure behaviour is ignored. Similarly, it is common practice in these approaches to draw statistics from a variety of sources, and to conduct an overview analysis without firstly identifying the basis upon which the statistics were compiled. This is the reason why statistics on leisure are often conflicting, evidenced by one source claiming that 'in home' leisure is declining, whilst another claims that it is on the increase.

Perhaps a more serious problem with these approaches for those wishing to understand leisure behaviour, is the fact that statistical sources like this are often used to make assumptions and predictions about leisure behaviour. This is problematic for two reasons. First, the collection of statistics on leisure is only able to describe the frequency and amount of leisure activities. Within the approach there is no basis for identifying the meanings and values which people attach to their leisure activities. For example, Mori (1990) statistics tell us that around three-fifths of the population go to a public house once a week or more, and half of these people go once a week. This information does not tell us which members of the population constitute this group, in terms of social class, gender, age, etc., nor why those groups engage in that behaviour. It cannot tell us what values the groups attach to pubs, or the types of pubs that they prefer to visit. We cannot assume that visiting the public house has the same importance and meaning for all groups in the population. It is also worth adding that these quantitative approaches are retrospective. Just because people have engaged in an activity in the past does not allow us to assume that they will do so in the future.

In summarizing these approaches, clearly what is absent from them is any conceptual framework which could allow some starting point to study the meanings and values which people attach to leisure, and the ways in which this facilitates and constrains their leisure choices.

In contrast to the quantitative approaches are the qualitative approaches. A feature of these is that they attempt to go beyond the statistical collection of data and offer some explanatory frameworks within which to study leisure. These approaches have been the prerogative of sociologists writing in the field of leisure.

QUALITATIVE APPROACHES TO LEISURE

By locating these approaches within sociological contributions we are in no way implying that all sociological approaches to leisure have the same methods, ideas or assumptions. In fact the opposite is the case. Within this field the whole area of leisure is surrounded with controversy and debate (Rojek, 1989). The factors which we do want to draw attention to in these approaches are the wider concerns of authors in relation to leisure, and the attempts which have been made to construct explanatory frameworks in order to study leisure behaviour.

Given the wide range of research, no comprehensive coverage is implied here. Rather what will be attempted is a selection of sociological approaches, and an evaluation of their strengths and weaknesses for students trying to make sense of a complex area of behaviour. Perhaps the first point to draw attention to is the way in which sociologists have tried to construct typologies, models and concepts with which to study and approach the subject of leisure (Moorhouse, 1989). The starting point in providing explanations of human behaviour as opposed to descriptions, is to select some theoretical framework. Within the sociology of leisure, authors have not yet reached the point of developing theories in the scientifically testable sense. Rather, contemporary research is at the stage of providing models or typologies of leisure behaviour, and much has yet to be done in the theoretical and conceptual treatment of the subject. It is necessary for this work to be undertaken so that theories of leisure will provide concepts which are empirically testable, which in turn will allow generalizations and predictability.

Despite these shortcomings, some of the typologies and models of leisure behaviour will now be examined for their value to students and to leisure operators.

WORK/LEISURE RELATIONS

Within sociological approaches to the study of leisure, no discussion could omit the work of Stanley Parker, who has been referred to earlier in the chapter (1983), and his typology of work/leisure relations. Parker's work has been the subject of much interest, prompting authors to write in critique. Briefly, Parker's work represents an approach in which leisure cannot be understood as separate from work. Parker (1983) argued that it is the experience of work which forms the context for the experience of leisure. This means that an individual's job impacts upon their leisure, both in terms of constraints and in the expression of leisure behaviour. Parker (1971) identifies three types of work/leisure relation.

1. Extension, in which activities in leisure are similar to those in work, and in which there is no clear demarcation between work and leisure. For example, business executives may combine work and leisure in playing golf to entertain clients. Hotel managers may engage in leisure activities in entertaining clients at the hotel bar.

2. The opposite pattern occurs according to Parker when leisure and work are clearly demarcated, and one activity does not stray into the other. This may occur in situations in which individuals choose activities which are deliberately unlike work, for example a hotel manager may participate in hang gliding at a club close to home.

3. Finally, the impact of work on leisure can be neutral. Here leisure activities are not deliberately different or the same as work activities. For example, a pub manager may choose to visit a nightclub on their night off.

For Parker, these types of work/leisure relations are correlated with job content, the role of work in people's lives and the functions of leisure for individuals. Students may want to consider various occupations and leisure activities and think about where they may fit into Parker's scheme. For example, if a lecturer reads novels outside the office, is that work or leisure? If a student on a hospitality management course visits a public house, is that work or leisure?

It is clear that the extension pattern is characterized by occupations which give job autonomy, and work is seen as the central life interest. Leisure is identified as being concerned with the personal development of individuals. Opposition patterns, by contrast, are associated with low job involvement, and leisure acts as a central life interest. The function of leisure is to recuperate from work. Neutral patterns are characterized by calculative job involvement and the purpose of leisure is purely one of entertainment.

There are obviously some strengths in examining the impact of work on leisure behaviour. However, Parker's typology also has serious flaws. The central problem with this model is that the vast range of meanings and experiences which affect work and leisure cannot be fitted simply into the typology, (Moorhouse, 1989). Students may have discovered this whilst fitting examples into it earlier. Also, it is the case that one occupation could give rise to all three types of work/leisure relation, and individuals may experience all three types of pattern at different times. As Moorhouse (1989) notes, Parker does not specify the conditions under which one pattern rather than another could be expected, nor the causes for this phenomenon. Parker also, it seemed, ignored the impact of wider societal variables upon leisure behaviour, such as class, age, gender and race, and the ways and effects that these factors might have on enabling or constraining choice (Clarke and Critcher, 1985).

Many feminist writers (Deem, 1986) have also challenged Parker for his neglect of the role of gender in leisure analysis. The central problem is that Parker's analysis of leisure is only understood in terms of its relationship with work, hence those who do not work have no leisure, or are, at the least, excluded from the model. Included in this list are housewives and househusbands who are not employed outside the house, the retired, and the unwaged (Deem, 1989).

There is no question that Parker's model has received a great deal of criticism. As it stands, it is limited in explaining leisure behaviour, but the central proposition that work impacts upon leisure is still worthy of consideration. One area in which Parker's framework may be useful is in relation to the leisure use of hotels. Hotels rely upon a combination of business and leisure markets. Since the 1980s many hotel companies have attempted to extend their product by introducing leisure centres as part of their provision. Leisure centres were introduced initially in an effort to increase occupancy by business and conference markets. The provision of in-house leisure also allowed companies to develop the short-break market, as the provision of such centres gave companies a competitive advantage (Hales and Collins, 1988). As the number of centres increased, companies also began to extend their use by tapping into local markets and allowing their use by non-residents. This was, of course, partly due to necessity, since competitive advantage was lost as more companies added leisure centres to their provision. Similarly, in the competitive environment of business markets, the tariffs could not always be used to recoup the cost of building and refurbishing for the introduction of the leisure centre. An additional problem has been that companies have found it difficult to manage the mix of resident and non-resident customers. Whilst hotel companies have recognized the possibility of converting existing business to leisure customers by the use of incentives, they have not fully recognized the opportunities open to them in the wider area of leisure.

Parker's model, or at least his central proposition, could be empirically tested in the hotel context by identifying the occupational groups who use hotels. Hotel companies could learn a great deal about the work and leisure behaviour of existing customers. The use of leisure within various customer groups could be investigated, as could the expectations of leisure which customers hold. This would allow companies to understand better the leisure orientations of the groups who use hotels, and to supply the types of products and leisure environments which various customer groups demand. One particular area in which this research could be of value to hotel companies is in the area of female customer markets. Hotel companies have slowly begun to recognize the importance of the female executive business market (Lutz and Ryan, 1993). This market now constitutes about 25% of the hotel business market. To date, the leisure orientation of this group with respect to hotels awaits systematic research.

Drawing upon sociological contributions to the study of leisure can, therefore, elucidate some of the issues surrounding the leisure use of hotels. Despite the inherent weaknesses of Parker's approach, it represents a contribution which has stimulated further research. This can also be claimed for an established approach within sociology of leisure, namely studies of the family and the life cycle process. Rappoport and Rappoport (1975) are the originators of pioneering work which examined the impact of the life cycle process on individuals' orientations to leisure.

THE LIFE CYCLE AND LEISURE

Drawing upon a biological analogy, they envisage an individual's life to be marked by significant stages in the life cycle. They conclude that the stage in a person's life cycle is the most important determinant of their leisure behaviour. The model argues that there are four stages in the life cycle: adolescence, young adulthood, establishment and retirement. These   stages will impact upon an individual's motivation towards leisure behaviours.

Within the adolescent stage (13–19 years) the central concern of individuals is to use leisure to satisfy an issue of personal identity. This can be related to spending on fashions by their group as a means of self-expression. Young adulthood is concerned with establishing relationships and identifying with social institutions. Within the pub retailing industry, operators have long since targeted this group and included a range of public house concepts within their portfolio designed to appeal to this group (McEwan, 1983). Many of these concepts have included theming and the provision of pub designs which facilitated social display and the opportunity to engage in social interaction. By the mid-20's, the Rappoports argue that individuals become more home centred as they take on the new social roles of marriage and parenthood. Clearly now, children impact upon leisure motivations both in relation to time, resources and choice of leisure activity and venue. Finally, in the retirement phase, motivations to leisure change as responsibilities for children reduce. The Rappoports argue that this stage offers an opportunity for fulfilling aspirations and trying out new identities.

Life cycle concepts (Buttle, 1988) have already been explored in general studies of consumer behaviour. Within the hospitality industry, the value of such concepts has been recognized by holiday companies such as Saga, who have operated a successful business by targeting their products to people over 50.

A major strength of the life cycle approach is the way in which leisure is related to other spheres of life and is influenced by wider variables. Added to this, the Rappoports do not marginalize social groups such as women and the elderly as is common in other approaches. On the negative side, this approach has flaws in providing an adequate framework within which to study leisure. A central weakness of the work is the conception of the family, and the assumption that all individuals will go through the same stages. This is compounded by the fact that there is no attempt to differentiate between families in terms of social class, culture or race. The conception of the family is one of the parents and children, and this may be considered outdated in contemporary society. The whole structure of families is changing, for example, the increasing number of single-parent families, families which consist of two men or women, etc. (BTA, 1992). This difficulty of the conception of family is recognized to the extent that sociologists now prefer to use the term household when discussing the living arrangement of the population.

Families or households are also stratified on the basis of social class, and this will affect access to leisure resources, regardless of stages in the life cycle.

CLASS CULTURE AND LEISURE

Featherstone's (1978) analysis has powerfully demonstrated the influence of class cultural differences on how stages in life are regarded. For example, young adulthood within working class culture can be a phase of responsibility and coping with marriage and children, whereas within middle class cultures, young adulthood may be a phase of identity exploration. Featherstone's arguments are supported by Coatler and Parry (1982) who argue that the social worlds of working class and middle class women are very different. Indeed, these social worlds relate to the leisure behaviour of those women. Recognizing these differences within families is an important issue for leisure providers. The changing composition of the household and the types of group structure which are found in contemporary households cannot be ignored. For example, the BTA survey (1992) indicates a decline in the number of households with pre-school children and an increase in the number of households with teenagers.

In terms of selecting leisure venues, the size and structure of the group is important. Households with pre-school children have different demand patterns from households with teenagers. This knowledge can assist leisure operators to pursue a successful strategy for targeting particular markets. An area where this issue can be demonstrated is in the area of theme parks, as they have historically targeted families as their main market. Clearly, the term theme park covers a wide range of products from large-scale parks such as Alton Towers and Disneyland, to themed attractions dealing with heritage, watersport and zoo concepts. Theme park operators are faced with a changing composition in their traditional markets as changes in the family structure progress. This will require them to restructure their products in line with these changes. This necessitates a knowledge and understanding of the role of leisure within the family and household group, including issues such as how much leisure time families spend together, if indeed they spend leisure time together at all. It has been noted that often the ways that families spend their leisure is a result of compromise. Therefore, the challenge for leisure operators will be to identify the social structure of leisure and the values and ideas which specific individuals and groups hold about the types of leisure environments they wish to frequent. They will also need to identify the significant others who will be involved in the decisions and activities.

Theme parks are well established in the product life cycle, and are a popular activity among segments of the population. The issue for theme park operators is to establish more product differentiation in the face of competition from both the UK and from Europe. This may be assisted by greater segmentation, and a recognition that segments will exist within particular household types. Phillips (1992) has already noted the possibilities of developing theme parks for the over-50s markets.

The changing structure of the household and the role of leisure within specific social groups, is also relevant to pub retailing companies. Within these companies, the development of pub catering concepts has been an important area over the last few years. Indeed, food accounts for 25% of profits among UK brewing and pub retailing companies (Slattery and Johnson, 1991). In order to maintain and extend this growth, additional research in the area of eating out will be necessary. For example, the role of children in the decision-making process in respect of the venue to eat in is important. The same can be said for the meanings and expectations of group members within households. Pub operators have to go beyond considerations of menu price and design, taking on broad issues of adding to the meal experience. For example, households with young children can experience mealtimes which are fraught with difficulty, and the eating out experience can overcome this. Play areas are a useful idea, and perhaps the staging of meals for adults and children. The point is that success in this area will be the result of what operators can add to the meal experience, which cannot be substituted at home.

The typology of work/leisure relations and the concept of life cycles have been used to demonstrate the value of sociological contributions to the study of leisure. These two approaches were selected, the critiques of them not withstanding, because they attempt to offer an approach to leisure which is empirically testable. This is not the case with other sociological approaches within the field.

The sociology of leisure continues to be an emerging area of study with a variety of contemporary strands and perspectives. For example, Marxist contributors (Clarke and Critcher, 1985) continue to examine the impact of capitalist structures on leisure behaviour. Feminist writers (Henderson, 1991) are concerned to examine societal constraints on female leisure behaviour, and to establish a more conceptual treatment of leisure activities. Finally, within another strand, writers are seeking to establish the role of class culture on leisure behaviour.

The issue of leisure has been investigated from a multidisciplinary approach in an effort to aid both students and leisure operators in an understanding of the factors which influence leisure behaviour. Individuals' perceptions and values about leisure are clearly important and can influence an individual's choice and activity. At the same time, studies of leisure behaviour cannot be divorced from the wider societal forces which impact upon both the supply and demand characteristics of leisure. Thus, for individuals involved in leisure industries, a recognition of the relationship between leisure behaviour and wider societal forces is a prerequisite to understanding the behaviour of leisure customers.

SUMMARY

In this chapter we have attempted to outline the difficulties in defining the concept of leisure, and have outlined the historical development of the notion of leisure behaviour. Three models that attempt to relate leisure to different influences have been presented – work/leisure relations, leisure and the life cycle, and leisure and class culture. The major strengths and weaknesses of these approaches have been identified. These strengths and weaknesses may result from an overemphasis or underemphasis on either the individual, or on social structures that influence leisure behaviour. Clearly, individual perceptions of leisure are important determinants of behaviour and consumption but, as we have demonstrated, to understand fully this behaviour, they must be located in the wider social context in which leisure behaviour occurs.

DISCUSSION QUESTIONS

1. Describe the concept of leisure.
2. How can different approaches to the analysis of human leisure behaviour be of use to a hospitality manager?
3. Identify factors of importance in understanding leisure behaviour.

FURTHER READING

Martin, J. (1989) *Leisure Centres in Hotels*, Hotel and Catering Research Centre, Huddersfield Polytechnic, Huddersfield. This provides a comprehensive analysis of the supply of leisure centres in the hotel and catering industry. It gives information with regard to financial and operational issues.

Rojek, C. (1989) *Leisure for Leisure: Critical Essays,* Macmillan, Basingstoke. This collection of essays explains and critiques the variety of approaches towards leisure in contemporary society.

REFERENCES

BTA (1992) Survey of Leisure Attractions. *Tourism insights.*

Burns T. (ed.) (1969) *Industrial Man: Selected Readings*. Penguin, Harmondsworth.

Buttle, E. (1988) *Hotel and Food Service Marketing,* Cassell, London.

Clarke, J. and Critcher, C. (1985) *The Devil Makes Work: Leisure in Capitalist Britain*. Macmillan, London.

Coatler, F. and Parry, N. (1982) *Leisure Sociology or the Sociology of Leisure,* Polytechnic of North London, London.

Cunningham, H. (1980) *Leisure in the Industrial Revolution 1780–1880,* Croom Helm, London.

Deem, R. (1986) *Women and Leisure.*

Dumazadier, J. (1974) *The Sociology of Leisure*, Elsevier, Amsterdam.

Featherstone, M. (1978) Leisure, symbolic power and the life cycle, in *Sport, Leisure and Social Relations* (eds J. Hone, D. Jary and A. Tomlinson). Sociological Review Monograph, Routledge & Kegan Paul, London.

Hales and Collins (1988) Hotel leisure a spring in the step or a lead in the dark. *Leisure Management*, **8** (8), 46–52.

Henderson, K.A. (1991) The contribution of feminism to an understanding of leisure constraints. *Journal of Leisure Research*, **23** (4), 363–377.

Lutz, J. and Ryan, C. (1993) Hotels and the business woman, an analysis of business women's perceptions of hotel services. *Tourism Management*, **14** (5), 349–356.

McEwan, J. (1983) Cultural forms and social processes, the pub as a social and cultural institution, in *Leisure and popular cultural forms* (ed. A. Tomlinson), Brighton Polytechnic, Eastbourne.

Moorhouse, H. (1989) Models of work, models of leisure, in *Leisure for Leisure, Critical Essays* (ed. C. Rojek), Macmillan, Basingstoke.

Parker, S. (1971) *The Future of Work and Leisure*, McGibbon Key, London.

Parker, S. (1983) *Leisure and Work*, Allen & Unwin, London.

Phillips, J. (1992) 'An evaluation of theme parks for the over 55's' Unpublished report, Bournemouth University.

Rappoport, R. and Rappoport, R. (1975) *Leisure and the Family Life Cycle,* Routledge & Kegan Paul, London.

Roberts, K. (1978) *Contemporary Society and the Growth of Leisure.*

Rojek, C. (1989) *Leisure for Leisure: Critical Essays,* Macmillan, Basingstoke.

Slattery, P. and Johnson, S.M. (1991) *Quoted Hotel Companies: the World Markets*, Kleinwort Benson securities, London.

Choosing a hotel 13

Aims

This chapter aims to:

1. illustrate and explain the concept of attitude;
2. identify and explain two psychological models of attitudes and their relation to behaviour; and
3. illustrate the utility of the concept of attitude in relation to consumer choice of hotel.

Outcomes

At the end of this chapter you will be able to:

1. outline different hospitality contexts where a knowledge of the concept of attitudes would be useful; and
2. describe the complexity of the relationship between attitudes and behaviour, and outline the implications for hospitality management context.

THE CONCEPT OF ATTITUDE

You will find it useful to write down what you understand by the term attitude, with some examples of attitudes that you hold, or that other people hold.

Perhaps the area most common to the experience of individuals in formal social science attitude research is being approached in the street by someone carrying out a market survey, and wanting to ask you questions about your knowledge and experiences of different brands of beer, a different chain store, etc. It is an experience we will all have gone through, and one in which you may experience the difficulties that researchers may face first hand, i.e. getting a sample of people that are willing to answer the questions. In the area of hospitality management courses, it is likely that the area of attitudes will have been implicitly, if not explicitly, considered through the issue of customer satisfaction and its measurement.

Now write down what you understand by the term belief. Try to include some examples of beliefs that you hold, or that other people hold. Do the same for the term value.

Compare your comments for each of the three terms – you may find that there are some repetitions. It is often difficult to distinguish between these terms and, for the layperson, differentiation in academic terms may not be important. However, as an investigator of human behaviour, with the need to separate and search for explanations and causal links between variables, it may be crucial to understand the differences and, importantly, to understand how each concept may lead to very different choices and behaviours for different individuals. In social science, the terms can be defined and explained as follows.

Beliefs

Our experience of the world and other people allows us to generate beliefs. These beliefs are concerned with what will happen in certain circumstances and when events will occur. Thus we can develop assumptions about the likelihood or probability that an object exists, that it has certain characteristics and that it is likely to be related to other things in particular ways. Beliefs can, thus, act as a guide for behaviour in situations. Some of my beliefs may include:

- I believe that the sun will rise in the morning.
- I believe in reincarnation.
- I believe in God.
- I believe that the sky is blue.

The interesting thing about beliefs is that they are purely cognitive. Although there may be beliefs that are common to many people (e.g. I believe in God), they are not necessarily shared by other people. Beliefs are, in fact, purely a product of an individual's thought processes or cognitive mechanisms. Similarly, I can hold a belief, without necessarily feeling anything about it, nor acting upon it. I believe that nightclubs exist, but do not have any feeling towards them one way or another, and do not intend to enter one. Clearly then, having a belief does not mean that there is any emotional feeling either for or against the object that the belief is directed towards.

If you think about some of the things that you may have listed as beliefs, you will see that they may include some indication of desire, or wishful thinking. For example, 'I am going to get straight A grades throughout my time at college', 'I am going to become head of a major hotel chain immediately upon graduating', etc. These are not strictly beliefs as they involve some kind of wishful thinking, as well as an honest assessment of the probability of their occurrence.

Values

Values represent the idea of what individuals think is desirable or undesirable. They give us an indication of what the individual wants to be true and why they want something to be true. The example above illustrates this fact, in that the move from a belief to a value is one in which you move from what somebody realistically thinks is true, to what somebody would desire to be true, and the reasons for that desire.

Consider the things that you have included in your lists for value. It seems that there are general values that individuals can hold, for example the value of happiness, or specific values, e.g. the value of being able to eat when hungry. Rokeach (1968) carried out a survey to investigate people's values and identified 36 widely distributed and relatively non-overlapping values. Consider what these might have been, and how might variables such as culture, age, gender affect lists.

Thus, individuals have beliefs about the world and behaviour, that is assumptions about the actual state of things or existence of things. They also have values – some kind of criteria for judging the worth of things in terms of their level of desirability. As well as this, however, we also have positive or negative feelings about many of the things in which we believe. We believe in certain things, we have criteria for judging things and, for some of those things and in some circumstances, those concepts become blended. This is what constitutes an individual's attitude.

It can be seen that it is difficult to distinguish these things, but when considering a rigorous analysis of human behaviour this may be crucial. How might you investigate an individual's motivation to work? Which of the concepts outlined would be important? What difference would it make to your investigation to differentiate between the concepts?

Although there is disagreement on the actual definition of an attitude by psychologists – and this is no surprise given different psychologists' perspectives and focuses on different aspects of behaviour – there are some commonly agreed and widely taught models of attitudes. Two that may be of use to a hospitality student or manager are the three-component model by Rosenburg and Hovland (1960), and a model proposed by Ajzen and Madden (1986) – a recent contribution to the attitudes literature. Before outlining these, it is important for you to think about the exact nature of the relationship between an attitude and a behaviour.

THE THREE-COMPONENT MODEL

The three-component model of attitudes (Rosenburg and Hovland, 1960) suggests that an attitude is, in fact, comprised of three inter-dependent components – a cognitive component, an effective component and a behavioural component.

The cognitive component refers to that part of an attitude which relates to the cognitive mechanisms and aspects, the way that we think and develop ideas about something. The effective component refers to that part of an attitude which we feel, the part towards which we have some positive or negative emotional reaction. The behavioural component is that part of an attitude relating to the actual action or behaviour that the attitude leads us towards.

Take one of the attitudes that you have listed earlier and work out its three different components. If I have an attitude towards equal opportunities in employment, the situation may be 'I feel strongly that women do not have equal opportunities in employment'. The cognitive component here is the actual thinking process behind that, the way that this idea has developed and the ways in which I develop arguments around this issue. The effective component is the way that I feel towards this issue – in this case I may experience anger, frustration, etc. The behavioural component is the actual behaviours that I exhibit as a result of having this attitude. Here, it might be that I actively campaign for equal opportunities, become a member of a union and so on.

This three-component view of attitudes can go some way towards answering questions about the relationship between attitudes and action. As you can see in the example above, having an attitude towards equal opportunities does mean that I take actions directly related to that. Perhaps the most readily available examples of attitudes and their relation to behaviour can be seen through prejudice and discrimination. Prejudice is the attitude that an individual might hold towards people of different races, sexes and ages and discrimination would be the behaviour that is exhibited as a result of that. It is clear, when considering examples such as that, that attitudes cannot only be directed at many different objects of principles, but can also vary in the strength with which you hold them and the degree to which that conviction will lead to action. For example, I might also hold an attitude concerning the privatization of the health service, but in fact do not act according to those beliefs in order to change anything in health situations.

COGNITIVE DISSONANCE

Imagine that you hold an attitude relating to equal opportunities, and desire to do something actively about that. In your current job you are the union representative for the unit and do attempt to ensure that equal opportunities policies are put into operation. Thus, you hold this attitude and are inclined to act and behave in accordance with that. You have been offered a new position as manager of a hotel, in which the employment package is a considerable improvement on your current position. However, it is clear that you could not continue your union activities and it is apparent that within the organization offering you the post, equal opportunities policies are not a priority. You have a feeling that despite their existence, they are not strictly adhered to. What would you do, how would you feel, and how can the three-component model of attitudes help explain all this?

Festinger (1957) proposed the idea of cognitive dissonance which, in relation to attitudes, means that the three components of the attitude are not in harmony with each other. If this occurs a feeling of unease or discomfort is likely to arise, and as this is not a desirable feeling, something is likely to happen in order to reduce that pressure and restore the equilibrium between components. This change can, of course, be in either the cognitive component, effective component or behavioural component of the attitude.

In the above situation, it might be difficult to refuse a job with considerably higher benefits than your current one, but taking it would involve some discomfort. Your attitude towards equal opportunities would still exist, but in the new work context, the behavioural component would not be in harmony with the other two components. You would still hold the cognitive ideas and effective feelings, but would be restricted in your behavioural actions. It would even be possible to imagine a situation in which you were promoting people and clearly not adhering to your principles. If this dissonance is to be reduced, something would have to be changed. It might be that you begin to change your ideas and feeling about equal opportunities, so that your behaviour at work is, in fact, now a reflection of those changed beliefs, or it might be that you construct a rationale that allows you to campaign for equal opportunities outside the workplace.

CHANGING ATTITUDES

If you now consider one of the attitudes that you have, and one that you feel particularly strongly about, how would you go about changing that, or how would somebody else go about changing that? This is not an idle question – you may find, for example, that your staff hold attitudes towards other people that are detrimental to staff relations, or customer service, how could you try to change that, and how difficult would it be? This presents us not only with a practical difficulty – attitudes are likely to have developed over time and through all manner of cultural experiences, in which case individuals may be extremely reluctant to change them – but also presents us with the difficulty that attitudes cannot be directly observed. If the three-component model is a sensible one, it is clear that the only observable aspect of an attitude is the behavioural component and, as we have seen, that does not necessarily have to reflect the cognitive and effective components. The implication of this in terms of employment practices might be that it is possible to legislate to prevent discriminatory behaviours, but extremely difficult to legislate to prevent thoughts or feelings towards individuals or groups.

It should be clear that attitudes are complex sets of ideas developed by individuals as a result of experiences of different kinds. The relationship between the attitudes that people hold and their behaviour depends on many factors, including the strength of that attitude, its origins and, often, the actual situation that individuals find themselves in at points in time.

CHOOSING A HOTEL

Imagine that you wake up one morning to find that you have won a competition for a holiday for two weeks in London. Your budget is unlimited, and all you have to do is write to the competition organizers and inform them of the dates on which you wish to take up this offer and the hotel in which you want to stay. You can choose any hotel in the centre of London, the only constraint being that once you have chosen a hotel, you are obliged to stay there for the full two weeks. Where would you choose to stay and why?

What we are really asking here, is how and why do customers make choices about selecting a hotel for leisure purposes? One of the ways in which we might analyse this decision-making process for individuals would be through the use of the concept of attitudes. Explanations can be given through the use of a further psychological model of attitudes.

Assume for a moment, that I have been given the above opportunity. How could my choice be explained in terms of attitudes? I would consider all the options available to me and, given that I have an unlimited budget, I know that I have the opportunity to stay in luxury hotels that I would not under normal circumstances be able to do. However, I know that given this situation, I would not choose a luxury hotel, but would go for a choice where I would feel more comfortable. How can a social scientist explain this phenomenon.

Ajzen and Madden (1986)

A model of attitudes proposed by Ajzen and Madden might help explain my choice and behaviour. In this model of attitudes, there are three components that influence my intention to act and my subsequent behaviour. These are shown in the diagram below.

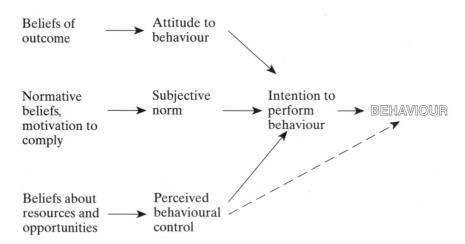

Source: Stephenson, G.M. *The Psychology of Criminal Behaviour;* published by Blackwell, Oxford, (1992). Reproduced with permission.

Clearly, I have an attitude towards the choice of hotel and the ways in which I would feel and behave in that situation. I also have a subjective norm connected to that, i.e. some idea of how significant others would view my actions, whether they would approve or disapprove. But there is also another important factor in this model of attitudes (which was developed from Fishbein and Ajzen's (1975) original theory of reasoned action), and that is concerned with my perceived behavioural control. This is the extent to which I perceive that I have some sense of control over the situation and behaviours that I would perform. In this example, I would quite like to experience a stay in a luxury hotel and feel that if any of my friends had the same opportunity they would also feel that way. In other words, my attitude and subjective norm towards the choice of hotel in some way suggest that I would have the intention to choose the Savoy. However, as I have said, I know I would not do that, as I would experience discomfort in such surroundings. Clearly, it is possible to explain this by the factor of perceived behavioural control. If I were to stay at the Savoy, I would find it difficult to know how to behave in situations, and would be unhappy with the level of deference that I expect the staff would show towards me.

By carrying out an analysis of my own behaviour in this way, it should be apparent that this model of attitudes can have a lot to offer to a manager trying to investigate consumer choices. It would be valuable for that manager to consider the nature of attitude formation, the role and influence of significant others on the individual and, of course, the issue of perceived behavioural control.

It is also interesting at this point to consider the roots of my perceptions and the foundations of my knowledge and attitudes. I have no experience of a luxury hotel, hence all the information I have on which to formulate an attitude and make a choice must have come from another source. I do, in fact, hold a stereotypical picture of the way such a hotel operates, the manner in which people interact and the ways in which it would be appropriate for me to behave. This view may have developed from talking to other people or from representations in the media and it is interesting to note that, despite the fact that it may be a wholly incorrect perception of reality, it is still that perception that determines my choice.

Hence, it is possible to see that a model of attitudes, and the consequent relationship to behaviour – in this case choice of hotel – can go some way towards understanding consumer choice. The important feature in using such theories and models is that the exact nature of the relationship between decisions, attitudes and behaviours can be investigated. It is clear that in relation to hospitality contexts, operators need to be aware of the different influences on customers' attitudes towards their product or service and, indeed, need to know if those attitudes actually influence customers' behaviour.

SUMMARY

Attitudes are relatively complex evaluative judgements towards people or objects. They represent a combination of our values and beliefs with regard to the world around us. Attitudes can vary in the degree to which we hold them and in their relationship to actual behaviour. Holding an attitude does not necessarily mean that actions can be predicted from it, nor that our behaviour will necessarily indicate it. Two models of attitudes have been presented and it is argued that such models can inform research into the behaviour of individuals within hospitality contexts.

DISCUSSION QUESTIONS

1. Compare and contrast two approaches to the concept of attitude.
2. Describe the value of the three-component model of an attitude for a manager trying to change an employee's attitude towards customers.
3. Identify the strengths and weaknesses of an analysis of an individual's hotel choice using the concept of attitude.
4. How might a hotel manager investigate the attitudes of guests towards the hotel services.

FURTHER READING

Eiser, J.E. and Van der Plight, J. (1988) *Attitudes and Decisions,* Routledge, London. The first chapters in this book illustrate the theories and concepts that surround attitudes and attribution theory. The text explicitly links these concepts to decision-making by applying them to particular areas, i.e. health, medical judgement and nuclear energy. It is a useful book for students to look towards when considering the application of theories in everyday life.

Brigham, J.C. (1991) *Social Psychology* (2nd edn), Harper Collins, New York. This is a general social psychology text which introduces readers to issues in social psychology. The section on attitudes outlines the key models and uses everyday examples to illustrate points.

REFERENCES

Ajzen, I. and Madden, T.J. (1986) Prediction of goal directed behaviour, attitudes, intentions and perceived behavioural control. *Journal of Experimental Social Psychology*, **22**, 453–474.
Festinger, L. (1957) *A Theory of Cognitive Dissonance*, Row, Peterson and Co.
Fishbein, M. and Ajzen, I. (1975) *Belief, Attitude, Intention and Behaviour: An Introduction to Theory and Research.* Addison Wesley, London.

Rokeach, M. (1968) *Beliefs, Attitudes and Values*, Jossey Bass, San Francisco and London.

Rosenberg, M.J. and Hovland, C.J. (1960) Cognitive, affective and behavioural components of attitudes, in *Attitude organisation and change, an analysis of consistency among attitude components* (eds M.J. Rosenberg, C.J. Hovland, W.J. McGuire, R.P. Abelson, J.W. Brehm), Yale University Press, 1–14, 2.

Stephenson, G. (1992) *The Psychology of the Criminal Justice System*, Blackwell, Oxford

Hospitality Scenarios, Questions and Answers

PART

3

This final section allows students to engage in their own analysis of hospitality situations. We hope that this will allow students the opportunity to monitor their understanding of the material covered in this text. We also hope that this will allow the development of the use of the multidisciplinary approach when attempting to understand human behaviour in hospitality.

First, in Chapter 14, we present a number of scenarios within a hospitality context. Students are encouraged to undertake analysis of these using the guidelines provided. Second, in Chapter 15, we present three sets of questions and answers relating to pieces of work within the hospitality area. We hope that this will allow students the opportunity to develop their analytical abilities.

Scenarios $\boxed{14}$

Aims

This chapter aims to:

1. provide students with a number of scenarios in which social scientific concepts and theories can be used to assist an understanding and explanation of behaviour;

2. provide guidelines for the procedure by which these scenarios should be undertaken; and

3. provide suggested answers to some of the scenarios.

Outcomes

At the end of this section you will be able to:

1. identify and make a case for the appropriate perspective/s with which to analyse the scenarios;

2. identify and make a case for the appropriate concepts with which to analyse the scenarios;

3. analyse and describe each scenario in terms of the concepts previously identified; and

4. consider and describe the implications of that analysis for the participants and others in the scenario.

The following scenarios have been written with the intention that students should work through them and attempt to identify the role that social sciences can play in assisting the understanding and explanation of the issues that they raise. Some of the issues have been worked out so that students can use these as guidelines for their own analyses. We suggest that a logical sequence of working would follow the procedure below.

1. From the issues that the case raises, identify the most appropriate discipline that can act as a framework for explanation. That may reveal the need for multidisciplinary treatment, or occasionally an emphasis on sociological or psychological explanations.

2. Identify the range of possible conceptual or theoretical frameworks which could be used in the analysis, that may reveal gender, social stratification, discrimination, etc.

3. Identify and list the main behavioural considerations that need to be understood and explained in the scenario. Suggest how these can be analysed using the appropriate conceptual framework.

4. Describe a rationale for using a particular conceptual framework.

5. Use the concepts to expose the problem and its origins, and highlight the significant issues.

6. Discuss the implications of the issues for all those involved. This may include staff, customers, management, other units, etc.

7. If further research of the problem is necessary, indicate the rationale for this and describe the ways in which that research may best proceed.

BLAIR HOTELS PLC

The situation posed in this scenario has been presented in the introduction to the book on p. xvii.

SUGGESTED ANSWER

Analysis and identification of the problem

This scenario relates to gender relations in the workplace. In this scene we have two members of staff, neither of whom has expectations which have been met in the allocation of positions within the company. We also have an approach by management in allocating these tasks which we must consider for the future implications for each party in the issue.

Identification of theory and conceptual framework to be used

The question raised by this scenario is whether there has been any unequal treatment of Jean Smith in relation to Tom Pine, or if, in fact, Jean has been treated more favourably than Tom. We are, therefore, able to cast this issue within the context of sex discrimination and employment. The concepts we will draw upon will be gender and discrimination.

Conceptual treatment of the issue

We might deduce from the issue, the fact that both employees entered the company with the same qualifications and prior experience. There is no indication in the issue that one individual performed better during the training period than the other, so we must assume that the employees were equal in ability. In allocating the tasks, the manager's judgements about the work roles are based upon differentiating Jean's expectations from Tom's. The manager evoked social stereotypes when allocating the housekeeping job to Jean, as he assumed that Jean was seeking a work role that could be combined with her present or future domestic commitments. These assumptions were not applied to Tom and, in fact, a different set of assumptions were put forward in relation to Tom's career progression, and not his domestic arrangements. However sympathetic the manager might have been in relation to Jean's future, he is guilty of discrimination. Jean herself expressed no desire for a role which allowed combination of work and domestic responsibilities. In fact, her desire to work in food and beverage indicated her willingness to work unsociable hours. There could have been many justifiable reasons for allocating Jean to the housekeeping department, and Tom to food and beverage. These include:

1. the manager had noticed that Jean was better able to cope with the demands of this department;
2. Jean performed this role better than Tom in the training period; and

3. Tom proved to be more competent in the food and beverage area than Jean.

In fact, none of these reasons are put forward. The rationale for placing Jean in housekeeping is given in relation to her present or future domestic arrangements. An additional factor is also relevant here – within the hotel and catering industry, housekeeping departments have traditionally consisted of all-female staff. The assumption was that Jean would be happy to follow this tradition and that head housekeeper was the limit of her career aspirations. Gender role segregation is apparent when the manager indicates that food and beverage is a staging post to management in a way that housekeeping is not. This is reflected in the fact that housekeeping was considered a permanent position for Jean – the role was ideal for her future.

There is no case for considering this as positive discrimination, as there is no indication that housekeeping would lead to a future position as general manager. Tom has no case to argue that Jean was more favourably treated than himself. He did not ask for domestic arrangements to be taken into account in his career progression, and this was not an assumption made by the manager in his case. Furthermore, if the general manager progressed within the company (as is indicated), the flexible hours offered in the housekeeping role did not equate with what would seem to be the opportunity for faster career progression.

Implications for the parties

Jean could pursue a case of discrimination against the company, as discrimination has been practised. However, it may be better as a first step to discuss the housekeeping role with the manager. This may bring the discriminatory nature of the allocations of the jobs to his attention and he may then be willing to reconsider. Secondly, Jean could resign from the post. This may not be a good alternative, given her limited experience in the job market and finding another job may be difficult. Jean's position is also hampered by a lack of female role models within hotel management; these, if present, could assist her in dissuading the manager from his stereotypical approach.

Within the issue, Tom did not gain the position he was seeking either, and future relations between the two members of staff might become antagonistic. For the general manager this could lead to problems in the work relations between Jean and Tom. Furthermore, were Jean to resign, this would in effect mean that the company had lost resources on her training programme. In addition, were Jean to take the case to an industrial tribunal, there could be damaging consequences both to the general manager and to the company.

Overall, the behaviour of the general manager was problematic in the following areas:

1. he made no attempt to discover the aspirations of the members of staff;
2. the basis for his decision was discriminatory;
3. he failed to communicate the information to the members of staff in an appropriate manner; and
4. his decisions could result both in legal action and in labour turnover.

Clearly the general manager has to resolve this issue. It will be necessary for him to base his decisions on something other than gender stereotypes. He must institute a more formal approach to staff appraisal, in order to establish a more objective means to identify the skills and competencies of staff. In the given situation, he might be best advised to follow through with his decision in the immediate future, but to reconsider within a relatively short time period. Perhaps he might best discuss with Jean and Tom the possibility of their changing departments, thus ensuring equal treatment.

INTERNATIONAL HOTELS INC.

You are the management team of a 300-bedroom city centre hotel which is owned and operated by a multinational hotel company. A fax has arrived from head office stating the following:

> Ms Wilson, a customer staying at your hotel two weeks ago, is bringing a legal action against the company for sexual harassment. Ms Wilson alleges that when she stayed at the hotel, she reported a faulty TV to reception. A member of service staff (off duty at the time) arrived to repair the TV. Ms Wilson allowed this member of staff, Ian Brown, into her room, because he was wearing a company uniform. Ms Wilson alleges that Mr Brown then sexually harassed her.

You are required to compile a report for head office to be received by them in two days' time. The report should indicate how the company should proceed in this case.

SUGGESTED ANSWER

Identification of issue/problem

This scenario involves a range of issues for discussion. These include the question of Ms Wilson's treatment at the hotel and if, in fact, the events occurred as she described them. There is also the issue of Mr Brown's credibility and his version of events. In simple terms, this appears to be a customer bringing a complaint against a member of staff. However, this complaint goes beyond the internal complaints system of the hotel, because the issue is to be the subject of possible legal action. Therefore, it is not only a customer complaint, but a complaint about sexual harassment which could have legal implications for the company. The issue could be cast within the area of the treatment of female customers in hotels, and this would bring us to analyse the scenario using gender as our framework. While this would be an important area in our analysis, there are additional problems in this case. These include staff and customer management and communications, which places our issue within the framework of organization and management.

Identification of theoretical and conceptual framework.

This issue directs our attention to the management of customers and staff within the hotel. It will include an analysis of gender relations between female customers and male staff. Therefore, an appropriate concept to use is that of gender relations. Added to this, the organizational context will be important to investigate issues of authority, organization structure, communications and management information systems. An additional area which it is necessary to discuss is the relationship between the unit management of the hotel and the corporate management. As this is a hotel owned by a company, actions occurring in one unit may have implications for the other hotels within the company.

Assessment of the issue

The starting point for the management team will be to determine the events which occurred. Areas to consider would be if Ms Wilson is a regular or first-time customer in the hotel. If the former is the case, she could have experienced no problems in the past and she might be known to the staff. If the latter is the case, the issue becomes more difficult. Either way, Ms Wilson's value as a customer has the same degree of importance. The management team would also be interested in Mr Brown's employment record, e.g. length of service and reliability. Mr Brown could, in theory, be a long-serving employee with no previous complaints against him; alternatively, he could be a part-time member of staff of three weeks duration. In either event, Mr Brown's account should be heard and recorded, preferably in the presence of a staff or trade union representative.

It may be difficult for the management team to reach a conclusion about Mr Brown and there may be disagreement within the team with regard to his guilt or innocence. The general manager – the only person with the authority to do so in this case – will ultimately have to make a decision. It is often the case that management decisions have to be taken without a full knowledge of the facts and in areas where it is difficult to prove a case one way or another.

Here, the manager may decide to suspend Mr Brown until a decision is agreed with head office. It is worth noting that time restrictions often apply to decision-making and, in this situation, the general manager must reply within two days.

It is likely that, as part of the general manager's enquiries, he or she will attempt to find out why Mr Brown was allowed to go to a customer's bedroom, since this was a problem for the maintenance department. The maintenance manager will have to explain this situation, which is likely to lead to conflict and disagreement as to areas of responsibility and communications. Furthermore, the management team must be concerned with the lack of communications within the hotel, and why this problem was not brought to their attention before the fax. With regard to this, it may be that Ms Wilson was too distressed to report the incident, desiring to leave the hotel as soon as possible. However, reception staff should have asked her if she had experienced any problems when she checked out, as this is an important area in which to receive customer feedback. The management team will be aware of the bad publicity which could be generated by this case and their investigations may reveal some problems in the management of the hotel. It might be the case, therefore, that the management team would conclude that paying some compensation to Ms Wilson is worth considering.

The management report will, therefore, recommend that Mr Brown is suspended pending further investigations and that, as the management team cannot determine the accuracy of the charges one way or another, some compensation is recommended for Ms Wilson.

As the corporate management team, you have received the report from the hotel, and must now decide what action to take. The scenario clearly raises issues of company policy in relation to staff and customer management, which need to be addressed. The corporate team may agree or disagree with the conclusions of the unit report, however, their concern must be to ensure that company policies and practices are implemented to ensure that the company is protected from the possibility of issues like this occurring in the future. This means that policy changes must be implemented in all the hotels.

The first area of policy change has to be in the area of staff management. Off-duty staff must not be allowed to remain on the premises in uniform when they are off-duty. Secondly, the system for reporting maintenance problems must go through reception to maintenance, with the duty manager being informed so that he or she might follow up the complaint. (Note, direct calls to maintenance by customers do not solve this kind of problem, in that sexual harassment could still occur if guests are alone in the room with staff.) Thirdly, reception staff must improve their reporting skills and encourage customers to complete comment cards to record problems experienced during their stay at the hotel. Clearly, if Ms Wilson had completed a card indicating that there were no problems with her stay, this would have implications for a future legal action. Customer care programmes should be introduced for all customers.

With respect to female customers, surveys of female customers' usage of hotels (e.g. Expotel, 1993) indicate that female customers feel uncomfortable with male room attendants. However, it would clearly be impractical and not cost effective to have only female customers served by female staff. Given that this is the case, when female customers experience problems the guest services manager should accompany staff to the customers room. Alternatively, the duty manager could accompany staff to deal with the problems of female customers. The particular approaches that companies adopt will depend largely upon the value that they place on customers.

Finally, the corporate management team should recognize that a lack of company policy in these areas does invite problems of the type discussed in the scenario. Clearly, actions occurring at the hotel in the example, raise problems of how best to deal with Ms Wilson's complaint. If legal action is pursued, this could be damaging to all of the hotels in the company. It could lead to a reduction in occupancy, especially by female customers. On the other hand, if the company agree to pay compensation, this may still attract press coverage, with even more damaging results.

Although the action will be taken against Mr Brown as an individual, Ms Wilson is suing the company for not ensuring her safety. Ultimately, the legal department of the company will have to decide which course of action is less damaging. Their decision will also be influenced by the company's corporate culture and approach to customer management. The suspension of Mr Brown is closely related to the outcome of the board's decision. He must remain suspended, despite the resentment this may cause to other staff, until the corporate management team receive legal advice. If the company decide to defend the action, he must remain suspended until the case is settled to avoid any further publicity which might accrue from the final outcome of the case.

■■■■■ HARE AND HOUNDS, BEECH COMMON ■■■■■■■■■■■■■

John and Beth Ridley have operated the Hare and Hounds, near Beech Common, for a period of five years. Every August, a local fair comes to the common near by for two weeks. The fair owners consist of what the local press call 'travelling people'.

Since the Hare and Hounds is the only public house within the area, the travelling people become regular customers for this two-week period. As yet, these customers have not broken any laws or caused any problems in the pub. However, their appearance and boisterous behaviour tends to put the local customers off visiting the pub during that period.

As August approaches, John decides to act and prevent the loss of revenue from his local custom. He places notices on the entrance to the pub reading 'NO TRAVELLERS'.

Analyse what you consider to be the implications of this action.

SUGGESTED ANSWER

John's actions were clearly confrontational and might have provoked more serious trouble at the Hare and Hounds. As the landlord, he had the right to refuse entry to customers as he pleased, but since the travellers had not caused any trouble in the past, his grounds for refusing admission were rather thin. Imposing dress restrictions as a solution may have offended regular customers and would not have solved the problem of boisterous behaviour.

Was John, therefore, guilty of discrimination by posting his notice, and could this have led to prosecution? You might be surprised to find that the action he took was not, in fact, illegal. Even though his behaviour seems to carry all the aspects of discrimination and prejudice, the law relating to discrimination is complex.

The scenario for this discussion was based upon an actual case (CRE vs Dutton 1989 IRLR 8 CA), where the judge ruled as follows:

> 'Travellers' are not synonymous with gipsies. Therefore as notice in a pub stating 'no travellers' did not indicate an intention by the licensee to discriminate on racial grounds, since the prohibited class included all those of a nomadic way of life and all nomads were treated equally whatever their race.

Hence, if John had used the term 'Gipsies' on his notice, he would have been guilty of discrimination on the grounds of ethnicity.

> Gipsies, using the narrower meaning of the word 'gypsies' as 'a wandering race (by themselves called Romany), of Hindu origin' rather than the larger, amorphous group of 'travellers' or 'nomads', are an identifiable group defined by reference to 'ethnic origins' with the meaning of the definition of 'racial group'.

THE VEGETARIAN RESTAURANT

Catherine had been working for a small vegetarian restaurant for four weeks before the following incident with the owner/manageress occurred. Catherine was employed as a part-time waitress, to work on Friday evenings and Saturday – the times at which the restaurant was at its busiest. She was 17 years old, with some previous waiting experience, and was paid £3 per hour.

On the first few occasions that she worked, she was eager to impress her new boss, worked hard and seemed to provide an excellent service to the customers. This did not go down well with the other two waiting staff, who had been there for three years. By the end of one shift she overheard a conversation between them:

'It's all well and good having another pair of hands to help, but this is taking things too far.'

'Yes, something will have to be done before long. It's all well and good being nice to the customers, but when it comes to shining already clean glasses and helping the potwash, I mean that really is taking things too far.'

'I guess she is new though, maybe given time she will learn the ropes and we'll be back to normal.'

'By which time, we may be out of a job, you know what Madam's like with this new cost-cutting here and cost-cutting there. It's alright for these students to come and work here part-time for a bit of pocket money, but this is our livelihood. Not only are our perks being taken away, which after all we deserve, but if this carries on, we may well end up on the dole or doing the potwash job as well.'

Catherine went home, and returned for the next shift determined to try and make some kind of amends and gesture to the other two staff. She worked hard with the customers once more, but when asked by the potwash to help, tried to find some excuse to get out of it, and by the end of the evening was given short shrift by him. As she was tidying the table for the following day, the manageress approached Pam, one of the other waitresses, and Catherine overheard the following:

'It's been a good night again hasn't it? I expect you got plenty of tips tonight.'

'I guess so.'

'I'm thinking of trying a few new dishes over the next couple of weeks. I thought you and Karen might like to have a look over the new menus and tell me what you think.'

'Fine, maybe we could do that tomorrow before we get the rush on.'

'Look, let's sit down and have a cigarette and a chat, we've been so busy lately and I just don't get the time to gossip like we used to.'

At which point, Pam sat down with the manageress, handed out her cigarettes, and began to talk. Karen joined them within two minutes, leaving Catherine to do all the work; it wasn't until she had finished that they stood up to get ready to leave. Catherine wasn't too bothered about this, after all it would help her get on with everyone else over the next few weeks. When she'd been there long enough, she would make it clear that she would not stand for this.

Little by little, it became clear to Catherine that things had been, and were, changing in the restaurant. All the staff were informed one day that they were no longer to eat food on the premises unless they brought their own in, or unless they paid for it; breaks were becoming strictly timed and wages docked unless they were adhered to and staff were punctual; more and more of the cleaning and odd jobs were expected of the waiting staff. The manageress actually got all the staff together at the end of a Saturday shift, and explained to them that unless she could cut costs quite drastically over the next few months, then she would have to take some serious measures.

'She's said all this before, we are the only vegetarian restaurant for miles around, we have a steady flow of regulars, there's no way she can get rid of us', said Pam as the manageress left.

And things carried on much as before. The only difference was that when the staff were hungry now, they had to make sure that the manageress did not see them eating. Between them, Karen, the potwash and Pam carried out subtle techniques in order to fool the manageress. They would order the wrong meals, eat whilst she was out and so on. The manageress, if she had noticed this, displayed no sign of it, and continued to be friendly with the staff. On occasion she offered to buy them a drink after the restaurant has closed, and made the effort to sit down with them for a smoke at the end of the night.

The manageress was out one evening; Pam was getting the change for a customer's bill out of the till, when Catherine saw her take out £1.50 and put it in her pocket. She said nothing at the time, but later on decided to ask Pam if she had made some kind of mistake. Pam denied any knowledge of the incident and got a bit haughty at the suggestion that she would do such a thing. However, later she said to Karen:

> 'We need to be a bit careful now you know, that new girl has eyes like a hawk, and watches us at the till at every opportunity.'

> 'So, what can she do or prove? And anyway, we only take what's due to us. By the end of the night Madam must have scrounged a packet of cigs off us.'

Catherine finished work one Saturday evening, and was told by the manageress that she would no longer be required in the restaurant. When she asked why, she was told that since she had started work, the tills had been down on each occasion she had been present, that this was too much of a coincidence and unacceptable. The manageress made it clear that she was not to be trusted, that she was also causing problems with other members of staff. They were increasingly complaining about how they had to cover up for her in front of customers. Similarly, since she had started, the restaurant had lost a number of valued regular customers and the staff were becoming uncooperative.

Identify:

- the difficulties faced by Catherine in this context;
- the difficulties faced by other participants; and
- the general issue raised by this particular scenario.

Remember that all these should be thought of in some kind of framework. By doing this, potential courses of action that the manageress might take can be identified.

■■■■■ THE DOG AND GUN, TOWNSEND ■■■■■

You have just been appointed as the manager of a public house in a rural area. It is, in fact, the only public house in a small village, and the main custom during the week seems to be the male workers from the surrounding farms. The weekends bring in a mixture of couples, walkers and again the regulars from the week. After a few months settling in, during which time you have encountered difficulties with some of the customers, you appear to have smoothed things over, and the business is running much the same as with the previous manager.

The nearest town is 10 miles away. Within that town, a university is in the process of expanding its student numbers. As part of this move, the university has bought an old warehouse within the village, and intends to convert this to be used as student accommodation. Whilst the complex itself, when finished, will have its own bar facilities, there is clearly an opportunity for you to increase your custom.

Local response to this development has been mixed. Some people think it will be the worst thing that can happen to the village, and the community will be destroyed. Others see it as positive in the sense that the students will be using the facilities and shops in the village. A small proportion of residents feel neither one way nor the other about the event. Listening to the customers in your pub reflects this range of attitudes, but you have heard comments such as, 'we'll be overrun by them all', 'we'll have women coming in here wanting to drink pints', 'I bet he puts the beer prices up', 'we come here after a day at work wanting a bit of peace and quiet'.

Consider the following questions. What might the difficulties have been for the new manager in the first few months after taking over the pub? Interpret these using social science perspectives. What should the manager consider when thinking about the issues of the student accommodation? If he or she were to attempt to increase sales with these potentially new customers, what difficulties do you think may be encountered, and what if any, courses of action can the manager take? Again, think about these in relation to some social science frameworks or concepts.

■■■ CONTROL STRATEGIES ■■■■■■■■■■■■■■■■■■■■■

The landlord and landlady of a public house on the edge of town have gone out for the night and left you with a phone number where they can be contacted. This phone number has a code that indicates it is not within 20 miles of the pub. You are 21 years old, and have worked in this pub for three years. The clientele are predominantly regular customers whom you know well.

By 8 pm you have five of these regulars in the pub, and are chatting with them. At 8.15, ten customers walk in that you have not seen before, and order a round of ten drinks. It looks as though they may be on their way into town, and several of them are staggering around as if they are already drunk. You serve them with the first round of drinks, and they wander off into the pool room. This room is not within sight of the bar, but you can hear abusive language, and what appears to be an argument between two people, You go into the pool room, and ask them to keep the noise down a bit, expecting and getting a torrent of abuse. At this point one of the regular customers comes into the pool room and repeats the request to keep the noise down, and for some reason this seems to calm the situation down and you both return to the bar. By 8.30 they have finished their drinks and leave the premises, much to your relief.

At 9.30, by which time you have more customers in the pub, they return, and order another round of drinks. They are by now clearly drunk, and a number of them are staring at the regular who helped you out in the pool room earlier. There appears to be a ringleader to the group, and it is him who has come to the bar to order the drinks.

What would you do? Again, consider the scenario from a social science point of view, and arrive at what you feel to be an appropriate course of action as a result of that information.

GREENFIELDS HOTEL

You are the manager of the leisure complex in a 300-bedroom hotel in a prosperous business city. Your hotel has excellent conference facilities which are in demand from customers, and these customers tend to use the leisure facilities fairly extensively. It has always been the hotel's policy to allow staff to use certain of these facilities, for example the swimming pool, at specified times of the day, and it has been assumed that this is a useful way to keep staff morale high.

You have been sent a memo from the general manager informing you that over the past two weeks there have been a number of complaints from customers. These range from customers who claim that they have not been able to use the gym, as staff members are already using the equipment, to customers who have said that they find it unacceptable that they should be sharing the swimming pool with members of staff. The general manager requests that you 'deal with this matter'.

What would you do? Would you want to know how useful it is in terms of morale to allow staff to use the facilities? If so, devise a method of investigating that issue.

Would you want to know the proportion of complaints that are received compared to the total users of the facilities? If so, devise a method of doing this. What other factors might you need to take into consideration before recommending a course of action?

Using social scientific concepts, why might these complaints be made by some customers in the first place?

SWAN HOTEL, READING

You are the newly appointed manager of The Swan Hotel in Reading. This is a 200-bedroom hotel owned and operated by a UK company. You have been appointed to this position after a 4-year university course in hotel management, 2 years' experience as a department head, and 3 years' experience as a general manager with a competitor company.

You have been informed at interview that the previous manager was sacked, but were given no reason for this dismissal. On arrival, you are going through your in-tray when you discover a letter of resignation from the previous assistant manager. Also, in the tray is an anonymous letter indicating that a system of pilfering is going on in the hotel, which involves all the department heads. You have decided to ignore these letters as they appear to be unfounded and wish to make a fresh start with the staff. There are also three letters from customers indicating that they have not yet received a reply about items of jewellery that were stolen from their rooms

Your brief from the chief executive is to sort out the problems at the hotel, which he does not specify. This is one of the most profitable hotels in the group. You are told that head office have also received some anonymous letters. You have also been instructed to appoint a new assistant manager from the existing hotel team.

In your previous job your approach to management was based upon giving staff a degree of autonomy, consulting and including them in decision-making. Generally, you managed the hotel with the help of the department heads. You feel that this approach is an appropriate one, and works best. Therefore, within six weeks you have set up a committee structure for the hotel, which allows staff grievances to be aired, and you have delegated responsibilities to the department heads in the usual way. This meant that the staff were consulted about the position of assistant manager, and ultimately were allowed to vote on the most likely candidate. In the event, the staff gave the restaurant manager the majority vote, and you appointed him to the post.

Some six weeks after the assistant manager's appointment, a stocktake within the food and beverage department revealed a significant discrepancy in revenue. Furthermore, a number of customers have made appointments to see you with regard to claims that items have been stolen from their rooms.

Consider the issues that this case raises in relation to management style, decision-making, group dynamics and customer management.

REFERENCE

Expotel (1993) Hotels and the female business traveller. *Dial Magazine*, Autumn.

Questions and answers 15

Aims

This chapter aims to:

1. present three exercises that represent themes and issues in the text;

2. guide students through the issues using questions and answers.

Outcomes

At the end of this section you will be able to:

1. work through the questions and answers for each piece of work;

2. recognize and describe the strengths and weaknesses of these articles in relation to an understanding of the contemporary hospitality industry;

3. undertake similar critical evaluation of other research in the hospitality area.

Each of the following pieces of work have been chosen for evaluation as we feel that they represent themes and issues that we have raised throughout the text.

- Slattery, P. *Social scientific methodology and hospitality management* has been chosen as it represents an attempt to summarize the role of social sciences in relation to the hospitality industry. The article comments on alternative explanations, and introduces the debate surrounding the inclusion of social sciences on hospitality management courses.

- Whyte, W. *The social structure of the restaurant* has been chosen as, despite its age, it remains a landmark work in the conceptual treatment of hospitality issues.

- Hall, S. *Quest for quality* has been chosen as it combines both conceptual and methodological issues.

Students can approach these tasks in a number of ways. However, we would suggest that readers attempt to read these articles and answer the questions as fully as possible before looking at the answers we have provided. It may be that students will want to refer to earlier chapters in order to complete the exercises. Similarly, students may also find it useful to use the exercises for the basis of discussion.

Social scientific methodology and hospitality management

Paul Slattery

Department of Catering Studies, The Polytechnic, Queensgate, Huddersfield, U.K.

The hospitality industry is frequently presented as a people industry. This paper argues that accepting this view requires our understanding of hospitality management to be social scientifically informed, because the social sciences alone are able to offer theoretically grounded interpretations of people and social events in hospitality. The success of these interpretations is dependent upon the methodology employed, and the paper identifies three areas of methodology crucial to the resolution of social issues in hospitality management.

Keywords: Social science, theory selection, application, evaluation

Introduction

The high manpower density of the hospitality industry and the service nature of the work, in which the crucial relationship is that between the people involved in the provision and consumption of hospitality, are among factors often identified in support of the commonplace and popular point that the hospitality industry is a people industry. This paper starts from this point and argues that its acceptance requires our understanding of hospitality management to be social scientifically informed. This in itself is not a new or radical assertion since most academics in our field are aware of it. There is a social scientific presence in all of the hotel and catering degrees and higher TEC diplomas in Britain, in the senior hotel schools of continental Europe (Slattery, 1980) and in the hotel and restaurant degrees in Australia, Canada and the U.S.A. In spite of this, and the fact that four out of the ten topics covered in the aims of this journal are explicitly social scientific, there are uncertainties among many concerned with the teaching and practice of hospitality management about what the social sciences are, how they operate and the contribution which they can make to our field. This paper is an attempt to deal with some of these uncertainties.

Why the social sciences?

The social sciences are a family of disciplines including psychology, sociology, economics, politics and sub-disciplines such as industrial psychology, organisation theory, social psychology and econometrics. Through these disciplines social sciences are concerned to offer interpretations of the human condition, of people and the lives they lead. In a field such as hospitality management the predominant approach to the social sciences is interdisciplinary (Slattery, 1980). That is, students invariably do not study single social scientific disciplines, rather their approach is centred on drawing from across the social sciences to explore, understand and interpret the hospitality industry. From the outset, however, it must be made clear that in the strictest terms the people industry observation does not mean that we must pursue social scientific interpretations of hospitality management. The social sciences are not alone in laying claims to understanding people, there are at least two other contenders.

The humanities, through the writings of novelists, poets, essayists and dramatists are involved in highlighting features of the social world. Indeed, there are many novels which portray life in hotels, none better than Orwell's exposition of his experiences as a *plongeur* in Paris (Orwell, 1933). There are also many plays such as Wesker's *The Kitchen* (Wesker, 1960) which can provide insights into the hospitality industry. However, no one makes serious claims that students of hospitality management should study humanities because the industry is concerned with people.

The other contender is the commonsense view that we are people who live in a social world and therefore we understand social life. The influence of this view on hospitality management cannot be underestimated. Examples of the

ARTICLE ▰▰▰▰▰▰▰▰▰▰▰▰▰▰

platitudes which are derived from this view include the notions that chefs are autocratic and hate waiters and that the more luxurious the hotel the more customers will enjoy themselves.

The social sciences, the humanities and the commonsense position all deal with the same bedrock data of human behaviour. The social sciences, however, are different from the others because their interpretations are based on and proceed from some explicit theory or concept. When social scientists assert that the interpretations which they offer are theoretical, they mean that the matter which they interpret is defined in terms of the theory, that the kinds of questions which they ask about it are derived from the theory and that the answers to the questions are bound within the theory. The humanities and the commonsense view on the other hand present personal descriptions without explicit theoretical foundations or the logical rigor of theoretical interpretations. This is not to say that they cannot be accurate. People can sincerely recount what for them are the facts of any situation. In contrast, social scientific interpretations of any event, being theoretically underwritten cannot be all encompassing, there can be as many interpretations of a given situation as there are theories on which to base the interpretation. To change the interpretation, change the theory. Thus the situation is defined differently, different questions are asked about it and different answers are produced. With the other contenders, to change the description of any situation, it is necessary to get someone else to describe it.

The value of theoretical interpretations and their need in the field of hospitality management has been identified more generally by Nailon (1981) who believes that 'only through the development of a theoretical framework, the competent can become effective, while those who are truly able can achieve excellence'.

Unlike the humanities and the commonsense position, social scientific interpretations can lead somewhere and this is part of their value. An example of where they can lead can be seen in my own particular interest in studying the hotel as an organisation which makes available the whole of organisation theory on which to draw to identify organisational features of the hotel. It is possible to analyse the goals of the hotel, its organisation structure, compare it with other organisations, examine the differences, speculate on the implications for our understanding of the hotel in organisation terms and so on. This is a departure from the commonsense wisdom about hotels which consists, almost totally, of anecdotes about hotels. They are gossip which, although enjoyable, has constrained the understanding of the hotel at the level of the man in the street. They are mere recollections which lead nowhere and are not in themselves social scientific. The promise held out by a social scientific perspective on hospitality management is that it can provide useful interpretations of people, their relationships and social events in the hospitality world. Moreover, such interpretations are necessary to understand the hospitality world and to solve social and administrative problems within it. The question now is how is the promise fulfilled? The answer requires us to consider the methodology of the social sciences and is in three parts: the selection of a theory, its application to a hospitality issue and the evaluation of the interpretation offered.

The selection of a theory

Not all of the social sciences are useful or relevant to hospitality management and thus we have to reduce the total stock of social scientific theories to those which are. The theories we select depend on the problems or issues in which we are interested. Puzzles such as: What motivates hotel customers? Are hotel workers committed to their jobs? How are hotels organised? illustrate that the theories of motivation, commitment and organisation, respectively, are necessary bases. This, however, does not resolve the matter of selecting theories because the range of puzzles about the hospitality world which are social scientifically orientated is vast. In fact, it does not matter what the puzzle is so long as it relates to the hospitality world and thus the range of theories which are useful is still vast. Academics have provided some help in reducing the range to a more manageable number. There are three areas of emphasis which appear more frequently than any others in the social science components of hospitality management courses – organisation, customers and workforce (Slattery, 1980). In those courses which are less explicitly social scientific the same three areas appear under the headings of management, marketing and personnel. These areas of emphasis are not exclusive but they do indicate the priority of issues and thus contribute to a narrowing of the range of theories.

Even with this narrowing of choice it is still not at all possible to produce a catalogue of theories which are useful and relevant and another catalogue of those which are not. In the practice of their work scholars must argue for the relevance of any theory and illustrate its value by using it in the service of hospitality management. For example;

theories of child development at first sight appear to provide little field for hospitality management. Yet for those interested in school meals, theories of child development might supply insights into the behaviour and social relations of their customers and therefore pinpoint the package of food and services which will most readily attract school children.

There are two final caveats about the selection of theories which are important. First, social scientific theories have been developed in a variety of different contexts. Useful contributions have been made, for example, to theories of motivation by researchers who have studied the motivations of lower order animals, criminals, school children, homosexuals, workers and car buyers. The factors which motivate any of these groups cannot be taken as indicative of the motivations of hotel customers because the context is different. In short, we cannot easily transpose such theories to hotel customers and expect that they will work effectively. If this were not the case people would behave similarly when working, breaking the law, buying a car or staying in a hotel. The successful use of a theory of motivation to interpret hotel customers as a result not only adds to our understanding of that part of the social world but also alters the state of the theory itself.

Second, as Potter *et al.* (1981) have recently attested, the social sciences are characterised by major theoretical disputes and controversies. There are different versions of most theories because they are based on assumptions about people and are constructed by scholars who have their own beliefs. Different assumptions and beliefs lead to different theories. Theories of intelligence are a case in point. There are two main opposing theoretical camps about intelligence (Kamin, 1974). One camp supports the assumption that intelligence is genetically determined in people. It is hereditary, so that our level of intelligence is fixed by the time we are born. The other camp maintains that this assumption is profoundly wrong and that our intelligence is influenced by the environment in which we live. The assumption which forms the foundation for their theory is that irrespective of the level of intelligence with which we are born it can be developed or retarded by the social environment in which we live out our lives. Both theories can muster strong support among social scientists and produce opposing interpretations of intelligence, Whichever version of the theory we choose will determine the kind of understanding of intelligence which we get.

The intelligence example is part of a more general controversy which cuts across the social sciences and has received attention from many of the major thinkers (Cohen, 1968; O'Neill, 1973; Popper, 1974) are indicative. The controversy revolves around the puzzle, does man create society or does society create man. The manifestations of this dispute are widespread. They are represented in the ideological positions of different political parties, in different views on the management of economy and in the understanding of the ways in which society works. Theoretical disputes are part of the life blood of the social sciences and arise from the complexity of the social world and the elusiveness of easy explanation. Failure on the part of social scientists to address these kinds of disputes detaches them from the foundations on which their interpretations rest. The task for the scholar is not only to select the theories which can underwrite the puzzles which interest him but also to study the theories and the controversies which surround them. Once the theory is selected and studied the scholar can then experiment with its application to hospitality management.

Applying theories

Talk about applying social scientific theories to the hospitality industry is talk about developing hospitality versions of the theories. The theory provides the perspective from which to interpret a hospitality puzzle and the events in the hospitality world which we study in turn influence and reform the theory we use. Application is thus crucial to our endeavour because without it there would be no social scientific interpretations of hospitality management. The venture of applying the theories to hospitality puzzles is an empirical task and there is a range of methods which can be employed to collect the data we need. We can conduct formal experiments which involve making comparisons between two sets of circumstances which match each other in all respects except one. We can use a questionnaire to collect the responses of people to prepared questions about a given topic. We can interview people to gain their views on some issue. We can undertake participant observation in which the researcher is an active participant in the social situation which he is studying and reports on his experiences. We can undertake non-participant observation in which the researcher is not an active participant in the situation being studied, rather he observes actions and reports whatever he observes. We can undertake a statistical analysis in which we can count the items or parts of the items being researched and finally we can conduct documentary research in which existing literature about the topic being studied is reviewed.

It is important to stress that in social scientific interpretations the empirical task cannot occur until the hospitality puzzle has been identified, a particular theory has been selected and questions about the puzzle, framed in terms of the theory, have been asked. To accept anything else would be to deprive the interpretation of its theoretical, and, thus its social scientific, character. Interpretations of people and social events in the hospitality industry which do not conform to the methodology of the social sciences not only pay insufficient attention to the theoretical base, but also the questions which they ask and their methods of data collection are indiscriminate. In their approach the questionnaire is ubiquitous. The topic of customer preferences is a case in point. What passes as our knowledge about customer preferences rests heavily on data collected by questionnaire. There are countless examples of hotels which place a questionnaire in customer bedrooms, undergraduates who question hotel customers and potential hotel customers in project work for their courses and hotel marketeers who conduct feasibility studies. Their efforts are like those identified by Ryan who 'hope that big samples and a good computer will reveal the hidden laws of the social order' (Ryan, 1981). Data about customers has been accumulated but little about customer preferences has been explained. The approach has been insensitive to the position (Phillips, 1973) that the 'collection of social scientific data constitutes a social process' which produces the result that questionnaire respondents exhibit the tendency to 'deny socially undesirable traits and admit socially desirable ones' and that they also 'agree or disagree to questions independently of their content'. The special methodological difficulties of teasing out accurate and relevant data from customers in the intense social context of hospitality have not been debated publicly or thought through fully. The value of the masses of questionnaire data collected about customer preferences is thus diminished.

The proper empirical task involves the collection of data about the particular aspect of the hospitality world which will answer the questions which the theory allows us to ask. For the application of theory, the choice of collection method is crucial since the wrong method will fail to deliver data, or will deliver data which will not answer the question, or deliver the wrong data. No method of data collection is universally applicable.

In the construction of social scientific interpretations gross errors in the choice of method can be avoided since the appropriate method is conditioned by the particular hospitality puzzle on which attention is focussed, the theory we use and the questions we ask about it. This in turn means that social scientific interpretations which are in effect the answers to the questions asked about the puzzles are not all of the same kind. Different answers produce different kinds of interpretations. Moreover, the different kinds of social scientific interpretations which result from the empirical process are influenced by the position adopted by the researchers on the following three issues. First, the kind of interpretation depends on whether the questions about a hotel and catering puzzle are answered by collecting fresh data from the hotel and catering world or by using data which already exists. To collect fresh data we must conduct experiments, observe events, interview people, have questionnaires completed or count things. This process involves, in addition to the construction of the appropriate empirical method, the identification of the exact context in which the data is to be collected. That is, the researcher must identify: the subjects of the experiment; the location, time and components of the event; the criteria on which people are chosen for interview or to complete questionnaires and the precise characteristic of that which is to be counted.

On the other hand, to proceed by using data which already exists involves documentary research. Material to be analysed can include official documents such as government reports, parliamentary papers and the documents of organisations. It can include academic literature such as research reports, learned articles and textbooks and it also includes popular literature such as books, plays, poems, songs, newspapers, magazines and advertisements. Interpretations which rely on this kind of data are different from those which draw on fresh data.

Second, the kind of interpretation depends on whether the data used to answer the question is factual information or a value judgement. Factual information is data which can be proven true or false. Information such as 'the Hotel Ritz, Paris, has 200 bedrooms' is factual. It can be proven true or false by, for example, going to the Ritz and counting the bedrooms. At the end of the exercise the information will be available to prove the statement true if the count reveals 200 bedrooms or false if it does not. A feature of factual information is that it can be measured accurately in mathematical and statistical terms. Interpretations which rely on factual information can thus achieve high degrees of precision. Not all interpretations, however, can draw on factual information. In contrast, there are value judgements, which differ from factual information since they cannot be proven true or false. They are called value judgements because they are interpretations based on the values, attitudes and beliefs of the individual. Their significance for us is that people think and talk about the hotel, predominantly, in evaluative terms. The vocabulary used to describe the hotel – good hotel, bad hotel, luxury hotel, hospitality, tasty food, fine wine, convivial atmosphere, friendly service – are all evaluative statements. That is, they are an expression of the values, attitudes and beliefs which people have about the hotel rather than a factual description of the hotel itself. A feature of value judgements is that they cannot be measured with the accuracy of factual information. Mathematical and statistical measures are unhelpful because in value judgements the same vocabulary can have different meanings for different people. For instance, the statement, 'I like good food' can have radically different meanings depending on who makes the statement and why he makes it. The statement itself does not enable us to identify the actual food which is good or is liked by the person. Value judgements play a major role in the way people describe and understand the world and accordingly a significant proportion of the data on which social scientific interpretations are based is in the form of value judgements, which, by their nature, preclude general agreement. Factual information on the other hand, requires and can achieve a consensus about the characteristics of the items being measured. It is this which allows factual information to be measured with the accuracy of mathematics and statistics. Value judgements cannot achieve this consensus and therefore cannot be measured with the same general accuracy as factual information. Interpretations which draw on value judgements are thus different from those which draw on factual information.

Finally, the kind of interpretation depends on the nature of the phenomena being researched. The social sciences are concerned with two kinds of phenomena, that which can be observed and that which cannot. Observable phenomena in the social sciences include social processes, events and activities. Phenomena which cannot be observed, on the other hand, includes aims, beliefs, meanings and experiences. The notion of phenomena which cannot be observed is peculiar to the social sciences. In the natural sciences the orthodoxy is that all phenomena is able to be observed and further, phenomena which cannot be observed are not part of empirical reality. To transfer this position to the social sciences would require us to illustrate that phenomena such as aims, beliefs, meanings and

experiences did not in fact exist. To achieve this would require us, for example, to believe that belief does not exist. In other words, we would have to use the process whose existence we were denying as the means by which we deny it. Such an exercise is an obvious nonsense. Unlike observable events, phenomena which cannot directly be observed produce doubts about the interpretations offered. How do we know that the interpretation offered is in fact about the topic we have studied? Let us consider the question, why does a particular customer make a return visit to a particular hotel? It can be interpreted that he believes the hotel to offer value for money. The problem is that his behaviour can also be influenced by many other factors which do not support this interpretation. There may be no other hotel, he may not be able to afford any other or the hotel may meet the aims of his visit. All that can be observed about the puzzle is that the customer returned. The fact in itself does not answer the question, why did he return? To answer the question we need to test the theoretical alternatives to our first interpretation, selecting relevant theories from which we can construct logical scenarios about how his behaviour can be interpreted. They might draw on widespread additional information such as the psychological and social characteristics of the customer, his own accounts of his behaviour, his economic position and so on. Interpretations about unobservable phenomena are invested with much more complex work by the scholar. He is involved not only in the exercise of applying theories but also in the examination of alternative interpretations which are produced to estimate their validity and worth for understanding the puzzle. This brings us to the last stage of the methodology of social scientific interpretations of hospitality management.

Evaluating interpretations

Social scientific practice does not end with the construction of an interpretation of a hospitality issue. The interpretation must also be evaluated and there are two distinct criteria for this: its logical rigor and its value to the hospitality industry. The concern with the logical rigor of any interpretation is to search for flaws and limitations in its construction. It is a basic criterion for acceptance in all science that an interpretation must be logically sound. An interpretation which is logically flawed is invalid, it is bad science and will contribute to bad hospitality management. By its nature, evaluating the logical rigor of an interpretation is the preserve of social scientists. It is part of their craft to assess whether the theory on which an interpretation is based has been analysed competently, whether the questions raised about the hospitality issue followed from the theory, whether the method of data collection was appropriate, whether the empirical work was sufficient and sensitive enough and whether the interpretation answers the questions raised about the hospitality issue. Only when this process of logical evaluation has been successfully completed should an interpretation be evaluated in terms of its worth to the hospitality industry.

Whereas the assessment of the logical rigor of interpretations is the preserve of the scholar, evaluation of the practical use of the interpretation requires hospitality managers also to be involved. A logically tight interpretation is of little practical use if it fails to persuade hospitality managers to use it. W. F. Whyte's landmark paper, 'The Social Structure of the Restaurant' (Whyte, 1947) illustrates the point. It has been accepted in the social scientific community as a fine piece of research, it has regularly been published in collections of readings yet its impact on the orthodoxy of hospitality management has been negligible. Managers have simply not been sufficiently persuaded by it. This highlights the position that to produce interpretations which are useful to hospitality managers, social scientists need to know much more about our field and to be more involved in our field than they have hitherto. Among the many social scientists who have made one-off sorties into the hospitality field are Goffman (1953), Bowie (1976) and Smith (1981a, b). Closer awareness and professional knowledge about hospitality management can contribute to the construction of more useful social scientific interpretations. The social scientist is then more able to persuade hospitality managers of the use of the interpretations. The vital point, however, is that at the end of the day it is the manager who must solve his hospitality problems, this is one of the ways in which his job performance is measured. Consequently, managers need a range of different interpretations of hospitality problems like a kit of tools from which they can select the interpretation which in their judgement fits the specific problem confronting them. They must take it on trust that the interpretations offered are logically sound, because their criteria for accepting an interpretation include factors such as the impact on their organisation if they implement an interpretation, the cost of implementation, the practicality of its use, and the time involved. The social sciences can only make a positive contribution to hospitality management if their interpretations are of practical value.

Summary and conclusions

I have argued in this paper that the popular conception of the hospitality industry as a people industry requires our understanding of hospitality management to be social scientifically informed because the social sciences alone are able to offer theoretically grounded interpretations of people and social events in hospitality. The success of these interpretations is dependent upon the methodology employed. Three parts of the methodology were identified and discussed: social scientific theories on which to base the interpretations must be selected; the theories must be applied to interpret the hospitality issues, and the interpretations must be evaluated. I conclude that without due attention to these methodological matters the myriad of hospitality issues which are social scientific in nature will not be resolved.

References

Bowie, A.M. (1976) *The Sociology of Organisations*. Hodder & Stoughton, London.

Cohen, P.S. (1968) *Modern Social Theory*. Heinemann, London.

Goffman, E. (1953) Communication and conduct in an Island Community. PhD thesis, University of Chicago.

Kamin, L.J. (1974) *The Science and Politics of IQ*. John Wiley, London.

Nailon, P.W. (1981) Theory and Art in Hospitality Management. Inaugural Lecture, University of Surrey.

Orwell, G. (1933) *Down and Out in Paris and London*. Penguin edn 1970, London.

O'Neill, J. (ed.) (1973) *Modes of Individualism and Collectivism*. Heinemann, London.

Phillips, D.L. (1973) *Abandoning Method*, pp. 20 and 70. Jossey-Bass, London.

Popper, K.R. (1974) *The Open Society and its Enemies*, Vols I & II. Routledge & Kegan Paul, London.

Potter, D., Anderson, J., Clark, J., Coombes, P., Hall, S., Harris, L., Holloway, C. and Walton, T. (eds) (1981) *Society and the Social Sciences*, p. 6. Routledge & Kegan Paul, London.

Ryan, A. (1981) Is the Study of Society a Science? in Potter, D. *et al. op. cit.*, p. 15.

Slattery, P.V.O. (1980) The Social Sciences in Hotel and Catering Undergraduate Courses: a review and a position.

Paper presented at the International Association of Hotel Management Schools Symposium on the Social Sciences in Undergraduate Courses, Huddersfield.

Smith, M.A. (1981a) *The Pub and the Publican*. University of Salford Press.

Smith, M.A. (1981b) *Work, Alcohol and the Public House*. University of Salford Press.

Wesker, A. (1960) *The Kitchen*. Jonathan Cape, London.

Whyte, W.F. (1947) The Social Structure of the Restaurant. *American Journal of Sociology* **54**, 302–310.

About the Author

Paul Slattery is a Senior Lecturer in Hotel and Catering Administration in the Department of Catering Studies at the Polytechnic, Huddersfield. He is Course Leader for the BA (Hons) degree in Hotel and Catering Administration. His teaching and research interests are in the development of a social scientific perspective on hospitality management. He is presently supervising three research projects on social and administrative issues in hospitality.

**Paul Slattery: Social scientific methodology and hospitality management
– Discussion questions**

1. Identify the approaches available to assist in the understanding of human behaviour.
2. Discuss the utility of each approach to an understanding of the hospitality industry.
3. For what reasons can the social sciences be construed as problematic to a hospitality manager?
4. Discuss the value of theories to a hospitality manager; what might be the limitations of such theories?
5. Identify the methods available within the social sciences to investigate human behaviour. Discuss the difficulties of such methods in research within the hospitality industry.
6. In a social science investigation, place the following terms in the correct order:

    evaluation, issue, empirical research, theoretical framework, theoretical reformulation, data analysis, theory identification.

   Illustrate this process with an example.

7. Illustrate and explain the difference between factual information and value judgement, with the use of two examples.
8. 'Argument and conflicting ideas are essential to the social sciences'. Discuss.
9. Discuss the implications of adopting each position on the nature/nurture debate when considering motivation of the workforce in the hospitality industry.
10. What do social scientists understand by the term 'logical validity', and does this always necessitate that conclusions are correct?

The social structure of the restaurant

William Foote Whyte

Abstract

The social structures of restaurants and factories are contrasted. Increasing size of organization is related causing difficulty in coordinating restaurant activities. The frictions occurring along the flow of work from kitchen to customer are analyzed in terms of formal structure, interaction, symbols, attitudes, and layout and equipment. Finally, this research is used to illustrate certain general propositions on method and theory.

While research has provided a large and rapidly growing fund of knowledge concerning the social organization of a factory, studies of other industrial and business structures are only beginning. Sociologists who are concerned with working out the comparative structures of economic organizations must therefore look beyond as well as into the factory. This paper represents one effort in that direction. It grows out of a fourteen-month study of restaurants.[1] We do not claim to have studied a representative sample of restaurants. In an industry having so many types of operations and sizes of units, such a task would have taken years. We did aim to find out, at least in a general way, what sort of structure a restaurant is and what human problems are found within it.

Here I shall present a schematic picture of the findings as they bear upon problems of social structures. I am also using the discussion of research findings to illustrate certain points of theory and methodology in studies of social structures. Discussions of theory and methodology,

divorced from the research data upon which the theory and methods are to be used, are generally fruitless. In a brief paper, discussion of our research findings must necessarily be sketchy, but that will provide a basis for at least tentative conclusions.

Characteristics of the restaurant

The restaurant is a combination production and service units. It differs from the factory, which is solely a production unit, and also from the retail store, which is solely a service unit.

The restaurant operator produces a perishable product for immediate sale. Success requires a delicate adjustment of supply to demand and skilful co-ordination of production with service. The production and service tie-up not only makes for difficult human problems of co-ordinating action but adds a new dimension to the structure of the organization: the customer-employee relationship.

The contrast between factory and restaurant can be illustrated by this simple diagram, representing the direction of orders in the two structures:[2]

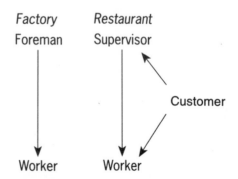

[1] The research was financed by the National Restaurant Association. The field work was done by Margaret Chandler, Edith Lentz, John Schaefer and William Whyte. We made interview or participant observation studies of twelve restaurants in Chicago and did some brief interviewing outside Chicago. From one to four months was spent upon each Chicago restaurant. In *Human Relations in the Restaurant Industry* (New York: McGraw-Hill Book Co., 1943), I report the study in detail. Since the book is primarily addressed to restaurant operators and supervisors, the sociological frame of reference given here does not duplicate the more detailed publication.

[2] This is, of course, an oversimplified picture, for many factory workers interact also with inspectors, engineers, time study men, etc., but the frequency of such interaction does not compare with that which we observe between customers and waiters or waitresses in a restaurant.

ARTICLE

The problems of co-ordination and customer relations are relatively simple in the small restaurant, but they become much more difficult as the organization grows. This may be illustrated structurally in terms of five stages of growth.[3]

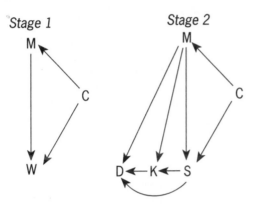

Stage 1

Stage 2

M – Manager
C – Customers
W – Workers

S – Service employees
K – Kitchen employees
D – Dishwashers

In the first stage, we have a small restaurant where the owner and several other employees dispense short orders over the counter. There is little division of labor. The owner and employees serve together as cooks, countermen, and dishwashers.

In the second stage, the business is still characterized by the informality and flexibility of its relationships. The boss knows most customers and all his employees on a personal basis. There is no need for formal controls and elaborate paper work. Still, the organization has grown in complexity as it has grown in size. The volume of business is such that it becomes necessary to divide the work, and we have dishwashers and kitchen employees, as well as those who wait on the customers. Now the problems of co-ordination begin to grow also, but the organization is still small enough so that the owner-manager can observe directly a large part of its activities and step in to straighten out friction or inefficiency.

As the business continues to expand, it requires a still more complex organization as well as larger quarters. No longer able to supervise all activities directly, the owner-manager hires a service supervisor, a food production supervisor, and places one of his employees in charge of

---

³ I am indebted to Donald Wray for the particular structural approach presented here.

the dishroom as a working supervisor. He also employs a checker to total checks for his waitresses and see that the food is served in correct portions and style.

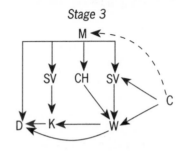

Stage 3

M – Manager
SV – Supervisor
CH – Checker
C – Customer

W – Waitress
K – Kitchen worker
D – Dishwasher

In time, the owner-manager finds that he can accommodate a larger number of customers if he takes one more step in the division of labor. Up to now the cooks have been serving the food to waitresses. When these functions are divided, both cooking and serving can precede more efficiently.

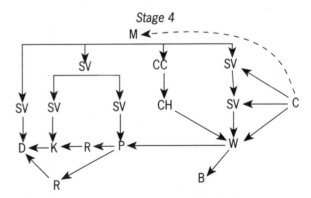

Stage 4

M – Manager
SV – Supervisor
CH – Checker
CC – Cost control
    supervisor
C – Customer

W – Waitress
B – Bartender
P – Pantry worker
K – Kitchen worker
R – Runner
D – Dishwasher

Therefore, he sets up a service pantry apart from the kitchen. The cooks now concentrate on cooking, the runners carry food from kitchen to pantry and carry orders from pantry to kitchen, and the pantry girls serve the waitresses over the counter. This adds two more groups (pantry girls and runners) to be supervised, and, to cope with this and the larger scale of operation, the owner adds another level of supervision, so that there are two supervisors between himself and the workers. Somewhere along the line of development, perhaps he begins serving drinks and adds bartenders to his organization.

Stage 5 need not be diagrammed here, for it does not necessarily involve any structural changes in the individual unit. Here several units are tied together into a chain, and one or more levels of authority are set up in a main office above the individual unit structures.[4]

The expansion process magnifies old problems and gives rise to new ones. They may be considered under three headings: administration, the customer relationship, and the flow of work. Whenever we lengthen the hierarchy, adding new levels of authority to separate top executive from workers, the problem of administration becomes more complex. However, this is true for any organization, and therefore these problems of hierarchy need not be given special attention in an article on restaurants.

The particular problem of the large restaurant is to tie together its line of authority with the relations that arise along the flow of work. In the first instance, this involves the customer relationship, for here is where the flow of work begins. The handling of the customer relationship is crucial for the adjustment of the restaurant personnel, and a large part of that problem can be stated in strictly quantitative interaction terms: Who originates action for whom and how often? In a large and busy restaurant a waitress may take orders from fifty to one hundred customers per day (and perhaps several times for each meal) in addition to the orders (much less frequent) she receives from her supervisor. When we add to this the problem of adjusting to service pantry workers, bartenders and perhaps checkers, we can readily see the possibilities of emotional tension – and, in our study, we did see a number of girls break down and cry under the strain.

Our findings suggested that emotional tension could be related directly to this quantitative interaction picture. The skilful waitress, who maintained her emotional equilibrium, did not simply respond to the initiative of customers. In various obvious and subtle ways she took the play away

from customers, got them responding to her and fitted them into the pattern of her work. She was also more aggressive than the emotionally insecure in originating action for other waitresses, service pantry people, and supervisor.

While in the rush hour the waitress works under a good deal of tension at best, the supervisor can either add to or relieve it. Here again we can speak in quantitative terms. In one restaurant we observed a change in dining-room management when a supervisor who was skilful in originating action for customers (thus taking pressure off waitresses) and who responded frequently to the initiation of waitresses was replaced by a supervisor who had less skill in controlling customers and who originated for the girls much more frequently and seldom responded to them. (Of the new supervisor, the waitresses would say, "She's always finding something to criticize"; "She's never around when you need her"; "She's always telling you; she doesn't care what you have to say"; etc.) This change was followed by evidences of increased nervous tension, especially among the less experienced waitresses and finally by a series of waitress resignations.

Here we see that the customer-waitress, waitress-supervisor, waitress-service–pantry-worker relationships are independent parts of a social system. Changes in one part of the system will necessarily lead to changes in other parts. Furthermore, if the people involved in the system are to maintain their emotional balance, there must be some sort of compensatory activity to meet large interactional change. For example, when wait-resses are subject to a large increase in the originations of customers (at the peak of rush hours), the supervisor allows them to originate action for her with increasing frequency and diminishes the frequency with which she gives them orders. This is, in fact, the sort of behaviour we have observed among supervisors who enjoy the closest co-operations with waitresses, as reported by the waitresses.

The customer relationship is, of course, only one point along the flow of work which brings orders from dining-room to kitchen and food from kitchen to dining-room. In a large restaurant operating on several floors, this is a long chain which may break down at any point, thus leading to emotional explosions in all quarters. The orders may go from waitress to pantry girl and then, as the pantry girl runs low in supplies, from pantry supplyman to cook. And the food comes back along the same route in the opposite direction. Where drinks are served, the bar must be tied in with this flow of work, but there the chain is short and the problem is less complex.

---

[4] The structural changes arising with union organization are beyond the scope of this article. They are discussed in the book, *op. cit.*, in the chapter, "The Rule of Union Organization."

We have here a social system whose parts are independent in a highly sensitive manner. Thus the emotional tension experienced by waitresses is readily transmitted, link by link, all the way to the kitchen.

I have already noted how a skilful dining-room supervisor may help to relieve the tension on the entire system at its point of origin. Here we may consider other factors which affect the relations among employees along the flow of work: status, sex relations, and layout and equipment.

I would propose the hypothesis that relations among individuals along the flow of work will run more smoothly when those of higher status are in a position to originate for those of lower status in the organization and, conversely, that frictions will be observed more often when lower-status individuals seek to originate for those of higher status. (This is of course, by no means a complete explanation of the friction or adjustment we observe.)

While more data are needed on this point, we made certain observations which tend to bear out the hypothesis. For example, in one kitchen we observed supplymen seeking to originate action (in getting food supplies) for cooks who were older, of greater seniority, more highly skilled, and much higher paid. This relationship was one of the sore points of the organizations. Still, we discovered that there had been one supplyman who got along well with the cooks. When we got his story, we found that he had related himself to the cooks quite differently from the other supplymen. He sought to avoid calling orders to the cooks and instead just asked them to call him when a certain item was ready. In this way, he allowed them to increase the frequency of their origination for him, and, according to all accounts, he got better co-operation and service from the cooks than any other supplyman.

Much the same point is involved in the relations between the sexes. In our society most men grow up to be comfortable in a relationship in which they originate for women and to be uneasy, if not more seriously disturbed, when the originations go in the other direction. It is therefore a matter of some consequence how the sexes are distributed along the flow of work. On this question we gave particular attention to the dining-room–service pantry and dining-room–bar relationships.

In the dining-room–pantry situation there are four possible types of relationship by sex: waiter–counterman, waiter–pantry girl, waitress–pantry girl, and waitress–counterman. We were not able to give much attention to the first two types, but we did make intensive studies of two restaurants illustrating the third and fourth types. Ideally, for scientific purposes, we would want to hold everything else constant except for these sex differences. We had no such laboratory, but the two restaurants were nevertheless closely comparable. They were both large, busy establishments, operating on several floors, and serving the same price range food in the same section of the city.

Perhaps the chief differences were found in the dining-room–pantry relationship itself. In restaurant A, waitresses gave their orders orally to the pantry girls. On the main serving floor of restaurant B, waitresses wrote out slips which they placed on spindles on top of a warming compartment separating them from the countermen. The men picked of the order slips, filled them, and put the plates in the compartment where the waitresses picked them up. In most cases there was no direct face to face interaction between waitresses and countermen, and, indeed the warming compartment was so high that only the taller waitresses could see over its top.

These differences were not unrelated to the problems of sex in the flow of work. One of the countermen in restaurant B told us that, in all his years' experience, he had never before worked in such a wonderful place. Most workers who express such sentiments talk about their relations with their superiors or with fellow-employees on the same job or perhaps about wages, but this man had nothing to say about any of those subjects. He would discuss only the barrier that protected him from the waitresses. He described earlier experiences in other restaurants where there had been no such barrier and let us know that to be left out in the open where all the girls could call their orders in was an ordeal to which no man should be subjected. In such places, he said, there was constant wrangling.

This seems to check with experience in the industry. While we observed frictions arising between waitresses and pantry girls, such a relationship can at least be maintained with relative stability. On the other hand, it is difficult to prevent blowups between countermen and waitresses when the girls call their orders in. Most restaurants consciously or unconsciously interpose certain barriers to cut down waitress origination of action for countermen. It may be a warming compartment as in this case, or, as we observed in another restaurant, there was a man pantry supervisor who collected the order slips from the waitresses as they came in and passed them to the countermen. There are a variety of ways of meeting the problem, but they all seem to involve this principle of social insulation.

The rule that all orders must be written also serves to cut down on interaction between waitresses and countermen, but this in itself is not always enough to eliminate friction. Where there is no physical barrier, there can be trouble unless the men who are on the receiving end of the orders work out their own system of getting out from under. Such systems we observed at one bar and at one of the serving counters in restaurant B. The counter in this case was only waist high. While the girls wrote out their orders, they were also able to try to spur the men on orally, and there was much pulling and hauling on this point at the bar and at the pantry counter.

The men who did not get along in this relationship played a waiting game. That is, when the girls seemed to be putting on special pressure for speed, they would very obviously slow down or else even turn away from the bar or counter and not go back to work until the offending waitress just left their order slips and stepped away themselves. Thus they originated action for the waitresses. While this defensive maneuvre provided the men with some emotional satisfaction, it slowed down the service, increased the frustrations of the waitresses, and thus built up tensions, to be released in larger explosions later.

One bartender and one counterman not only enjoyed their work but were considered by waitresses to be highly efficient and pleasant to delay with. Both of them had independently worked out the same system of handling the job when the rush hour got under way. Instead of handling each order slip in turn as it was handed to them (thus responding to each individual waitress), they would collect several slips that came in at about the same time, lay them out on the counter before them, and fill the orders in whatever order seemed most efficient. For example, the bartender would go through the slips to see how many "Martinis," "Old Fashions," and so on were required. Then he would make up all the "Martinis" at once before he went onto his next drink.

When the work was done this way, the girl first in was not necessarily first out with her tray, but the system was so efficient that it speeded up the work on the average, and the girls were content to profit this way in the long run. The men described the system to us in terms of efficiency; but note that, in organizing their jobs, they had changed quantitatively the relations they had with the waitresses. Instead of responding to each waitress, they were originating action for girls (filling their orders as the men saw fit and sending them out when the men were ready).

Along with our consideration of layout and equipment in the flow of work, we should give attention to the communication system. Where the restaurant operates on one floor, the relations at each step in the flow can be worked out on a face-to-face basis. There may be friction, but there is also the possibility of working out many problems on a friendly, informal basis.

When a restaurant operates on two or more floors, as many large ones do, face-to-face interaction must be supplemented by mechanical means of communication. We saw three such mechanical means substituting for direct interaction, and each one had its difficulties.

People can try to co-ordinate their activities through the house telephone. Without facial expressions and gestures, there is a real loss of understanding, for we do not generally respond solely to people's voices. Still, this might serve reasonably well, if the connection between kitchen and pantry could be kept constantly open. At least in the one restaurant where we gave this subject special attention, that solution was out of the question, as one call from kitchen to pantry tied up the whole house phone system and nobody could call the manager, the cashier or anybody else on this system as long as another call was being made. Consequently, the telephone could be used only to supplement other mechanical aids (in this case, the teleautograph).

The public address system has the advantage over the telephone that it can be used all the time, but it has the great disadvantage of being a very noisy instrument. Busy kitchens and service pantries are noisy places at best, so that the addition of a public address system might be most unwelcome. We do not yet know enough of the effect of noise upon the human nervous system to evaluate the instrument from this point of view, but we should recognize the obvious fact that surrounding noise affects the ability of people to communicate with each other and becomes therefore a problem in human relations.

The teleautograph makes no noise and can be used at all times, yet it has its own disadvantages. Here we have an instrument in the service pantry and one in the kitchen. As the pantry supplyman writes his order, it appears simultaneously on the kitchen teleautograph. The kitchen's replies are transmitted upstairs in the same way. The machine records faithfully, but it does not solve the problem of meaning in interaction. We may pass over the problem of illegibility of handwriting, although we have seen that cause serious difficulties. The most interesting problem is this: How urgent is an order?

When the rush hour comes along, with customers pushing waitresses, waitresses pushing pantry girls, and pantry girls pushing supplymen, the supplymen is on the end of the line as far as face-to-face interaction is concerned, and he is likely to get nervous and excited. He may then put in a larger order than he will actually use or write "Rush" above many of his orders. If he overorders, the leftovers come back to the kitchen at the end of the meal, and the kitchen supplymen and cooks learn thus that the pantry supplyman did not really know how much he needed. They take this into account in interpreting his future orders. And, when everything is marked "Rush," the kitchen supplymen cannot tell the difference between the urgent and not so urgent ones. Thus the word becomes meaningless and communication deteriorates. Stuck in this impasse, the pantry supplyman may abandon his machine and dash down to the kitchen to try to snatch the order himself. The kitchen people will block this move whenever they can, so, more often, the pantry supplyman appeals to his supervisor. In the heat of the rush hour, we have seen pantry supervisors running up and down stairs, trying to get orders, trying to find out what is holding up things in the kitchen. Since they have supervisor status, the kitchen workers do not resist them openly, but the invasion of an upstairs supervisor tends to disrupt relations in the kitchen. It adds to the pressures there, for it comes as an emergency that lets everybody know that the organization is not functioning smoothly.

It is not the function of this article to work out possible solutions to this problem of communication. I am concerned here with pointing out a significant new area for sociological investigation: the effects on human relations of various mechanical systems of communication. It is difficult enough to co-ordinate an organization in which the key people in the supervisory hierarchy are in direct face-to-face relations. It is a much more difficult problem (and one as yet little understood) when the co-ordination must be achieved in large measures through mechanical communication systems.

Implications for theory and methodology

In presenting our observations on the restaurant industry, I have discussed formal structure, quantitative measures of interaction, symbols in relations to interaction, attitudes and interaction, and equipment (including mechanical systems of communication). Data of these categories must be fitted together. The uses of each type of data may be summarized here.

1. *Formal structure.* – We have ample data to show that the formal structure (the official allocation of positions) does not *determine* the pattern of human relations in an organization. Nevertheless, it does set certain limits upon the shape of that pattern. Thus to analyze the human problems of a restaurant, it is necessary to outline its structure in terms of length of hierarchy, divisions into departments, and flow of work (as done in the five stages above).

2. *Quantitative measures of interaction.* – Within the limits set by the formal structure, the relations among members of the organization may fall into a variety of patterns, each of which is subject to change.

The pattern we observe we call the *social system*. A social system is made up of *interdependent* parts. The parts are the *relations* of individuals in their various positions to each other. This is simply a first description of a social system, but there are important theoretical and practical conclusions which flow from it.

The relations of individuals to one another are subject to *measurement,* sufficient to allow them to be compared and classified. We can, for example, count the number of times that a waitress originates action for her customers compared with the number of times they originate it for her in a given period and observe how often she originates action for her supervisor and how often the supervisor does so for her, and so on, through the other relations in the system. So far, mathematically precise measurements of interaction have only been made in laboratory situations involving interviewer and interviewee.[5] Nevertheless, in the present state of our knowledge, we can get, though interviewing and observation, quantitative data which, through only approximate, are sufficiently accurate to allow us to predict the course of developments or explain how certain problems have arisen and point the way to their possible solution.

As the terms are used here, *interaction, origination,* and *response* are abstractions without content, That is, they are indices which have no reference to either the symbols used or the subjective reactions felt by the interacting individuals. Such measures do not, of course,

5   Eliot D. Chapple, with the collaboration of Conrad M. Arensberg, *Measuring Human Relations: An Introduction to the Study of the Interaction of Individuals* ("Genetic Psychology Monographs," No. 22 [Provincetown, Mass.: Journal Press, 1940]); Eliot D. Chapple and Carleton S. Coon, *Principles of Anthropology* (New York: Henry Holt & Co., 1941), esp. first four chapters; Eliot I). Chapple and Erich Lindemann, "Clinical Implications of Measurement of Interaction Rates in Psychiatric Interviews," *Applied Anthropology,* I, No 2 (January–March, 1942), 1–12.

tell us all it is useful to know of human relations. Indeed, many students will think it absurd to believe that any useful data can come from abstractions which leave out the "content" of human relations. To them I can only say that science is, in part, a process of abstraction, which always seems to take us away from the "real world". The value of such abstractions can be determined only be testing them in research to see whether they enable us better to control and predict social events.

Since the social system is made up of *interdependent relations*, it follows that a change in one part of the system necessarily has repercussions in other parts of the system. For example, a change in the origin-response ratio between waitresses and supervisor necessarily affects the waitress–customer and waitress-service–pantry-girl relations, and changes in those parts lead to other changes in the system. Therefore, in order to study the social system or to deal with it effectively, it is necessary to discover the *pattern* of relations existing at a given time and to observe changes within that pattern. The nature of the interdependence of the parts of the system can be discovered only through observing how a change in Part A is followed by a change in Part B, is followed by change in Part C, etc. Therefore social systems must be studied *through time*. A static picture of the social structure of an organization is of little value. Science requires that we develop methods of study and tools of analysis to deal with constantly changing relations.

3. *Symbols in relation to interaction* – We cannot be content simply with quantitative descriptions of interaction. We need to know why A responds to B in one situation and not in another or why A responds to B and not to C. In part, this is a matter of habituation, for we respond to the people we are accustomed to responding to and in the sorts of situations to which we are accustomed. But we must go beyond that to explain the developments of new patterns and changes in old patterns of interaction.

We observe that individuals respond to certain symbols in interaction. I have discussed here status and sex as symbols affecting interaction (the problems of the originating from below of action for high status individual or by woman for man).

I have noted some problems of language symbols in the discussion of mechanical means of communication. That leaves the whole field of symbols in face-to-face interaction untouched, so that it represents only the barest beginning of an attempted formulation of the relations between symbols of communication and interaction.

Especially in economic institutions, it is important to examine the bearing of *economic symbols*[6] on interaction, but this is a large subject and can only be mentioned here.

As we analyze social systems, symbols should always be seen in term of their effects upon interaction. They are *incentives* or *inhibitors* to interaction with specific people in certain social situations. Thus, to put it in practical terms, the manager of an organization will find it useful to know both the pattern of interaction which will bring about harmonious relations and also how to use symbols as to achieve that pattern.

4. *Attitudes and interaction* – Changes in relations of individuals to one another are accompanied by changes in their *attitudes* toward one another and toward their organizations. In recent years we have developed excellent methods for attitude measurement, but the measurement in itself never tells us how attitudes came about. The whole experience of our research program leads us to believe that the dynamics of attitude formation and change can best be worked out as we correlate attitudes with human relations in the organization we study.

5. *Layout and equipment* – Here the sociologist is not directly concerned with the problems of the mechanical or industrial engineer. He does not undertake to say which machine or which arrangement of work space and machines will be most productively efficient. However, he cannot help but observe that, for example, the height of the barrier between waitresses and countermen or the nature of the mechanical communication system have important effects upon human relations. Only as these effects are observed do the physical conditions come in for sociological analysis. (Of course, human relations have a bearing upon efficiency, uses types of data and schemes of analysis quite different from those used by the engineer.)

A few years ago there was a great debate raging: statistics versus the case study. That debate is no longer waged publicly, but it still troubles many of us. On the one hand, we see that an individual case study, skilfully analyzed, yields interesting insights – but not

6 See Whyte's "Economics and Human Relations in Industry" to be published in *Industrial and Labor Relations* Review.

scientific knowledge. On the other hand, we find that nearly all statistical work in sociology has dealt with the characteristics of aggregates: How much of a given phenomenon is to be found in a given population? Such an approach does not tell us anything about the relations among the individuals making up that population. And yet, if we are to believe the textbooks, the relations among individuals, the *group* life they lead, are the very heart of sociology.

So let us have more individual case studies, but let us also place the individual in the social systems in which he participates and note how his attitudes and goals change with changes in the relations he experiences. And let us have more quantitative work, but let us have more quantitative work, but let us at last bring it to bear upon the heart of sociology, measuring the relations among individuals in their organizations.

Cornell University

William Whyte: The social structure of the restaurant – Discussion questions

1. Did Whyte study a representative sample of restaurants in his study? Discuss the implications of this factor for his conclusions.

2. What factors differentiate the restaurant from other production units? Identify the crucial relationship thus introduced into the organization structure, and comment on the extent to which this is applicable to other hospitality organizations and environments?

3. Identify and discuss the main variable Whyte contends as problematic for co-ordination and customer relations within the restaurant as an organization.

4. What do you understand by the term 'social system'? What are the factors that inhibit the optimal operation of this system in the restaurants Whyte studied, and what are the implications for organization goals?

5. Why must social systems be studied through time? Discuss the importance of this with respect to the contemporary hospitality industry.

6. Analyse the validity of Whyte's notion that many difficulties in human relations could be attributed to differences in authority based on gender relationships?

7. In large organizations, it becomes apparent that 'meaning in interaction' is crucial; what do you understand by this term, and what indicates its importance?

8. To what extent is Whyte's analysis useful to an understanding of contemporary hospitality organizations?

"Quest for quality": Consumer perception study of the American hotel industry

Sponsored by: The American Hotel and Motel Association

Preface

In 1981 in Kansas City, The American Hotel & Motel Association agreed to create the "Quest for Quality" Program. As an outgrowth of their decision, a committee was formed and two studies were commissioned to Stephen Hall and Associates. Citicorp Diners Club agreed to fund both these projects.

In 1984, the "Quest for Quality" Cost of Error Study was completed and presented to the Hospitality Industry. This booklet summarizes findings of the second study, "Quest for Quality" consumer Perception Study.

The contribution of those responsible for the completion of the "Quest for Quality" *Cost of Error Study* and *Consumer Preception Study* should be recognized.

I would like to thank the leadership of the American Hotel and Motel Association for their help, Bob Richards and Ken Hine for their support and coordination; Bill Pitts, who served as the first chairman of the AH&MA "Quest for Quality" committee; all the members of that committee; the many Hoteliers who so patiently completed extensive cost of error analyses forms; Lodging Magazine for its extensive coverage, the Educational Institute for undertaking the publication of a training manual on the subject; and, last but not least, CitiCorp Diners Club for providing the funding; and Doug Fontaine who, as president of AH&MA in 1982, had the foresight to initiate "Quest for Quality"

Stephen Hall

Introduction

"Quality" is something that almost every person and every organization thinks they have – and yet very few people can define what it means! Most people try to define "quality" by saying that it is "the best," or "the finest," or the "most outstanding." "Quality food," they will say, "is food that is excellent." "A quality car" is the "best" car made.

Another problem in using superlatives in defining "quality" is that we tend to equate "best," "finest," "most outstanding" with cost. We tend to think that things that cost more must be better and, therefore, higher quality. If this were the case, it would be impossible to run a "quality" hotel or motel that charged average rates and catered to the average American. And, the vast majority of Americans would be unable to afford "quality." This, of course, is not true at all. Quality is not a function of how much something costs but, rather, how well it meets the expectations of those who purchase it. The person who stays at the budget motel does not expect valet parking, an expensive lobby, extra-large guest rooms, room service, same-day laundry service and so forth. They do expect a place to park, a friendly, efficient room clerk, a clean, comfortable room, safety and security. If those expectations are met, the budget motel can be said to have delivered a quality product and service. On the other hand, the guest who wants more service and more lavish accommodations, and is willing to pay for them, would not feel that quality had been delivered if the room was dirty, the shower didn't work correctly, and the employees were not friendly.

Regardless of the type of accommodations, a guest stays there with certain expectations. When these expectations are met, he has received quality. When his expectations are not met, quality is absent. Now we have a definition of "quality" that we can use.

Quality is conformance to standards

Quality means everyone doing their job correctly each and every time. Quality is consistency of performance. People always return where the performance is consistent. We want our expectations met every time without surprises. When it doesn't happen – that is, when we have to argue and hassle to get what we expect, we simply do business with someone else the next time. Such is the case with the hotel and motel guest.

What is a standard?

Many people believe that "*standards*" are desired levels of *performance*. When a standard is set, it becomes a requirement and should be met each and every time the job is performed. To do otherwise is to render the standard useless. If we have a standard to provide our guests with a clean guest room, then, each and every time we room a guest, the room must be clean. Otherwise, the standard means nothing.

Standards are required levels of performance

Sometimes the guest receives a morning wake-up call on time, sometimes not. Sometimes the front desk has a record of the reservation, sometimes not. Sometimes the room thermostat works and other times it does not. The result of standards which are delivered in a haphazard fashion is simply a guest who does not return – and that hurts everyone who depends upon the hotel or motel for their livelihood.

"Quest for quality" cost of error study

Whenever a standard is not met, the result is an error. And errors always cost money. The cost may be in lost sales because the guest won't return. The cost may be in lost profits when we have to put a guest in an upgraded room at no extra charge because we "lost" the reservation. Errors always cost money and, thus, must be avoided if we are to be successful in running a business.

How much do errors cost?

As surprising as it may seem, this question has never really been answered in all the years that the Hospitality Industry has existed. It's not that hoteliers avoid the question, rather it's because there is not a good way to look at "cost of error." In 1981, when the American Hotel and Motel Association initiated "Quest tor Quality," an extensive, in-depth process was begun in which more than 40 leading North American hoteliers were interviewed in person. They were asked how much they thought "errors cost" and the average of these responses was 1.2% of total revenues.

In the "Quest for Quality" Cost at Error Study, selected hoteliers were asked to calculate the cost of 50 common errors. Some examples are: walking a guest, poor employee attitude, long check in/check out lines, etc. The result indicated that the total cost of 50 errors could well amount to more than 5% of revenues. When you consider the complexity of the Hospitality Industry and the fact that one property actually identitied 379 errors, you begin to see that errors could easily cost in excess of 10% of total revenues. In the manufacturing industry, it has been estimated that errors cost between 20% and 25%, of total revenues, so estimates of 10% for the Hospitality Industry seem conservative. In terms of dollar amounts, a 10 % cost of error in a typical 200 room property with 70% occupancy, an average rate of $60.00 and a ratio of room revenue to total revenue at .65, would amount to $471, 692 per year. And that does not take into account the increased sales that would result from an "error-free" operation. The cost of error' is really the "cost of opportunity".

How do you calculate the cost of an error?

By asking ten questions in order, it is possible for anyone to calculate what an error costs. The questions are:

1. What is the error?
   Identify the error accurately. For example, "unsatisfactory food service" would be too general because it could include many errors from unfriendly employees to long lines, to slow service. A more proper "error" might be a "guest served a wrong order – meal redone." It is easier to deal with specific descriptions of errors.
2. What Are the Consequences of the Error?
   List each consequence that could result from the error such as "guest will not return," "food is discarded," "waiter (waitress) loses time." "bill is discounted." etc. It is rare that you will have more than 6 meaningful consequences. but don't allow yourself to stop with only the most obvious. For example, whenever the property has to respond by letter to a guest complaint, the cost is easily $5.00.

ARTICLE ━━

3. What Would Each Consequence Cost If it Happened? Estimate the cost of each consequence as *if it* happened.

4. How Often Does Each Consequence Happen?

   Not every guest who is served a wrong meal will stay away from your dining room, and it is wrong to assume that they will. On the other hand, it is just as wrong to assume that every guest *will* come back. For each consequence, estimate the percentage of time it will happen. Perhaps you believe only 5% of your guests who receive wrong meals won't return. On the other hand, probably 80% or more of the wrong meals served will be wasted. Experienced hoteliers have a sense for such estimates. Until now, they have not had the format to use their experience.

5. What is the Expected Cost of Each Consequence?

   This is a simple multiplication of the consequence cost by the estimated probability that it would happen (question 3 times question 4).

6. What is the Individual Cost of the Error?

   The individual cost of the error is the total of the expected costs calculated in question 5.

7. How Many Times a Year Could the Error Happen?

   In the case of our wrong order, the error could happen each and every time we serve a meal.

8. What Percent of the Time Does the Error Happen?

   Again, we have to make an estimate, but you can be certain the chef has an idea of how often the error occurs – in the case of wrong orders. The waiters and waitresses will also have a good idea of frequency.

9. How many Times Per Year Does the Error Happen?

   Multiply the number of times per year the error could happen (question 7) by the estimated percent it does happen (question 8) to get the number of times the error occurs each year.

10. What is the Total Cost of Error (Opportunity)?
    Multiply the number of times per year that the error happens (question 9) by the individual error cost (question 6) to get the annual cost of error and thus the opportunity to save.

The above cost of error process helps all involved to identify the wide range of consequences that errors produce – it helps employees to visualize the individual error cost, the immensity of the volume of business done, and the total number of errors per year. By the time they get to the final cost, the value of the process has been gained – *Awareness* – it is the most important step in developing a proper attitude towards assuring quality.

Because quality has been defined as conformance to standards, every error occurs because either (1) there are no standards, or (2) standards are not being followed. That is the definition of "error" – standards not met. Guest's perceptions must be recognized. What better way to win a guest while influencing the bottom line results than to understand their demands and expectations. "Quest for Quality" Cost of Error Study concentrates on errors and their associated cost. "Quest for Quality" Consumer Perception Study looks from the consumer side of the question and lets the guest share with the industry their perceptions and reactions to quality, standards and error. "Quest for Quality" Consumer Perception Study is in effect an opportunity study for hoteliers.

"Quest for quality" consumer perception study

Findings of this study are based on 863 responses from a questionnaire mailed to Diners Club Cardmembers who are frequent travelers. In all, 25,000 questionnaires were mailed by Diners Club/Carte Blanche and responses were analyzed by Stephen Hall & Associates. The total return rate for the survey was 3.5% and while all respondents did not answer every question, the majority did. The questionnaire employed for the study is exhibited on page 199.

In terms of demographic finding, 80% of respondents were male travelers and the remaining 20% female travelers. Married travelers accounted for 74% of the groups while 26% were single.

MARITAL STATUS AND SEX			
	MALE	FEMALE	
MARRIED	62	12	74%
SINGLE	18	8	26%
	80%	20%	

EXHIBIT (1)

Annual income data is shown on the following table.

INCOME DATA			
	Total	Male	Female
	100%	100%	100%
	(842)	(671)	(171)
$20 – 35,000	23%	18%	41%
35 – 50,000	32	31	34
50 – 75,000	24	27	15
75, 000⁺	21	24	10

EXHIBIT (2)

It should be noted that income for male travelers clusters in the higher dollar ranges. Female travelers – reported lower incomes, as 41% said they earned $20,000 to $35,000 as compared to 18% for their male counterparts. While this situation may be unsatisfactory, it correlates with other industry studies.

Looking at the types of properties frequented by the respondent, economy hotel/motels were mentioned by 3%; 62% stated they stayed in a standard property and 35% answered luxury types. The following bar graph inspects these responses by sex and marital status and exhibits a higher concentration of single females – 75% – in standard properties.

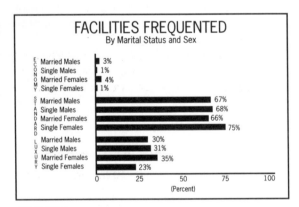

FACILITIES FREQUENTED
By Marital Status and Sex

EXHIBIT (3)

Some reasons for this deviation among single females may include:

- A different "price-value" standard.
- Relative inexperience in the marketplace.
- Or simply a skewed, or an "a-typical" sample.

"Employee Attitude" is very important to frequent travelers.

Respondents were asked to list their 3 greatest complaints encountered in their use of U.S. hospitality establishments. The following list–numbering seventy-five seems to be a large number of critical errors given that each respondent was limited to 3 unstructured choices. The complete list is exhibited below:

75 MOST MENTIONED ERRORS	
1. Poor Employee Attitude	39. Poor Room Location
2. Room Not Ready	40. Slow Room Service
3. No Record of Reservation	41. Poor Lighting
4. Check-in / Check-out	42. Security
5. Wake up Call-Early, Late, None	43. Air Conditioning
6. Dirty Guest Room	44. Parking Cost
7. Changing Room Type	45. Billing Request not Met
8. Noise	46. Poor Management
9. Tired Facility	47. Excessive Telephone Cost
10. Shoddy Overall Maintainance	48. Inadequate Parking
11. Dirty Facility	49. Poor Room Service Food
12. Poor Overall Service	50. Small Guest Rooms
13. High Room Rates	51. Valet Cleaning/Pressing
14. Inadequate Linen in Room	52. Poor Response to Complaints
15. Poor Food	53. Room Lacking Hangers
16. Overbooking	54. Noisy Maids
17. TV Or Radio out-of-order	55. Slow Elevators
18. Tired Guest Room	56. Asked to Vacate Early
19. Temperature	57. Room Not Held for Late Arrival
20. Check Out Process	58. Surprise Charges
21. Uncomparable Room	59. Insects
22. No Off-Hour Service	60. No Ice
23. Poor Housekeeping	61. Maids Move Belongings
24. Condition of Linen	62. Inadequate Electrical Outlets
25. Smokey/Stale Room	63. Misleading Advertising
26. Lack of Facilities	64. No Complimentary Gifts
27. Maids Enter Room Early/Late	65. Dirty Bathroom
28. Slow Service	66. Inadequate Food Outlets
29. Slow Check-in Process	67. Miscellaneous Food Problems
30. Message Not Delivered	68. Damaged Furnishing
31. Computer Problems	69. Door Key Problems
32. Plumbing	70. Safety
33. Noisy Guest Room	71. Poor Entertainment
34. Poor Telephone Service	72. Uniformed Employees
35. Billing Errors	73. Swimming Pool Problems
36. Inadequate Hot Water	74. Expensive Food
37. Heating	75. Expensive Room Service
38. Mechanical Problems	

EXHIBIT (4)

The top 10 complaints, in order of importance are:

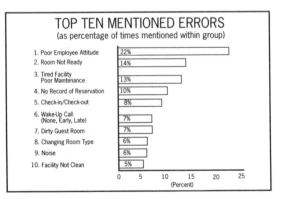

TOP TEN MENTIONED ERRORS
(as percentage of times mentioned within group)

EXHIBIT (5)

There seems to be little doubt that American travelers place high value on employee attitude. It is noteworthy that a previous study conducted by the writer as part of the AH&MA "Quest for Quality" project, asked managers to identify their biggest obstacle in the delivery of quality. Seventy percent of those interviewed stated "employee" in one form or another, almost all of which were critical of employee attitude, motivation and desire to excel. While the finger is pointed at employees for "not following," the possibility that management is "not leading" must also be considered. One question that must be asked is whether or not the hospitality colleges and schools of America are properly emphasizing the human skills or are they tending to over-emphasize "bottom line – profit and loss" considerations to the detriment of a proper balance given both the nature of hospitality and the desires of the consumers. If that is the case then the industry must review what it expects from the training schools. On the other hand, the schools may well be responding to what they perceive the needs of the industry are as communicated by hoteliers in the field, in which case, the industry must look more closely at both its product and its philosophy of management. In either case, many more questions should be asked and more answers evaluated.

Repositioning these stated errors by the hotel's functional areas, the front desk accounts for the highest number responses – 34%.

Other key areas include management, housekeeping, etc., and are shown in the following chart:

ERRORS BY FUNCTIONAL AREAS
(As a Percent of Total Mentions)

FRONT DESK
Room not ready, no record of reservation, check-in/check-out, overbooked, room not held, changing room type, high rates, message not delivered. — 32%

MANAGEMENT
Employee attitude, poor service, perceived poor management, slow service, misleading advertising, poor response to complaints — 23%

HOUSEKEEPING
Dirty, not enough linen, noisy maids, maids who enter too early or too late, condition of linen, dirty bathroom, smokey/stale, tired room. — 16%

OVERALL FACILITY
Noisy, tired facility, dirty, security, small rooms, safety, lack of facilities. — 13%

ROOM/MAINTENANCE
Shoddy Maintenance, TV/Radio out-of-order, temperature control, plumbing, heating, general mechanical problems, slow elevators. — 11%

FOOD & BEVERAGE
Poor food, slow service, inadequate outlets, expensive. — 4%

PARKING
Cost and Unavailability — 1%

100%

EXHIBIT (6)

How Does the Guest React to Hospitality Error?

Another question in the "Quest for Quality" Consumer Perception Study asked respondents to review a list of 10 errors and, having already indicated the frequency of their business and pleasure travel, indicate how often each of the 10 errors occurred in their travels. Further, respondents were asked to indicate, when each error was encountered. how many times the error caused them to change facilities on their next trip to that city. From the data, it is possible to establish the frequency of each error, and the rate at which the error will cause a decision to change facilities. The overall frequency and discontinuance rate for all 10 errors as a group is also shown.

OCCURRENCE FREQUENCY AND DISCONTINUANCE RATE
(By Sex)

	MALE		FEMALE	
	FREQ	DISC RATE	FREQ	DISC RATE
Unsatisfactory food service	19%	20%	13%	18%
Tired facility – poor maintenance	18	27	13	35
Slow check-in, check-out	18	15	18	31
Employees not friendly	12	32	9	48
Room not ready upon arrival	10	11	13	15
Poor overall service	9	48	10	58
Requested room type N/A	7	14	7	16
Morning wake up call not made	5	14	3	19
No record of reservation	4	31	5	27
Over booked – guest walked	2	59	1	81
Overall				
Frequency Rate Per Trip	1.035		.909	
Discontinuance Rate	24%		31%	
Trip per Discontinuance	4.0		3.5	

EXHIBIT (7)

The data raise some very interesting points. First, unsatisfactory food service ranks #1 among males and #2 among females, yet was not among the top 10 errors volunteered by respondents. While there is insufficient data to support a probable conclusion, it could be advanced, that unsatisfactory food service is frequently encountered but generally tolerated. The discontinuance rate for males is 20% and 18% for females.

Another interesting point is found in the discontinuance rate comparisons of male and female travelers. Although males, overall, encounter one or more of the 10 errors more frequently than females (1.035 frequency for males vs. .909 frequency for females), the overall discontinuance rate is seven percentage points higher for females than males (31% vs. 24%). This means that the emerging female traveler is considerably less tolerant of error than their male counterpart. For example, when unfriendly employees are encountered, males will change facilities 32% of the time, while females will change 48% of the time. Also, if you must have slow check-in and check-out lines, rooms not ready on arrival, and/or over booking such that guests are walked, it would be best to cater mainly to male travelers. Female travelers are far more apt to change when these 3 errors occur than are males.

Overall, the data indicate that male travelers will change facilities on average every 4 trips while female travelers will change every $3^1/_2$ trips. This seems to indicate a rather large body of "floating" consumers who are ready to be converted into loyal guests by the property that can eliminate or significantly reduce the ten errors listed. What the data would have indicated if the list of ten errors had been a list of 20 or 30 is pure speculation but it is reasonable to assume that the results would still indicate that there is a large body of dissatisfied travelers looking for a home. Jim Bennetts oft spoken quote that "We are only as good as our last 30 minutes" seems to be a good philosophy for the industry. Restated, the guest is only really ours when we deliver consistency.

How Did the Respondents Rate the U.S. Hospitality industry?

The question was asked in 2 ways. First, respondents were asked:

> "Using a scale of 1 (low) to 10 (high), I believe the level of "quality" (consistent delivery of standards) in the United States Hospitality Industry is:"

The overall rating of all respondents indicated a perceived quality level of about seven. The data was analyzed further by type of property frequented, income level, sex and marital status. and by frequency of business travel. All of the classifications resulted in virtually the same rating (between 6 and 8). The lowest rating came from more frequent business travelers and the highest came from those who frequent economy properties. This indicates a very consistent agreement on the level of quality delivery – a mean of 7 – but improvement is possible. It also says that hoteliers who can deliver levels at quality of 8, 9 or 10, stand to gain considerably in increased business.

The second question regarding quality delivery asked:

> "Versus the rest of the world, do you believe the U.S, Hospitality Industry is "better," "equal to," "worse" in the following five areas?"

The results were significant and clearly identify a great opportunity for the American Hospitality Industry.

U.S. VS. THE WORLD			
	BETTER	SAME	WORSE
RESERVATION SYSTEMS	60%	35%	5%
FACILITIES	51%	40%	9%
OVERALL SERVICE	34%	35%	31%
FOOD SERVICE	23%	34%	43%
EMPLOYEE ATTITUDE	16%	34%	50%

EXHIBIT (8)

Clearly the data indicate U.S. superiority in technical areas of "facilities" and "systems" but a clear opportunity for improvement in areas of "employee attitudes," "food service," and "overall service." It is important to note that the acquisition of technical ability is largely a question of purchasing or acquiring the expertise and that this can happen fairly easily and quickly. On the other hand, improving employee attitudes requires behavior modification which will take a much longer time. If this is true, and we believe that it is, the conclusion would be that non-U.S. hoteliers will become increasingly competitive in capturing the world tourism *if* good employee attitudes are, in fact, important to frequent travelers.

Conclusion

- So it's your move now. Your move – in keeping with all the conclusions our study reaches.
- Your chance to please an American traveling public that places a high value on the human side of Hospitality.
- Your opportunity to bring our worldwide Hospitality position up to snuff in areas of Human Behavior...
- and to meet the great expectations of American Travelers – who are so willing to switch if you don't.
- It's definitely your move – if you want to win the emerging female travelers, who appear to be less tolerant when errors occur – and more willing to change facilities than are male travelers.

- Now is the time to move against the full variety of errors – proving to be so much more top-of-travelers-minds.

- The Boca Raton Hotel and Club is already working on it – eliminating Errors and developing new standards.

- So is the Ritz-Carlton in Boston…

- the Hotel Utah in Salt Lake City…
the Sheraton in Arizona…

- and so is a combination of small and large hotels in Bermuda.

- We could name a lot more. Suffice it to say that this is the kind of activity, throughout the Hospitality Industry, that really justifies our Consumer Perception Study –

along with everything that AH&MA puts into its "Quest for Quality" Program…

This study, commissioned by The American Hotel and Motel Association and funded by Citicorp Diners Club, identifies many common errors which can easily be eradicated by quality and service oriented programs. To meet this challenge, Citicorp Diners Club offers the Club Hotel Services Program. Educational brochures are available for training hotel/motel staff to deliver the service guests expect. Request these materials or additional copies of the "Quest for Quality" Consumer Perception Study today by returning the enclosed business reply card.

Cost of error study

A Joint Project of the American Hotel & Motel Association and the Citicorp Diners Club as part of the Hospitality Industry – "Quest For Quality" study

	On Business	Not On Business
1.1 How many nights did you stay away from home in a hotel, motel, motor inn, resort, etc., in the United States, during the past 12 months?	(1.1.1)	(1.1.2)
1.2 What would you estimate to be your average length of stay in each property?	(1.2.1)	(1.2.2)
1.3 In your **non-business** overnight visits, what would be the average number of **other** individuals travelling with you?		(1.3.1)

2.
On all of your nights spent in lodging facilities in the United States during the past 12 months, both business and pleasure, did any of the following errors occur? Please indicate how many times. Also please indicate if **the error** caused you to stay elsewhere on your next trip to that city, or if a chain facility, to stay with a different chain on subsequent trips.

Error	How Many Times Did This Happen	How Many Times Did The Error Cause You To Change Facility Or Chain
2.1 Arrived at lodging facility and they had no record of your confirmed reservation.	(2.1.1)	(2.1.2)
2.2 Employees were not friendly.	(2.2.1)	(2.2.2)
2.3 Check in/Check out lines were too slow.	(2.3.1)	(2.3.2)

Error	How Many Times Did This Happen	How Many Times Did The Error Cause You To Change Facility Or Chain
2.4 Room not ready when you arrived.	(2.4.1)	(2.4.2)
2.5 Morning wake-up call not received at requested time.	(2.5.1)	(2.5.2)
2.6 Food/food service was unsatisfactory.	(2.6.1)	(2.6.2)
2.7 Facility seemed "tired" – maintenance not good.	(2.7.1)	(2.7.2)
2.8 Requested room type not available on arrival.	(2.8.1)	(2.8.2)
2.9 Facility overbooked – required to stay elsewhere	(2.9.1)	(2.9.2)
2.10 Overall facility service not satisfactory.	(2.10.1)	(2.10.2)

3.1
The 3 errors that upset me most when staying overnight in a lodging facility are:

(3.1.1)

(3.1.2)

(3.1.3)

4.1 Using a scale of 1 (low) to 10 (high), I believe the level of "quality" (consistent delivery of standards) in the United States Hospitality Industry is:	(4.1.1)

5.
If you have travelled to other countries within the past 5 years, how does the U.S. Lodging Industry compare? (Check the appropriate column)

	U.S. Is Worse	U.S. Is Equal	U.S. Is Better
5.1 Overall Service	(5.1.1)	(5.1.2)	(5.1.3)
5.2 Facilities	(5.2.1)	(5.2.2)	(5.2.3)
5.3 Reservations System	(5.3.1)	(5.3.2)	(5.3.3)
5.4 Employee Attitude	(5.4.1)	(5.4.2)	(5.4.3)
5.5 Food Service	(5.5.1)	(5.5.2)	(5.5.3)

6.
The demographics of the primary traveller responding to this survey. (Please check approriate response)

6.1 Sex	☐ **Male** (6.1.1)	☐ **Female** (6.1.2)
6.2 Marital Status	☐ **Single** (6.2.1)	☐ **Married** (6.2.2)

6.3 Average annual total income:
☐ Under $25,000 (6.3.1)
☐ $20–$35,000 (6.3.2)
☐ $35–$50,000 (6.3.3)
☐ $50–$75,000 (6.3.4)
☐ Over 75,000 (6.3.5)

6.4 Mostly stay in:
☐ Economy Properties (6.4.1)
☐ Standard Properties (6.4.2)
☐ Luxury Properties (6.4.3)

EXHIBIT (9)

Stephen Hall: Quest for quality – Discussion questions

'Quest for quality', as its title suggests, aims to assess quality in hotels in the USA. The study is divided into two parts: a cost of errors study, where errors are talked about as the absence of quality, and are argued to cost the company in terms of lost sales and customers not returning; second, the article presents results from a survey attempting to assess customers, perceptions of standards and quality.

Below is an evaluation of that investigation. The format follows that of the original article; therefore, some opening comments will be made with regard to general issues, and then an evaluation of each of the two parts of the study will be made.

Definition of quality

The study defines quality in terms of three variables:

- when guest expectations are met;
- everyone doing their job correctly each and every time; and
- consistency of performance.

Definition of standards

The study talks about standards, also in three ways:

- desired levels of performance;
- set standards become requirements, and should be met each time the service is performed; and
- haphazard deliverance of standards is a guest that does not return.

There are many points that can be raised with respect to these definitions. These include:

- What are guest expectations? How do you measure them? How do you know if they are appropriate?
- What does doing a job correctly mean? How would this be achieved in practice? Is it possible? What are the implications of this?
- What exactly is consistency of performance?
- What is a desired level of performance? How do you measure that? What does it imply in terms of working practices, etc.?
- How do you know why a guest has not returned?

So, you can see that even superficially, there are major questions that can be raised about the assumptions and definitions that are proposed as working parameters for the study. What is really needed is some kind of conceptual analysis of standards and quality that would more rigorously inform an investigation. However, as a result of these assumptions, it was decided that the cost of errors could be numerically calculated, hence the first survey.

Cost of errors survey

This was carried out with selected hoteliers, and they were asked to calculate the cost of 50 common errors. The maximum number of hoteliers that could have been involved was 40.

If you go through the list of points on how to calculate the cost of an error, there are immediate issues that arise, e.g.

- how to accurately identify an error?
- how to accurately identify the consequence of errors?
- how to accurately identify the cost of each consequence.

Clearly, although it may be possible to get an indication of these points, it is impossible to accurately quantify anything but the most simple of issues or complaints.

Assume the following scenarios, and try to work out for yourselves a sensible cost of error.

> A family of four, two adults and two children, walk into McDonald's on a Saturday afternoon. They queue for five minutes, have to wait two minutes until the required burgers are ready, and the process of serving and paying takes a further two minutes. They take the food to their table, which has not been cleaned, and begin to eat. They are constantly jostled by other customers trying to find seats, and within 15 minutes have left the premises.

> A business woman checks into a hotel in the area in which she is to do business the following day. The hotel is commonly used by her company for such work, and the room is pre-booked. She immediately asks for use of the business centre and, after leaving her bags in her room, sets off to find it. One of the lifts is not working, so she has to walk further than she would have expected, and on arrival at the centre finds that it is locked. She contacts reception, and they send someone with the key. The facilities are fine; she knows this because they have used them before, and she leaves within one hour. She returns to her room, and begins to prepare for her meeting the next morning. Housekeeping respond within five minutes to her request for an iron, and she retires knowing that her wake-up call will give her plenty of time for last minute details. All this occurs, and she sets off to her meeting at 8 am.

The main benefit of this exercise for Hall *et al.* was, in fact, awareness. It helped the hotelier to gain an understanding of possible consequences of errors and their cost. Of course, the main issue here is concerned with customer expectations. A factor mentioned previously, but not addressed here, is that of the appropriateness of expectations. In some way, the researchers recognized this as an issue, and set up the second part of the survey – a consumer perception study. The aim was to investigate guests' perceptions and reactions to quality, standards and error. Below is an evaluation of that exercise.

1. *Population and sample*
   (a) Return rate from 25 000 questionnaires was only 3.5%. Why would those 3.5% respond? How can researchers claim representativeness of the population?
   (b) Population was only to Diners Club card members. How representative is that of other hotel users?
   (c) All respondents did not answer every question.

2. *Demographic information*
   (a) What is the purpose of travel for the respondents, and who is paying for the stay?
   (b) Where do the 3 possible reasons for deviation among single females come from? Whilst they may present interesting hypotheses, they should be stated in this form, and there are many more reasons that could be cited. Perhaps if the questionnaire were shown, it may be possible to deduce such statements from comments made by this segment of the population, but as it is, the information given is virtually useless.

3. *Perceptions of standards and quality*
   (a) List of complaints.
   - What do some of these mean? e.g. Shoddy overall maintenance, slow elevators, noise, poor entertainment?
   - Of the top ten complaints, the most important is poor employee attitude. What does this mean? If asked, you could probably get 75 responses to the question of what constitutes a poor attitude.
   - Assuming that we take these at face value, why not analyse the responses in terms of gender, income etc?
   - Given that this issue of attitude is constantly referred to in some way by guests, and by management themselves, it seems that it may require more comprehensive treatment. How might you do this?
   (b) Errors by functional areas.
   - Might it not be worthwhile breaking these statistics down once more by age, gender, income, reason for visit, level of hotel? As it stands, again it might give some indication that some form of treatment is required, but for a particular unit in a particular area, these data tells us nothing.

   In terms of customers' perceptions of standards then, there is some evidence to suggest that expectations are not always being met, but whether or not these are appropriate, and a clear explanation and understanding of these perceptions is not given. It would be very difficult to plan some kind of programme to overcome these problems unless the issues were tackled in considerably more depth.

4. *Reactions to errors*
   (a) Why do we not know the rates of business and pleasure travels? In relation to discontinuance rate, this could be a key variable.

(b) When unfriendly male employees are encountered, females change facilities more of the time than males. Hence for Hall, the female traveller is considerably less tolerant of error than the male counterpart.

- How do we know it is the male counterpart?
- This would seem to be a highly contentious issue. What is the nature of unfriendly employee in this kind of gender relationship?

5. *Rating of US hospitality industry*

(a) There is an issue about the way that respondents will answer a question of a ten-point rating scale. What do the responses mean to different people, how is the scale calibrated etc?

(b) Better, same, worse?

General issues raised

1. Who funded the research and why? Do you want to go on the Club hotel services programme?

2. Basic methodological weaknesses. Poor response rate, population, poor analysis of results, results that may be construed as meaningless. Is there any analysis of the times in which no mistakes were made?

3. Poor conceptual treatment of quality, perception, expectations etc.

4. Can you compare the USA with other countries without a cultural analysis?

SUGGESTED ANSWERS

Paul Slattery: Social sciences in the hospitality industry

These answers represent a brief guide to some of the answers that are required.

1. Humanistic, common sense and social scientific approaches.

2. Some reference must be given to the personalized, descriptive nature of common sense and humanities approaches, and to the informed, rigorous, logical nature of the social scientific approach.

3. There are many different theoretical interpretations to similar issues. Consequently, a manager must decide which theories are not relevant at a given point in time. Similarly, if one changes one's interpretation of a situation, the theory may also need to be changed.

4. Some discussion of the value of theories in providing logical, informed analysis is required. There may be difficulties arguing for the relevance of a particular theory, and further, in the application of that theory to hospitality situations and customers.

5. Formal experiments, interviews, questionnaires, observations, statistical analysis, documentary evidence.

6. Issue, theory identification, theoretical framework, empirical research, data analysis, evaluation, theoretical reformulation.

7. Factual information can be proven true or false; information can be measured accurately in mathematical or statistical terms. Value judgements can both be proved true or false – they are interpretations based on values, attitudes or beliefs of individuals. As such, they cannot be measured with the accuracy of factual data.

8. Some reference must be given to the fact that arguments and debate are inevitable in the social sciences due to issues such as subjectivity, the fact that different interpretations of particular situations occur, etc.

9. The nature view on the debate suggests that our capabilities (i.e. intelligence) are inherited; the nurture view suggests that they are environmentally determined. The ultimate logical argument if the nurture argument is adhered to is that individuals are essentially passive, awaiting a stimulus to promote action. If this were true for example, punishments or incentives would be effective as performance determinants. A similar argument could be constructed for the nature side of the debate.

10. Logical validity is concerned with the competent analysis of an interpretation, the logic of enquiry, the correct data collection method, etc. This does not always necessitate that the conclusions are correct.

William Whyte: The social structure of the restaurant

1. No, the sample was not representative. The research consisted of interviews or participant observations studies of twelve restaurants in Chicago. Some reference to the difficulty of generalizing from this research and cross-cultural problems should be mentioned.

2. The restaurant is a combination 'production and service' unit. The crucial relationship thus introduced is that of the customer/employee. The extent to which this relationship is applicable to other hospitality organizations is affected by the type of organization, the level of service, and the particular function of the employee.

3. The main variable was the size of the organization. The specific difficulties size gives rise to are concerned with authority relationships, for example, how a large restaurant ties together its line of authority and the relations that arise along the flow of work.

4. A social system is one which is composed of interdependent parts. The factors Whyte identified inhibiting optimal operation of the social system of the restaurant were sex relationships, status, layout and equipment. Some discussion of the realization of organization goals (i.e. profit, customer satisfaction) would be expected here.

5. Social systems are dynamic. Some reference should be made to the factors which contribute to this dynamism. For example, nature of the labour force, nature of the business environment.

6. Some discussion of the validity of Whyte's comments from within his research is needed, and reference to other factors which may be important, i.e. market level of the restaurant.

7. 'Meaning in interaction' relates to the different channels of transmission of information in interaction. A lack of accurate communication indicates its important when face-to-face interaction is not possible.

Stephen Hall: Quest for quality – revisited

We have demonstrated that Hall's article was an example of a piece of research in which the title did not accurately represent the study. Hall claimed to be examining consumers' perceptions of quality in the American hotel industry. This was not, in fact, achieved in the article, because the concept of perception was not introduced into the study as the framework within which to phrase the question, collect and analyse the data. The result, therefore, was that the term 'perception' was actually used by Hall to mean views about the sources of error or dissatisfaction that certain customers held and experienced when using hotels.

If the article did intend to study quality, and how quality is perceived by American consumers, then the starting point should have been introducing quality within some conceptual framework. Remember that the use of theories and concepts in the study of human behaviour allows us to set parameters for the investigations. In this context then, it allows us to set out what can be included in the concept so that it means the same thing to the researcher/s when questioning individual consumers. The use of concepts also allows us to generalize data from the study rather than simply being an individualistic account of a particular set of people. Furthermore, the use of a conceptual framework should produce definitions which are empirically testable. Hall's definitions fitted none of these criteria, as the study was based upon a subjective statement, namely consumer expectations. Not only do consumers' expectations vary, but they may vary at different times and under different circumstances. This means that they are difficult to study empirically.

To be able to study perceptions requires an in-depth focus in the area of perception; the key factors which affect perceptions need to be identified. This would allow us to identify those factors within hotel and catering contexts which influence customers' perceptions, and would further allow us to investigate and measure the importance of those influences. We would expect to be concerned with the ways in which perceptions are related to environmental variables, and the ways in which they are connected to the values which individuals hold about hotels. Similarly, it might be that we would be concerned with the ways in which individual's perceptions are processed and categorized, and linked to social variables, such as the groups who use hotels.

Turning to the issue of quality, the approach taken within Hall's article is really to identify quality from the operator's point of view, rather than from the perspective of the consumers. This is apparent as quality is defined in relation to the standards set by operators for the delivery of hotel products. In this sense, quality is technical and is not necessarily related to the ways in which consumers might define quality. Thus, it is possible to see that consumers may enjoy their stay in hotels, even if some aspects of the technical product are not up to the operator's standards.

Therefore, there may be a disparity between consumers' and operators' definition of quality. Students will be able to see now, that often this issue can mean that quality audits in hotels have weaknesses, and may not actually address the question that the operators are seeking to answer.

It seems then, that when looking at the area of customer satisfaction, quality may not be the appropriate term to use. When an organization is attempting to consider satisfaction or dissatisfaction with a product or service, the operator needs to be able to identify the groups who use the facility, the purpose of use, and how demand patterns are influenced. An operator must always be aware that what they consider to be quality and therefore determinants of satisfaction, may not be the same as their customers' considerations of quality or satisfaction.

Author index

Subject index

OwL

Generating Social Stratification: Toward a New Research Agenda